African
Masks and
Emotions

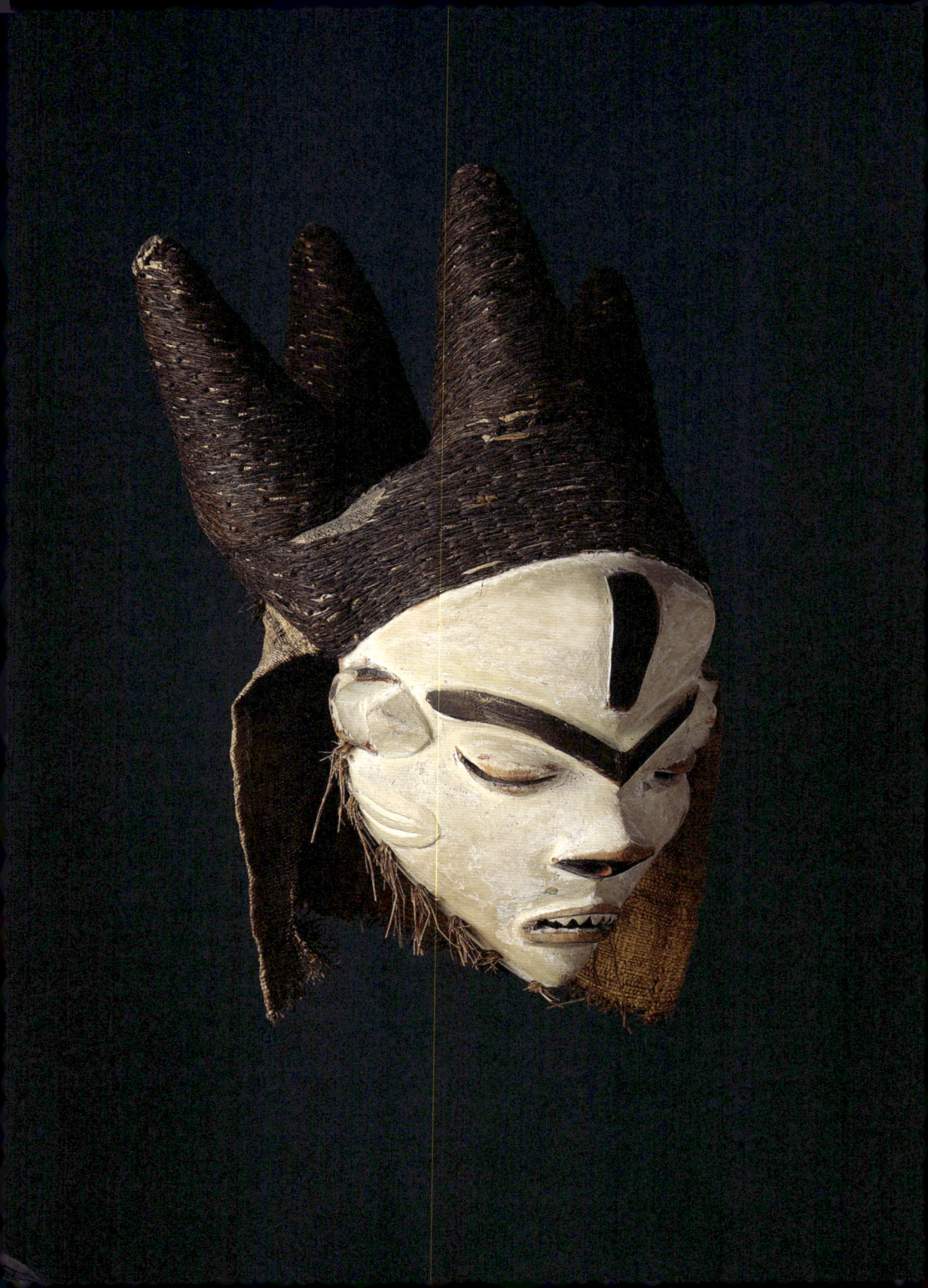

African Masks
Masks and
and Emotions
In Theory
Emotions
and in
Practice

Getty Research Institute, Los Angeles

Z. S. Strother

In memory of a cherished colleague,
Nzomba Dugo Kakema
(4 September 1956–31 May 2024)

Contents

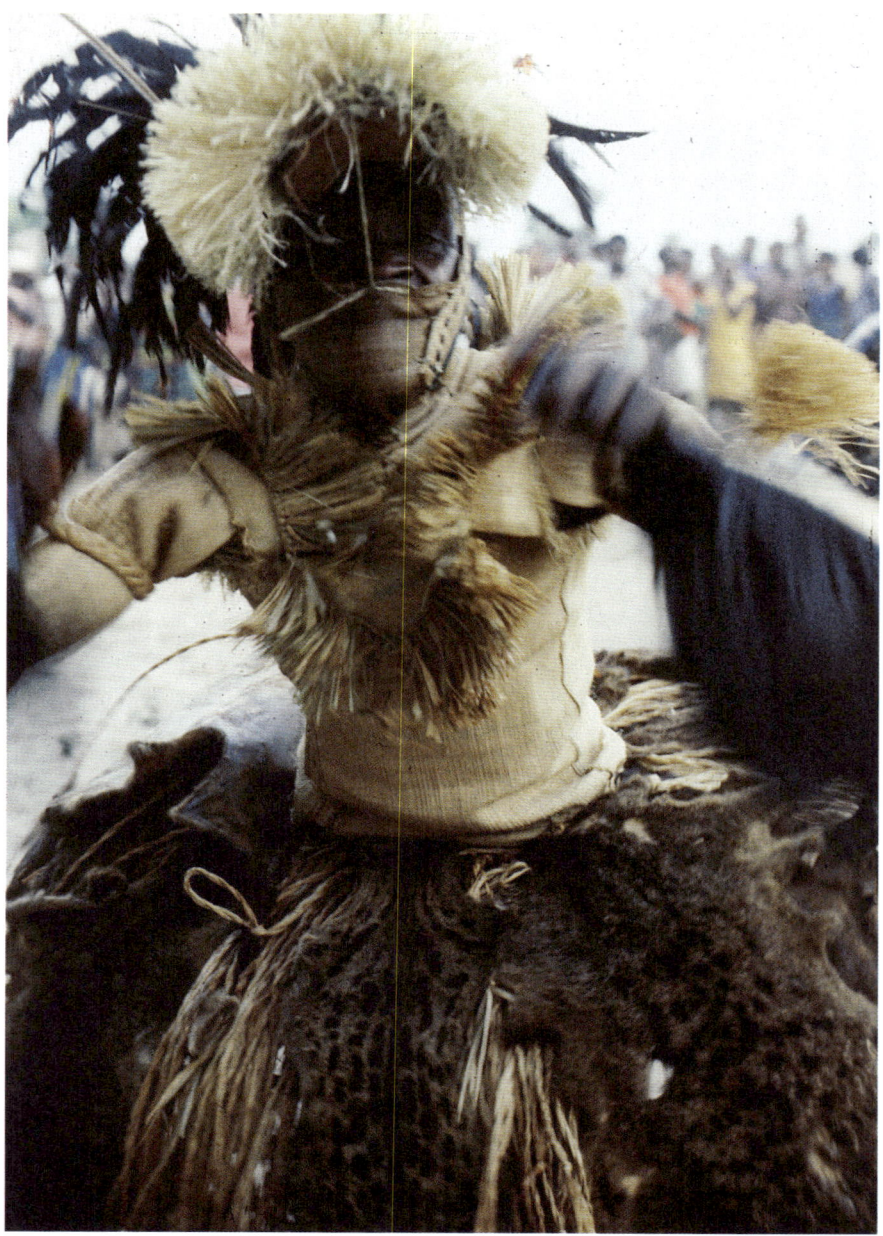

The Mask Is Not
a Face Fragment

For all the wrong reasons, Hans Belting declares "the mask" to be "the most brilliant invention that ever occurred in the making of images." As an art historian, he defined images as material representations whose existence points to an absence: The mask is compelling because it substitutes one face for another. It creates a new "presence" by replacing or "hiding" what is "perishable" with what endures.[1] This view rips the mask off the body of the performer and overlooks what makes masquerade distinctive among representational practices (fig. 1). Like so many European and North American theorists, Belting conflates the mask with the face. In large part, however, masks are powerful because they shift emphasis elsewhere.

In this text, the term *mask* refers to the conceptual package of face mask (if there is one), costume, and performer (in action). As a species we are hardwired to home in on the face to read expression; indeed, within forty-three minutes of birth, newborns respond to face-shaped objects marked with schematic eyes.[2] What is brilliant about masks is how they interfere with this process and reverse the expected figure-to-ground

Fig. 1   **The famed dancer Masuwa Léon performing as the Central Pende mask Muyombo.**
The "face" sits on top of the head, permitting the dancer to see and breathe freely.
Nioka-Munene, DR Congo, 1989.
Photo by Z. S. Strother.

relationship. When the face is obscured, the body emerges as the primary site of communication. Consider this formulation from the Nobel laureate dramatist Dario Fo:

"It is the body which gives all expression to the mask. . . .

The whole body acts as a frame for the mask and transforms its inertness."[3] This ability to shift signifying capacity away from face and voice was one of the reasons many prominent twentieth-century dramatists advocated experience working in masks so that actors might stop relying exclusively on facial expression to convey emotion and rediscover their bodies.[4] The mask is not a face fragment, and it is not inert, given the energy broadcast through the human physique.

Vocabulary in a cross-cultural and cross-disciplinary study poses a challenge. In this text, I follow the more generalized Africanist practice of describing a gathering at which one or more masks appear as a "masquerade." Some theater professionals such as Julie Taymor take umbrage at the term *masquerade,* which they regard as trivializing.[5] *Performance*—"an activity by an individual or group in the presence of/ for another individual or group"[6]—applies, but it is too generic a term and implicitly reinforces in the mind of the speaker a separation of the actor from the audience that I wish to avoid. Some, like Belting, insist that the key feature is absence, the overshadowing of one face or body or identity by another. I argue instead that

masquerade is specifically a performance medium holding in tension two personae through the vehicle of the human body.

For spectators, the tension between personae comes alive through motion, sometimes even through the simple act of breathing.

Sensing the breathing body within the mask undergirds the emotional logic of masquerade, which often unsettles or disturbs spectators. Realizing that the person she took to be Saint Nikolaus during a Christmas celebration had her father's hands cemented a powerful childhood memory for Kim Richter, a German student and now a senior research specialist at the Getty Research Institute. "Suddenly," she recalled, "there was a loud knock on the door and in came Nikolaus all dressed up with his red-and-white outfit, long white beard, a big sack filled with goodies, and a fist full of branches [whips]. To confirm whether we had been good or not, he opened his big, silver book. And <u>in that moment</u> I recognized my dad's hands!"[7] When the three-year-old child spotted her father's hands, the identity of the visitor was doubled: Saint Nikolaus and her father, the two held in tension, each making the other strange. The uncertainty was frightening but also pleasurable and deeply memorable.

The child's experience with Saint Nikolaus, of <u>suddenly</u> recognizing the body in the mask, will resonate for many West and Central Africans. Contradictions in costuming can make the human dancer all too visible— something that scholars, in their preoccupation with what masks hide, have been loath to acknowledge. Writing on the symbolism of masks in West Africa, the anthropologist Germaine Dieterlen proclaimed that "the porter [of the mask] usually must be entirely disguised by the costume, to disappear completely behind the entity that he represents."[8] This is a curious statement, given that Dieterlen had years of experience among Dogon peoples in Mali and that Dogon masquerade practice was exhaustively documented by Dieterlen's close collaborator, Marcel Griaule, who recorded in drawings and photographs that Dogon masqueraders routinely exposed their shoulders, chests, and legs (fig. 2).[9] Noninitiates were kept at a distance of twenty to thirty yards but could clearly see the dancers' arms and legs. Perhaps, as Dieterlen goes on to reference, "certain masks" in the region were covered by long fibers or leaves that obscured the body, but here again the issue is not clear-cut.

In her glancing reference to masks dressed with masses of fibers or leaves, Dieterlen was likely referring to Bobo peoples in Burkina Faso, for whom the ethnographer Guy Le Moal insisted that "the clothing must do more than preserve the anonymity of the performer, it must render unimaginable the presence of a man inside the costume."[10] He repeats over and over again that the entire body must be hidden, seemingly as a guarantee for the authenticity of Bobo masquerade. And yet, what are we to make of the visible hands and feet, prominent no matter whether the performer is covered by leaves or by thick ropes of raffia thread, no matter whether he wears a helmet or face mask (fig. 3)?[11]

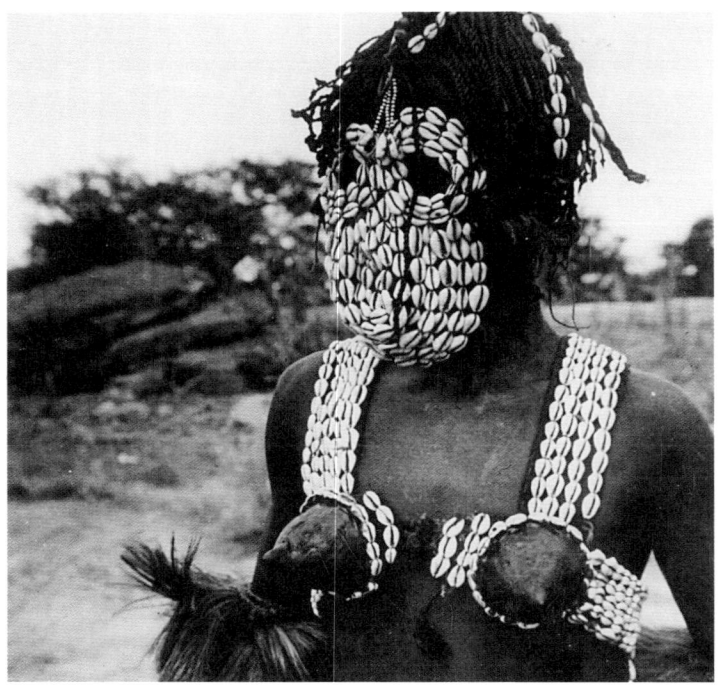

Fig. 2 **The Young Girl was a popular Dogon mask in Mali before it became controversial in the 2010s.**
The face covering is composed of cowries, and the breasts are made from baobab fruits.
Dakar-Djibouti Mission, 1931.

Masquerade within a defined social group has its *punctum* (if I may borrow a helpful term from Roland Barthes) when an individual spectator's reverie and absorption in the color, the spectacle, and the performance is punctured by a <u>sudden</u> awareness of the body of the performer. Maybe the hand or style of movement belongs to a school chum or a boyfriend, or maybe it is just undeniably human. Observation of the detail acts on a spectator's subjectivity and changes the experience irrevocably.[12] Should we

Introduction

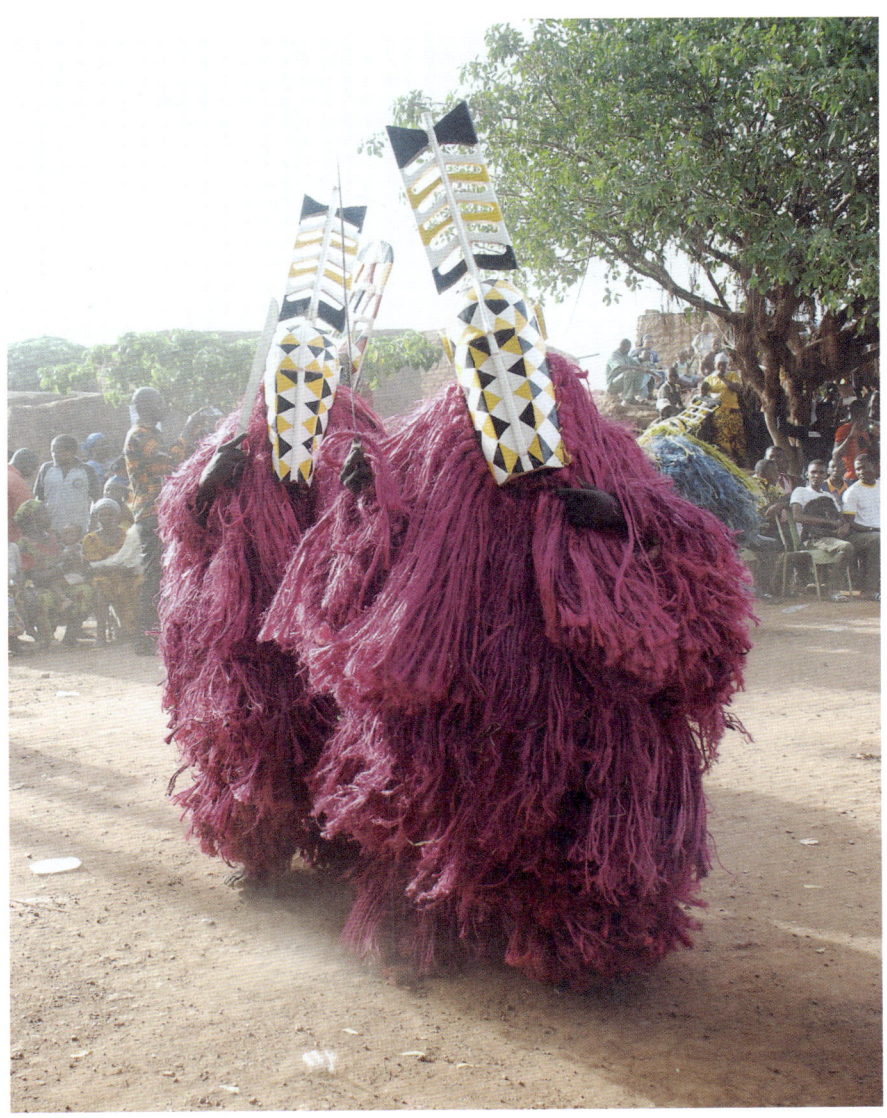

Fig. 3 **Bobo peoples.**
Pair of Kiele Pene masks.
Sya district, Bobo-Dioulasso, Burkina Faso, 2016.
Photo by Lisa Homann.

The Mask Is Not a Face Fragment

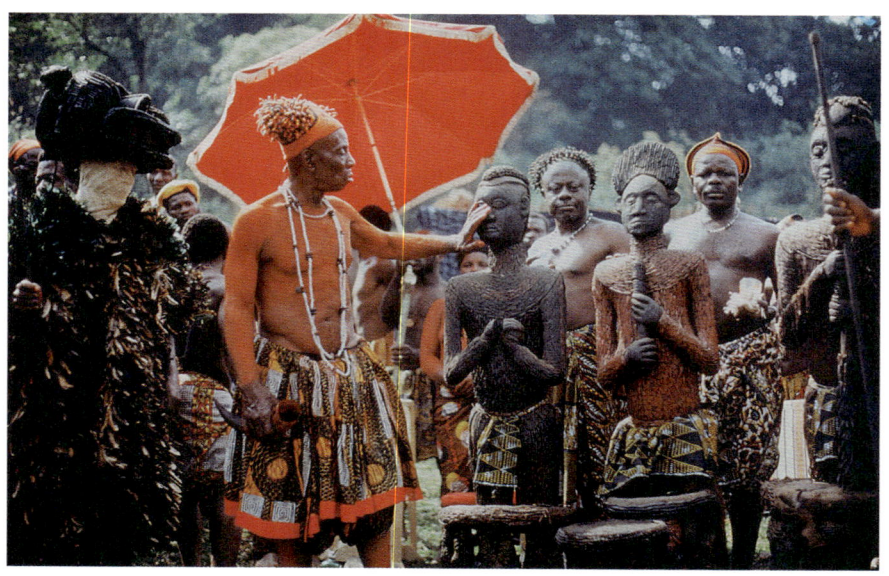

Fig. 4 **King Jinabo II in front of royal figures.**
Note how the features of the masquerader (far left) press
through the cloth covering his face.
Kom, Cameroon, 1976.
Photo by Hans-Joachim Koloss.
Berlin, Ethnologisches Museum, Staatliche Museen zu Berlin.

attribute the change in perception to a failure in disguise, as Le Moal seems
to suggest? Or, on the contrary, does the revelation point to the power of
masquerade itself?

While flipping through the pictures in this book, marvel at the many
ways a performer may disclose his or her identity despite voluminous costumes. In Kom, Cameroon, the masquerader is covered from head to toe,
but the face is so tightly banded that one can distinguish the eye cavity,
the nose, the chin—in fact, the face in all its specificity (fig. 4). And in the
delta of Nigeria, one savors the incongruity of a shark floating on top of
the human body. Again, the body is entirely clothed, but the feet are bare
and the walk is personalized, loose and limber, stamped with the imprint
of an individual personality (fig. 5). A Congolese mechanic critiquing some

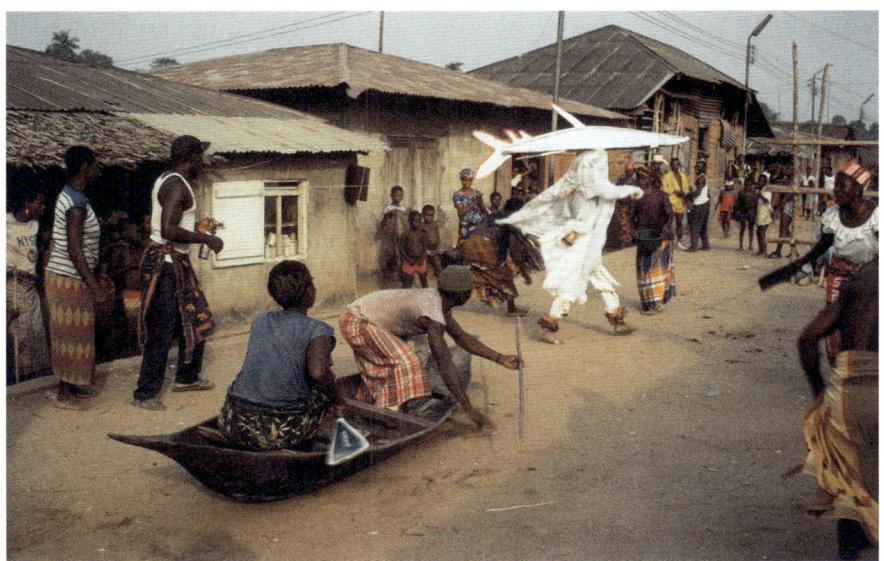

Fig. 5 **The Ofurumo masquerade.**
Ondewari, Nigeria, 1992.
Photo by Martha G. Anderson.

masquerade video in the Democratic Republic of the Congo (DR Congo) advised, "Change your style of walking so that no friend will recognize you from your gait."[13] In practice, it is hard work to change one's gait for any length of time, and few performers have the self-discipline. Besides, most performers seem to enjoy flashing clues about their identity.

There is good evidence to argue that the most common form of masquerade worldwide was and probably still is situated in social groups where the performer risks (or even toys with) being identified. Yes, audience members often recognize precisely who is performing, even though there might be strict rules prohibiting the voicing of such knowledge. As with dimming the lights in a theater, the prohibition on naming the performer during the performance helps audience members engage the illusion.

On occasion, spectators play with this convention. When the acclaimed Congolese masquerader Khoshi Mahumbu danced in the late 1980s, his wife would sometimes cry out, "Has anyone seen Khoshi? Where is he? He should see this dance—the performer is so gifted!" The crowd roared with laughter at her clever means of exposing what they all knew but dared not say.

What people say and what they do contrast sharply in Monni Adams's bravura studies based on four years of research among the Bo-speaking people (in the Wè cultural zone) of southwestern Côte d'Ivoire.[14] Referring to masked figures called *gela,* she noted that people could never say out loud that a human being was present.[15] Instead, her interlocutors told her that the "*gela* come from the forest, they are monstrous, dangerous, and obscure, they are ancient, they manifest the ancestors, they are the source of regenerative vitality, and they never die."[16] Nevertheless, everyone knew that young men "carrying" the *gela* could be so charismatic that women actively sought out the performers for sexual liaisons; some were even nicknamed "adultery *gela.*" Referring to a dancer admired for his ability to follow complex rhythms, the Bo elder Zoué François mused: "That *gela* wins girls, he can choose the woman he wants. It's like that with the young *gela,* all the girls can fall in love with them."[17]

Rather than "hide" or substitute one face for another, masks frequently draw attention to the artificiality of the relationship of face and body. In fact, the influential mid-twentieth-century mask theorist Georges Buraud (whose impact is addressed in chapter 3) attributed the "mystery" of the mask to the phenomenon of joining a face to a body with which it does not have a natural relationship.[18] Adams found that *gela* performers distorted their voices with a mirliton and wore bulky costumes of massed raffia, which floated over spindly human legs.[19] The "contradictory unions" of human qualities with other bizarre characteristics created what Adams called "a wavering line of affinity and estrangement."[20] Wrestling with some of the same contradictions in the context of Amerindian masks, Carlos Fausto argues in favor of a

"cognitive instability"

triggered in the mind of the viewer when "the face of a nonhuman entity" is visibly animated by another being who is all too human.[21]

Another strategy to promote cognitive instability in Africa occurs when masks are faceless, or when the carved face is displaced to another part of the body. Intimations of the human form will nevertheless periodically punctuate or disrupt the outward manifestation, often through movement. The most extraordinary example of this phenomenon may lie with the Nupe (Nigeria), although photographic documentation can be quite deceiving. Isolated images portray an enigmatic apparition, and it is not obvious that it can move or be moved.[22] However, film footage by Constanze Weise shows the tall cylindrical tube as it bends, bounds, spins, and rolls—indeed, it dances. There are even moments when the illusion is shattered, when the billowing fabric clings to a human backside or molds the outstretched fingers of the hand pushing the construction forward.[23] Similarly, when studying a still photograph of Bobo Kori masks, one may be absorbed by the mystery of the towering apparitions and wonder whether or how they move (fig. 6). During an actual performance, however, their absolute strangeness is enhanced by shock when the illusion is broken and the spectator gains a peek at human feet (fig. 7). These moments of slippage tend to be censored in the published photographic record because they conflict with the public's expectations that masks *should* conceal the body. That said, the scholar Lisa Homann has reminded me that my own use of her field photographs distorts the experience because it fixes in consciousness what should be fleeting in time. The flashes of the dancer's feet in Kori performance should be marked by their <u>sudden</u> appearance, whether in terms of visibility or in terms of rising to consciousness in the spectator's mind.

The importance of cognitive instability in masquerade practice has been underrecognized because the mask is such a powerful conceptual metaphor in Western languages. Thirty-two months of study with Pende chiefs, patrons, artists, and historians in (what is now) the Kasaï and Kwilu provinces of DR Congo (1987–89) followed by periodic visits, conversations, or emails with Pende patrons and artists since 2006 in DR Congo has prompted me to shift the focus of analysis from performer to audience-participant. A veil was lifted from my eyes when I read Chinua Achebe's words that for Igbo people in Nigeria, masquerade—"really an elaborated dance"—is "the art form par excellence for it subsumes not only the dance, but all other forms—sculpture, music, painting, drama, costumery, even

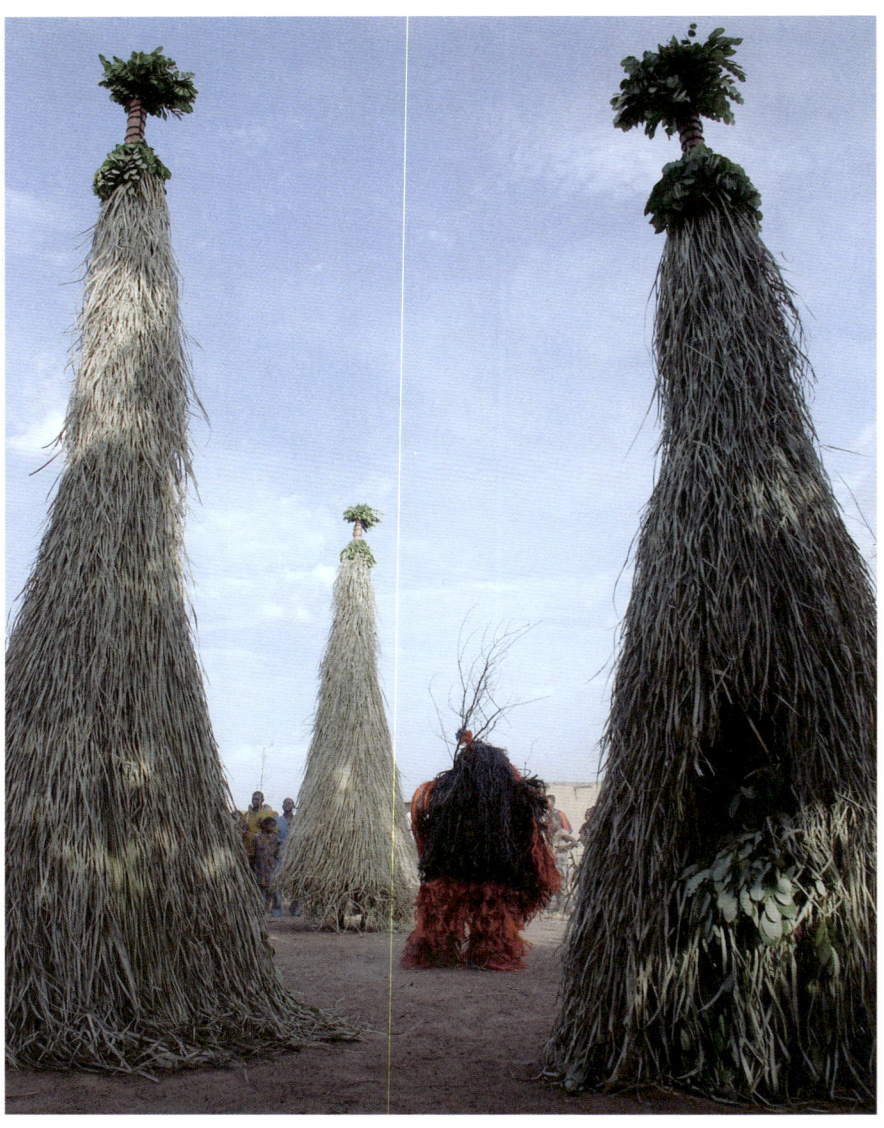

Fig. 6 **Bobo peoples.**
Three Kori masks with an attendant in charge of crowd control.
Tondogosso, Burkina Faso, 2009.
Photo by Lisa Homann.

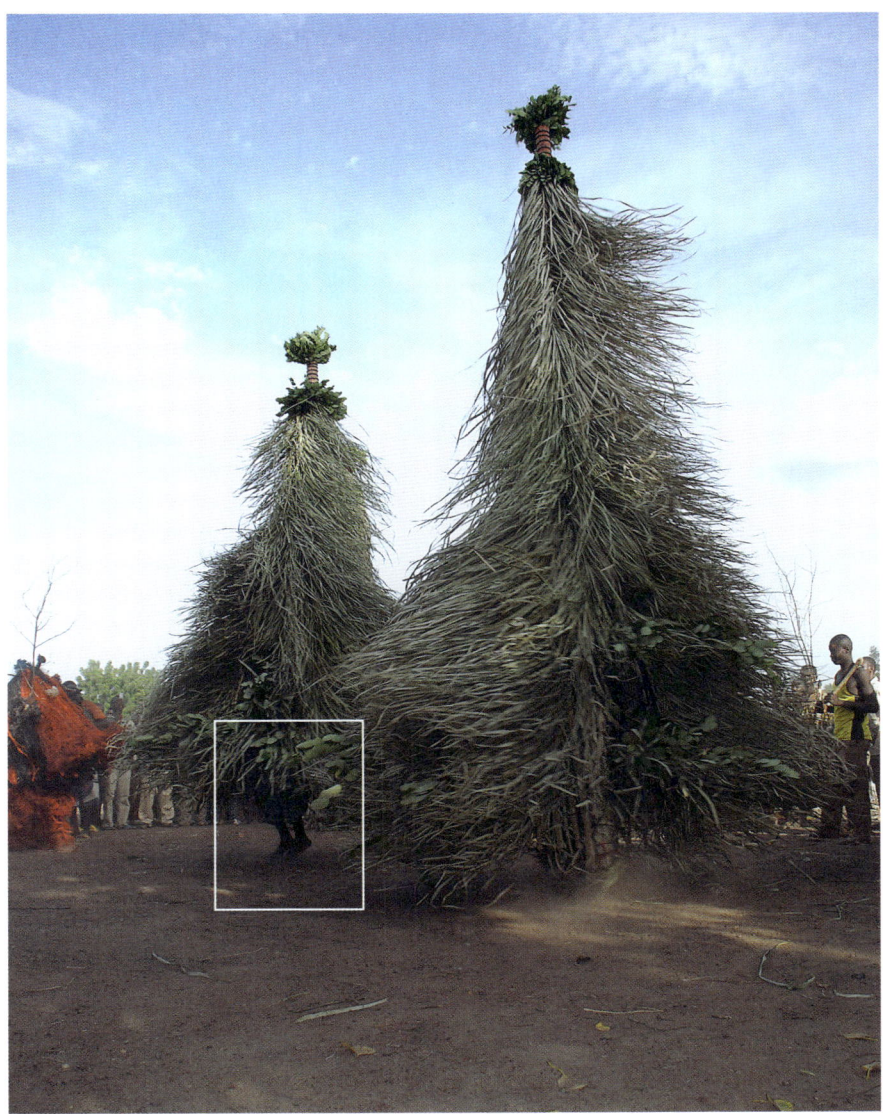

Fig. 7 **Bobo peoples.**
Kori masks dancing.
Tondogosso, Burkina Faso, 2009.
Photo by Lisa Homann.

architecture." An Igbo proverb summed up what to him made masquerade "so satisfying":

> " 'You do not stand in one place to watch a masquerade.'

You must imitate its motion. The kinetic energy of the masquerade's art is thus instantly transmitted to a whole arena of spectators."[24]

A Canadian visitor to DR Congo remarked in surprise that a Pende masquerade felt more like visiting a fair than watching a stage performance with the spotlighting on the actor. Generally, spectators stand and move from place to place, jostling for a better position, and there are multiple points of focus (see fig. 5). They may join the chorus, dance along, take videos, or even correct a performer's gestures. Achebe's argument is that this mode of viewing or interacting with masks has both a cognitive and psychological dimension. Audience members constantly adjust their perspective and also respond viscerally—through their bodies. I applaud the work of scholars who have worked closely with African performers[25] but believe that concentrating on audience participation is critical to engaging in a cross-cultural dialogue on the commonalities of masquerade experience.

In the Africanist literature, the disregard for performance and the insistence on disguise of the face has skewed the historical record, most seriously in regard to gender. For decades, members of the multiethnic women's Sande Association in Sierra Leone were described as the only women in sub-Saharan Africa who masqueraded. Now it appears that they merely number among the few in the nineteenth and twentieth centuries who covered their faces with a carved wooden headpiece. Researchers have identified numerous cases of women masquerading with cloth, twigs, fire, or other materials to conceal their faces and bodies.[26]

That said, the Ejagham in Cameroon draw no semantic or metaphysical distinction between men masquerading and women masquerading, even in cases where the women's faces are visible.[27] The anthropologist Ute Röschenthaler worked with cultural associations in the region in the late 1980s and learned that "women dancing with sculptures on their heads should be perceived as comparable to male masquerades" (fig. 8).[28] As Egbobha/Egpobha Association members explained to

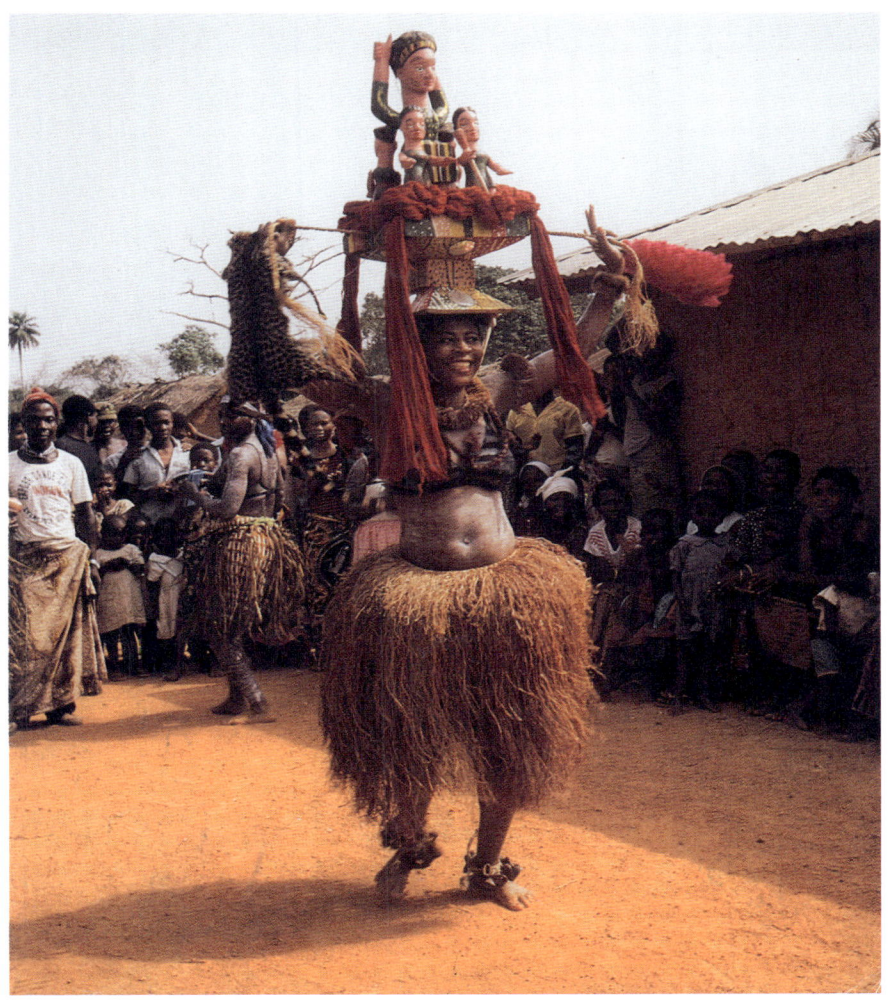

Fig. 8　**The principal dancer for the Ejagham women's
Egbobha Association.**
Ejagham consider women dancing with sculptures on their
heads to be a form of masking even though they do not cover
their faces.
Cameroon, 1988.
Photo by Ute Röschenthaler.

her, women do not obscure their faces, because they put a high premium on dance technique. Some of the men's masks had taken on retributory functions, for which reason it is good to create doubt in the mind of the target about who exactly among one's neighbors might be responsible.[29] The emotional impact of the judicial performances was different: One woman said, "men's dances are meant to create panic."[30] When women's associations took on a threatening and punitive role, their members did so by dancing as a group at night—naked—and the men hid locked up in their houses.[31] Even though the female performer's face was visible, it was still true, as Fausto writes in another context, that the performance presented "the face of a nonhuman entity," which was enlivened through the agency of the human porter.[32] The spectator's eye oscillates back and forth between the two personae, and the doubling creates the same cognitive instability that happens when the face is covered.

Part 1 of this text opens by exploring the Western European preoccupation with the intent of the performer. What emerges is a feedback loop by which age-old stories about masks in Europe centered on problems of disguise have been used to interpret African practices, which are then cited as proof for the pure ("primitive") and authentic practice of masquerade and offered as models for European or American dramatists to relearn authenticity in theater. While I strongly suspect that the feedback loop described is true for the study of many masquerading practices around the world, the literature is vast and requires cultural training to interpret. For these reasons, I restrict myself as an Africanist to African masks. In particular, the text has the most to say about Dogon (Mali), Dan and neighboring Wè/Guéré (Côte d'Ivoire; Liberia), Pende (DR Congo), and Chewa (Malawi), because their masked dances have attracted in-depth analysis over a number of generations from scholars trained in different disciplines and speaking different languages. They have also appeared frequently in a wider theoretical literature; I have tried to note the dates not just of the publications but of any field research in order to situate the performances historically. To the degree possible, the ethnic names used in the text reflect those in currency among self-identified members of the communities.[33]

Beloved stories told in English and, to a lesser extent, in French and German revolve around claims that masks lie, masks reveal, masks transform. I will not propose a fourth totalizing interpretation on masks—far from it. Mask practices are far too rich and creative for any universal interpretation to be anything but a mirage. Even within a single tradition, as Peter Probst concluded about Nyau performances organized by Chewa during funerals or initiations, masks mean "different things to different people … and these differences depend again on the time and the place, when and where, nyau appears."[34] Instead, I would like to prioritize a series of questions inspired by interlocutors in DR Congo:

What emotions do masks provoke? And how do they do it?

It is hoped that these questions will also inspire reflection on masquerade as a performance medium holding in tension two personae through the vehicle of the human body in the world beyond.

By engaging emotion, we are finally shedding the dehumanizing scientism decried by Léopold Sédar Senghor, Senegal's acclaimed poet and first president, for urging Africans "to despise emotion and to be guided only by discursive reason." Senghor wrote that the African diaspora students who launched the movement of Négritude in the 1930s in Paris sought to validate emotion and empathy as fundamental values of African art and civilization.[35] In the years since, emotions (particularly aesthetic emotions) have found scant support in art history, but the explosion of interest in the sciences in recent decades creates an opportunity to follow up on Senghor's lead.

Whereas a scientist might monitor changes in heart rate or brain scans to evaluate how subjects react to different stimuli, I rely on subjects self-reporting on their own emotional experiences, in person and in print, in fiction and in real life. Professional authors aside, most people do this more skillfully in oral exposition. Classical ethnography often employs narrative vignettes to illustrate patterns in human behavior grounded in cultural practice. My use is somewhat different. When individuals narrate significant emotional experiences, they often set the scene and sketch out how the experience unfolded in time—this way, they identify the trigger for the emotion and account for its intensity. It is striking how often narrators, both participants and scholars, mark abrupt transitions in their narratives. Constructed thus, these narratives serve to expand emotion beyond what the historian Robert Boddice calls the "neurobiological narrative": "Meaning always has to be made and it is always made in context, in culture, and in society."[36]

Because beliefs about masks are deeply engrained, the type and design of the text have been modified in several ways to engage the reader in reflecting on their assumptions. I use italics to mark my own (or another author's) emphasis.

The reader may have already noticed that throughout the text I also underline passages where abrupt transitions are marked in the narrative. Suddenly is an adverb calling attention to a swift change of action, as when a mask steals a baby, but it also communicates that the change aroused surprise and, quite frequently, a radical shift of perception. Recall the little girl's vivid memory of suddenly recognizing that Saint Nikolaus had her father's hands.

Suddenness signals surprise, recognized by clinical psychologists as a primary emotion associated with a spectrum of responses including bafflement, amazement, astonishment, wonder, marvel, and awe.[37] The sensation of surprise is extended in time through experiences of wonder or awe, but none of these responses have the stamina of other primary emotions—for example, sadness or anger. Nonetheless, David Doris captures the paradox that what is fleeting can have a profound impact:

"Wonder is more a feeling than a thought; it arrives unexpected, compels us by its immediacy, and soon moves on, leaving us changed."[38]

When associated with a radical shift of perception, experiences of profound surprise can live on in flashbulb memories that people like to replay in their mind's eye. It is surprise that will emerge as a foundational emotion to engage with masquerade (as opposed to the face fragment mounted on the wall).

Chapter 1
Truth and Deceit: Definitions of Masks in Europe and North America

A society which believes it has dispensed with masks can only be a society in which masks, more powerful than ever before, the better to deceive men, will themselves be masked.

—Claude Lévi-Strauss, 1961[1]

Strangely enough, the mask as metaphor has long warped interpretations of actual masquerade practices in Europe, Africa, and elsewhere. In English dictionaries, definitions of the verb "to mask" quickly shift from "to take part in a masquerade" to "to disguise one's true character or intentions."[2] The fear is that by disguising the face, the masquerader intends somehow to trick the viewer. In an iconography primer popular in the seventeenth and eighteenth centuries, the very personification of deceit is pictured as a "slyly smiling elderly woman [who] lifts a mask from her face."[3] In the modern period, Mikhail Bakhtin maintained, "the mask hides something, keeps a secret, deceives."[4] The imagery is updated, but the message remains the same in an advertisement for the horror film *Saw V:* There, tension is generated by contrasting the physicality (the truthfulness) of the body, the tactility of its flesh and hair, with the fitting of a fake face with a benign expression, which is designed to allow a murderous psychopath to draw near his victim (fig. 9).[5]

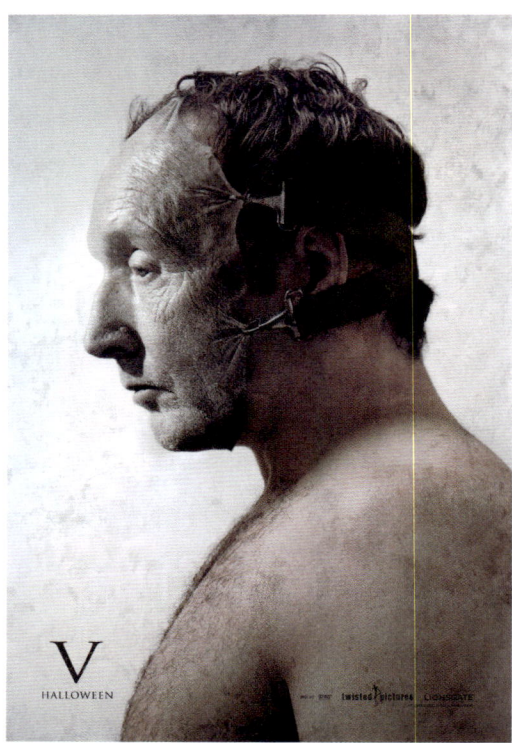

Fig. 9 **Advertisement for the horror film** *Saw V*, 2008.

The anxiety that English speakers feel about masking is reflected in their literature. In the novella *Behind a Mask,* Louisa May Alcott skillfully builds the reader's sympathy for Jean Muir, a pale and thin governess who suffers many slights at the hands of her well-to-do employers. The reader sighs with relief for the poor girl when she is allowed to escape to her bedroom. There, however, Muir undergoes an astonishing transformation.

> Still sitting on the floor she unbound and removed the long abundant braids from her head, wiped the pink from her face, took out several pearly teeth, and slipping off her dress appeared herself indeed, a haggard, worn and moody woman of thirty at least. The metamorphosis was wonderful, but the disguise was more in the expression she assumed than in any art of costume or false

adornment. Now she was alone, and her mobile features settled into their natural expression, weary, hard, bitter.[6]

We learn that Muir, a crafty hag of thirty, has assumed the mask of a nineteen-year-old in order to pursue her heinous intention: marrying above her social station (!). Muir is an accomplished governess. Her gifts in French, music, and the "art of making people comfortable"[7] are real. However, none of this matters, because she has fooled us. In terms of deception, Alcott is as brilliant as Muir, and her readers share the wealthy family's sense of betrayal.

Fear of what lies "behind a mask" is a trope that extends beyond the literary realm. The news media and everyday speech are saturated with references to masks engaged to misrepresent the facts for malicious purposes.[8] For speakers of English and French, "the mask" exists more vividly as a conceptual metaphor structuring the relationship of deceit and its exposure than it does as a performance medium—*even though Europeans and Americans engage in myriad forms of sanctioned masquerade.*[9] Consider Halloween, Saint Nikolaus, cosplay, the Ku Klux Klan, science fiction conventions, and avant-garde theater, to name only a few such venues.

In their paradigmatic book *Metaphors We Live By,* the linguist George Lakoff and the philosopher Mark Johnson demonstrate that "most of our conceptual system is metaphorical in nature."[10] As models or hypotheses, "metaphors may create realities for us, especially social realities." The danger is that the "power of the metaphor to make experience coherent" can turn metaphors into "self-fulfilling prophecies."[11] The metaphor feels "true" when it is internalized so that one sees "only those aspects of our experience that it highlights," downplaying other factors deemed inconsequential or even antithetical to the establishment of the category.[12] In this case, authors write as though truth were a treasure, something inert, that people hide or bury—and it falls on intellectuals to

> Uncover
>
> Unearth
>
> Reveal
>
> Unveil
>
> *And unmask the truth.*

No one loves the metaphor of the mask as a tool for deceit better than cultural critics. Friedrich Nietzsche first diagnosed this condition when he contrasted the artist's purported attraction to the beauty and mystery of illusion with the macho intellectual's commitment to reveal what others would like to hide, no matter the cost: "Whenever the truth is unveiled, the artist will always cling with rapt gaze to whatever still remains veiled … but the theoretical man gets his enjoyment and satisfaction out of the castoff veil. He finds his highest pleasure in the process of a continuously successful unveiling effected through his own unaided efforts."[13]

I challenge the reader to find a major modern(ist) critic writing in English or French who does not adopt at some point the posture of the hardheaded realist exposing what others conceal. As the small sampling in chart 1 demonstrates, masks in the theoretical literature are what neurotics, psychopaths, capitalists, colonialists, anthropologists, art historians, and bad artists use to fool us. The intellectual's mission is to rip off the mask of false ideology. By this logic, interpretations of masquerade will be persuasive when they make claims to expose some crucial reality that usually escapes detection. The desire to lay claim to authenticity or realness becomes an obsession.

Modern satirists have gone even further than critics: They delight in exposing the hypocrisy of social masks, making liars of us all. Even a foundational anthropologist such as Claude Lévi-Strauss waved aside the importance of myriad ongoing practices in favor of mocking the falseness of social masks (see epigraph). The satirists maintain that we all masquerade every single day when we present ourselves with a decorum, or integrity, or competence that we do not feel on the inside. In "The Masks" (1964), one of the most acclaimed episodes of the American cult television series *The Twilight Zone,* written by Rod Serling and directed by Ida Lupino, a bitter old man obliges his four heirs to don masks during Mardi Gras under threat of being disinherited. He has made face masks for them that reflect who he thinks they really are: a sniveling coward, a narcissist, a miser, and a sick buffoon. The heirs complain and are relieved to take off the masks at the end of the evening until they discover, to their horror, that their faces have taken on the form of the physical mask they had been forced to wear. Henceforth, their true character will be forever exposed to the world.

The Masks of False Ideology¹⁴

NEUROTICS & PSYCHOPATHS

Joan Rivière, "Womanliness as a Masquerade"
Hervey Cleckley, *The Mask of Sanity*
Frantz Fanon, *Black Skin, White Masks*

CAPITALISTS & COLONIALISTS

David Harvey, *The Condition of Postmodernity*
"Money and market exchange draws a veil over, 'masks' social relationships between things.
This condition Marx calls 'the fetishism of commodities.'"

John Berger, *Ways of Seeing*
"Publicity helps to mask and compensate for all that is undemocratic in society."

Pierre Bourdieu, *The Logic of Practice*
"So it would be wrong to see a contradiction in the fact that violence is here both more
present and more *masked*."

Homi Bhabha, "Of Mimicry and Man"
"Mimicry conceals no presence or identity behind its mask."

ANTHROPOLOGISTS & ART HISTORIANS

Johannes Fabian, *Time and the Other*
"But one should not forget that behind the mask of the modest, candid, and tentative
bricoleur hides a player *who is out to win*."

Donald Preziosi, *Rethinking Art History*
"Art history has all too commonly been a coy semiology in the service of a theologism
masquerading as a humanism."

BAD ARTISTS

Friedrich Nietzsche, in *The Birth of Tragedy*, reproaches Euripides: "Thy very heroes have but
counterfeit, masked passions, and utter but counterfeit, masked words."

Rosalind E. Krauss, in "Reinventing the Medium," attributes to Walter Benjamin the
sentiment that kitsch is the "fraudulent mask of art."

Chart 1   **The Masks of False Ideology.**
This chart lists texts featuring common tropes
related to masks and masking.

The readers of this text are presumed to be friendly to masquerade and may feel frustrated by the emphasis on deceit in Western European languages. Do not despair. A counternarrative in the modern period posits that donning a physical mask is liberating. The terms are reversed, but the dialectical tension between truth and deceit continues. Masquerade might free the individual to be oneself, or, paradoxically, it might grant a delicious "release from self."[15] Superheroes in cinema often play with a reversal of expectations about the social mask. Batman poses as a socialite in everyday life but reveals the implacable strength of his authentic self when he conceals his face and assumes the costume of a crime fighter. When Batman tells his girlfriend that his "mask is just a symbol," she demurs, stroking his face: "No, *this* is your mask. Your real face is the one that criminals now fear."[16] Similarly, the hero T'Challa's gentle and thoughtful demeanor in the film *Black Panther* dissimulates steely determination as communicated through his hard, faceted head mask.[17]

The redemptive power of concealing one's face is also a very long-lived literary trope. According to Henry Fielding, writing in 1728, to "masque the face" was "t'unmasque the mind."[18] Another writer reflected for *Lady's Magazine* in 1777 that it was only during masquerades that people revealed their true natures when they lay aside the "borrowed feathers" of their social roles.[19] Although it can feel good to reveal what lies hidden under one's everyday mask, this gesture relies on the same duality of truth and deceit evident in *The Twilight Zone* episode discussed above.

The potential that a mask might "free" an actor to discover who he really was inspired a number of twentieth-century dramatists, including Jacques Copeau, Jacques Lecoq, Konstantin Stanislavski, and Peter Brook.[20] This paradox derives from the view that liars are skilled at manipulating their expressions *but not their bodies*.[21] As George Bernard Shaw quipped, "Give a hypocrite a mask to wear, and he will be rendered incapable of further lying."[22] Copeau, among others, has recommended mask training for actors, claiming that it would "teach sincerity since in a mask one cannot deceive."[23] With avant-garde training, Western performers often do feel "liberated" psychologically when they mask, but it is far from a universal experience.[24] I have never heard anything remotely like it when talking to mask performers in DR Congo or Nigeria; there, performers are more likely to sound oppressed, complaining of heat, headaches, and, most importantly, difficulty breathing.

The counternarrative that physical masks are emancipatory also has an impressive scholarly lineage, eloquently encapsulated in Bakhtin's formulation of the carnivalesque as a liberating zone in which oppressive social norms are riotously overthrown.[25] Herein lie the roots for Judith Butler and for the social critique of the 1990s that presented gender as a masquerade and singled out figures like the film actress Marlene Dietrich in her top hat and bow tie for making people conscious of gender as a construction that might therefore be manipulated and changed.[26] Entertainers Little Richard and Prince also became favorite subjects of study for both scholars and artists, as their self-presentation scrambled codes "of race, gender and sexuality" so that spectators became aware of the "cultural constructedness ... of the sexual roles and identities we inhabit."[27]

In addition, the liberating potential of donning a mask captured the imagination of those who consumed more private expressions of popular culture, referenced even on greeting cards. In one example, viewers are coached by the addition of a quotation from Oscar Wilde to perceive that a little boy playing at Zorro, the swashbuckling defender of the downtrodden, is able to live his "real life" only when adopting the domino mask and cape.[28] And it was not only men and boys who could take advantage of this freedom. In the 1990s, the masquerade ball became a site of empowerment for women in romance novels where they could cast off oppressive class and family expectations to do what they would not have otherwise dared to do.[29]

The history of blackface demonstrates the impact of masking as a figure of speech on representations of flesh-and-blood masquerade. In the prizewinning book *Love and Theft: Blackface Minstrelsy and the American Working Class*, Eric Lott documented the origins of blackface in the United States in the 1830s, far from the southern plantations where most African Americans lived. In fact, blackface was born in Boston and Pittsburgh among Irish American and other immigrant groups struggling as proletarians to qualify as white. The actors studied African American speech and musical forms quite seriously, and Lott argues that the ugly racist caricatures in minstrelsy disguised a genuine attraction to—nay, a love for—African American culture among white working-class men.[30]

According to this dialectic, the actors dissemble their desire to be Black, but Lott rips off their masks to expose class anxiety, same-sex desire, and cross-racial desire.

What is the impact of class, gender, racial privilege, and other cultural constructs on how individuals interpret the sensations that they feel in wearing a physical mask or even how they engage the metaphor of the social mask? Many African American authors express acute ambivalence. On the one hand, the "mask of meekness" (as Ralph Ellison called it) has promised African Americans protection and privacy from race-based oppression.[31] However, in his poem "We Wear the Mask," Paul Laurence Dunbar voices the searing pain provoked by the necessity of living a lie:

> We wear the mask that grins and lies,
> It hides our cheeks and shades our eyes,
> This debt we pay to human guile;
> With torn and bleeding hearts we smile
> And mouth with myriad subtleties.
>
> Why should the world be over-wise,
> In counting all our tears and sighs?
> Nay, let them only see us, while
>   We wear the mask.[32]

The phenomenon of "passing" is also sometimes perceived in the United States as a form of masquerade in which raced individuals feel alienated from themselves by the role that they are obliged to play. The legal scholar Cheryl I. Harris tells the story of her grandmother who passed, in "the parlance of racist America," to order to be able to work in a large retail store in Chicago: "Each evening, my grandmother, tired and worn, retraced her steps home, laid aside her mask, and reentered herself."[33] Quoting Gunnar Myrdal, Harris interprets passing as the "deception of the white people," which relies upon "a conspiracy of silence" on the part of other Blacks who become aware.[34]

The contemporary artist Lorna Simpson captures the psychic cost of adopting a social mask in a hostile environment in *Vantage Point* (1991) (fig. 10). She photographs herself from behind and constructs a diptych

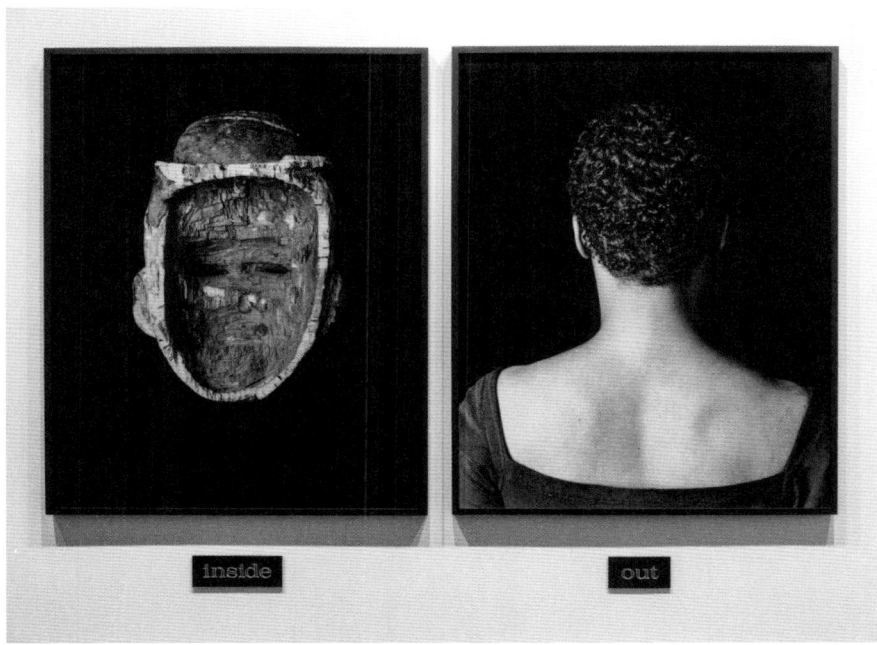

Fig. 10 **Lorna Simpson (US American, b. 1960).**
Vantage Point, 1991, gelatin silver prints, 50 × 70 in.
Raleigh, North Carolina Museum of Art.

with an image of what appears to be an African mask, photographed from the inside, floating in space. The labels "inside" and "out" along the bottom suggest an allegorical reading about interiority, but the visual juxtaposition raises questions about whether the mask is something to be fitted over the face or whether it has just been removed. The eye slits are uneven and the wood on the "inside" is chipped and splintered. It would hurt to wear this mask. Vision would be skewed. Does the coarse surface imply that it was difficult to remove—that it had become glued to the face of the young woman over the course of time? The juxtaposition of the coarse surface with the artist's own soft skin recalls Dario Fo's "sensation" when he removes his mask after a long performance that part of his "face has remained stuck to it."[35] The black paint on the inside of the mask raises further questions. Does the tinting imply that the facepiece is discolored from repeated use (as connoisseurs assume when they check for signs that an African face mask has been danced)? Or does the heavy impasto paint point to the adoption of a "Black" identity constructed for public consumption? And what is the relationship of this African relic to the elegantly dressed and coiffed subject? By generating a plethora of unanswerable questions, Simpson disrupts clichés about the play between truth and falsehood in social masks.

The rich and deeply internalized conceptual life of masks in modern European and North American discourse revolving around metaphors of deceit and exposure, truth and lies could not fail to have an impact on the study of masquerade in other civilizations, particularly as they were initiated within colonial campaigns of knowledge production.[36] The next two chapters trace how European language metaphors have warped the study of masking in Africa.

Chapter 2

The Mask in Africa: Hiding? Revealing? No, Hiding!

Masking Viewed from a German Armchair

German speakers were among the first to recognize the importance of masking as a subject of academic study in the 1880s. Their interest may well have been sparked by the vitality of Central European practices around them. Familiarity with their own masking fraternities sometimes granted authors insight into individual customs elsewhere. Although the German language does not often make use of masks as metaphors for disguise and deceit,[1] early German theorists nevertheless associated these qualities with masks, at home and in Africa,[2] granting scholarly plausibility to European hypotheses about African masquerade practices.

The ethnologist Adolf Bastian made a wide-ranging, cross-cultural comparison of the uses of masks around the world for a journal devoted to "folk psychology" (1883). Bastian's examples derived from the ancient Greeks and Romans, the Americas, the Pacific, Austria, and China.[3] He argued that despite their colorful diversity, masks spring from a single root, a reserve of terror and dread akin to the fear of God (*Gottesfurcht*)— masks serve "to scare and to scare off."[4] Bastian was influenced by popular interpretations of European carnival masks, which continue to circulate today. For example, Slovenian *kurenti* are said to roam with whips and bats and generate a deafening din of cowbells to frighten away winter so that spring may return (fig. 11). Although Bastian admitted that other kinds of masks appear in dances and games and theatrical performances,[5] his

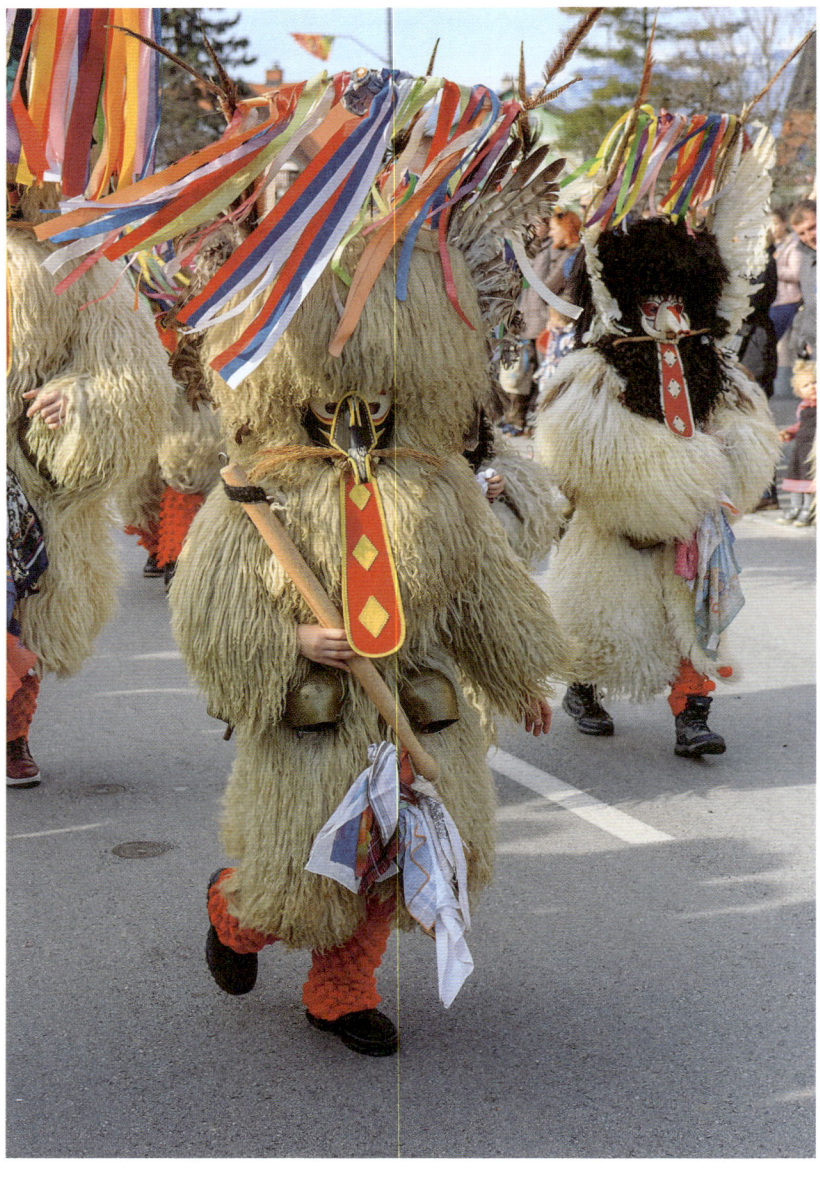

Fig. 11 **Many European masqueraders, including these Slovenian kurenti, carry whips, bats, and bells.**

concluding summary reads as though penned by a ranting medieval theologian: masks "conceal," "disguise," "disfigure," and render "grotesque" the beauty of the human form through their "unnatural" costumes.[6] Bastian believed that humans found the frightfulness of masks instrumental in scaring away malicious spirits and the souls of the dead. Conversely, one might honor a terrifying being by adopting his persona.[7]

Whereas Bastian was interested in the psychology of masquerading, his friend the encyclopedist Richard Andree aspired to be the first to codify masks by the contexts in which they appear: religion, war, mortuary rituals, tribunals, and theater and dance.[8] Andree located the major mask cultures in East Asia, Melanesia, and the Americas, and he observed that they were "not absent from Africa."[9] In most cases, he accepted Bastian's interpretation of the frightening aspect of masks enriched by his own study of European witchcraft. According to Andree, the same mask could be perceived as defensive or aggressive, depending on one's point of view. For example, a vulnerable party might protect oneself by driving away a threatening demon "by confronting him with a terrible, grimacing face."[10] (This is the logic behind the Slovenian kurenti masks: be as large, outlandish, and noisy as possible [see fig. 11].)

Andree's most interesting insight lay in the category of judicial masks. Here he drew on his knowledge of Haberfeldtreiben, a notorious vigilante ritual in Upper Bavaria. In the eighteenth and nineteenth centuries, men who were masked or who blackened their faces surrounded the homestead at night of a neighbor accused of moral, social, or economic transgressions. Granted anonymity by the mask, men could administer penalties in small communities without incurring resentment or revenge. The accused certainly had suspicions but could not be sure. Andree saw the same principles applying to the use of masks in African "secret societies"—for example, in Bastian's reports about the Ndungu ("Sindungo") association in Loango (Congo-Brazzaville). The leader of this organization received complaints from lenders about debtors failing to honor their obligations. If he deemed the accusation just, he would send masked initiates with oversize faces and huge ruffs of feathers to seize goats or chickens or other property from the defaulting debtor. As in Bavaria, the maskers relied on their anonymity to escape retribution.[11]

"Secret societies" were rife in Europe and the United States in the late nineteenth and early twentieth centuries. In the United States alone, between 1900 and 1927, the number of fraternal orders rose from 568 to 800, after which the number declined.[12] Many kept their memberships secret and required nominees to undergo elaborate initiation rites. Some, like the Masons, wielded serious political and economic clout, making them a source of envy and anxiety. Given this history, many Europeans and Americans were eager to document African organizations with restricted membership that seemed to resemble their own. Curiously, with time, the memory of fraternal orders in Europe and the United States has faded while the literature on Africa never dies.

Objects from Africa began to flood Europe during the 1870s and 1880s. In 1898, Leo Frobenius compiled the first monograph devoted to the subject of African masks. Only twenty-four years old, Frobenius had not yet traveled on the continent and worked entirely from travelogues, expedition reports, and early museum collections. He proposed various routes of diffusion for raffia (straw), wood, and composite masks in sub-Saharan Africa. Although Frobenius's theories have been discredited, the map that he compiled is useful in locating clusters of masquerading practices (fig. 12).[13] Masks continue to be created and abandoned today, but this map helps visualize the fact that (at most) a quarter of African societies masqueraded in the late nineteenth century. European modernists like Pablo Picasso made African masks famous, but mask-making was and is far from a universal practice.

The title for Frobenius's tome promised cloak-and-dagger scholarship: "Die Masken und Geheimbünde Afrikas" (The masks and secret societies of Africa).[14] The presumed "secret" justified a methodology of looking for what was hidden, and readers were probably disappointed that the author was himself more interested in tracing an evolution of forms. Commentators have summed up Frobenius's argument in the dictum "masks represent spirits of the dead."[15] Would that it were so simple. Frobenius hypothesized that masks emerged from the ritual apparatus of ancestor worship. Studying the rare drawings reproduced in field reports, he concluded that masks did not spring from any desire to reproduce the human face.[16] Instead, it seemed to him that the face was differentiated very little from the "mask-body" (that is, the fully costumed performer)

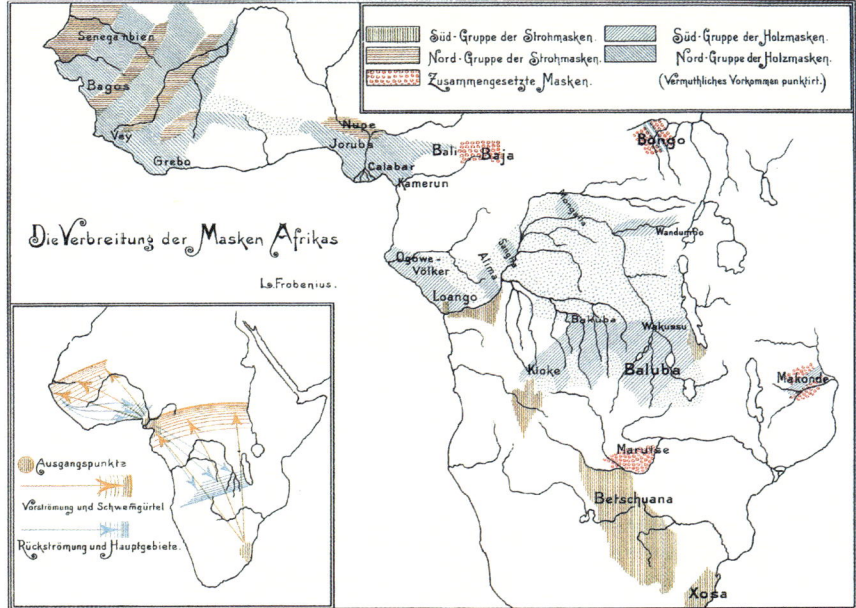

Fig. 12 **Leo Frobenius (German, 1873–1938).**
Die Verbreitung der Masken Afrikas (The diffusion of African masks), 1898.
Map showing the locations of recognized masking practices in sub-Saharan
Africa in the late nineteenth century. According to the key, blue = [face]
masks made of wood (*Holzmasken*); yellow ocher = raffia (*Strohmasken*);
and orange circles = composite materials (*Zusammengesetze Masken*).
From Leo Frobenius, "Die Masken und Geheimbünde Afrikas," *Nova
Acta: Abhandlungen der Kaiserlichen Leopoldinisch-Carolinischen Deutschen
Akademie der Naturforscher* 74, no. 1 (1898): plate 14.

in what he took to be the oldest forms (fig. 13).[17] Frobenius hypothesized
that the performers' crocheted body suits were made from the same
materials as mortuary houses and that carved face masks only developed
over time.[18]

Conceiving of the mask-body as an ambulating "spirit-house,"
Frobenius was flummoxed by eyewitness reports of masks used for dances
and games. In particular, the travelogue of Max Buchner shook him.
Between 1879 and 1882, Buchner crossed Angola, and he had multiple

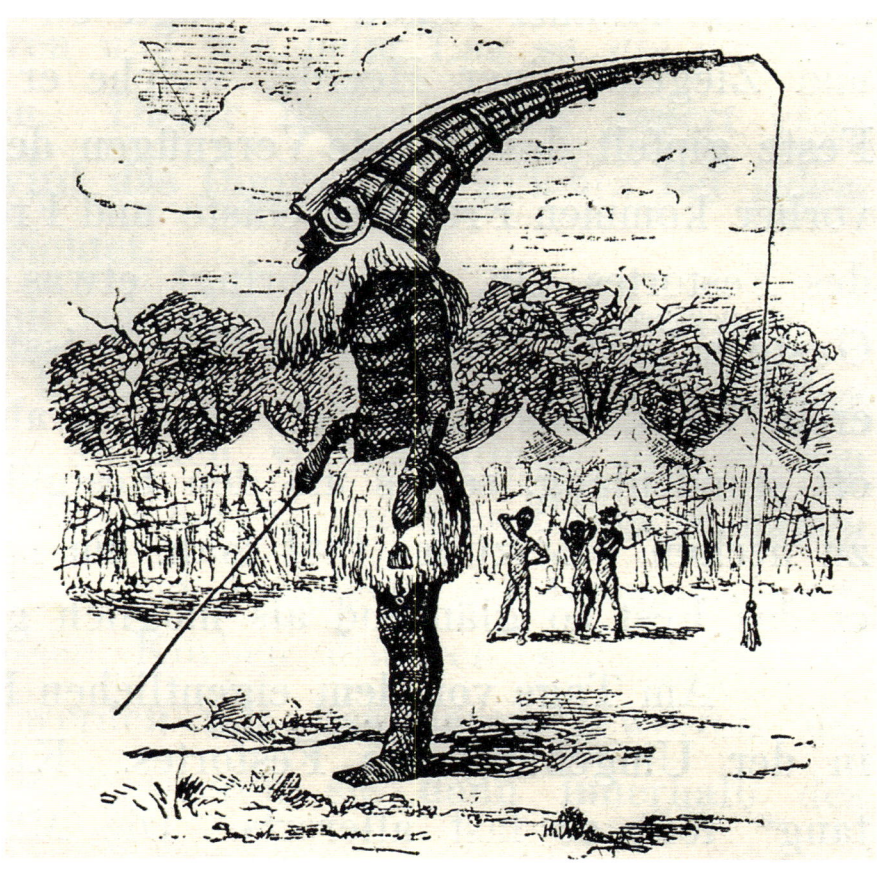

Fig. 13   **Leo Frobenius (German, 1873–1938), after Max Buchner (German, 1846–1921).**
A whip-toting Chokwe Chikunza Mukishi masker from Angola. Despite there being similar practices in Central Europe, Leo Frobenius was flummoxed by eyewitness reports of the pleasure and merriment experienced by boys running from initiation masks.
From Leo Frobenius, "Die Masken und Geheimbünde Afrikas," *Nova Acta: Abhandlungen der Kaiserlichen Leopoldinisch-Carolinischen Deutschen Akademie der Naturforscher* 74, no. 1 (1898): fig. 10.

opportunities to observe Chokwe Mukishi maskers in action. Although Buchner assumed that Chokwe believed that they were ghosts (the spirits of their ancestors),[19] he recognized that "a good part of the enjoyment they offered lay in the thrill of shuddering." Buchner was not bothered at all by the "merry howls" with which people ran from Mukishi, comparing that behavior to what "street urchins do at our own masquerades."[20] Perhaps Frobenius had never run down the street himself as a boy, taunting whip-toting masqueraders, or perhaps he believed too much in his theory about mortuary houses. In any case, forced to acknowledge the pleasure experienced by the audiences of Chokwe masks, he could only ask, "Where does belief end and trickery (or fraud) begin?"[21]

Frobenius expected Africans to venerate or fear their masks, and the perception of (what seemed to him) irreconcilable emotions provoked doubts. He concluded that his readers would be left with a series of unanswerable questions: "Do blacks believe they see spirits in the masked men or rather people possessed by spirits? Moreover, do the masked men consider themselves to be spirits, or to be possessed by spirits, or do they trick [*betrügen*] the people?"[22] He excused himself for not being able to answer by claiming that such discriminating questions were futile. One could hardly expect logic from a people "whose mode of thinking one can only describe as instinctual."[23] Frobenius voiced the anxieties about truth and authenticity that would continue to paralyze the development of scholarship on masquerade in the twentieth century. Subsequent authors, who most likely were unfamiliar with Frobenius's youthful text, gnawed at the very same questions that he posed:

> Is the masquerader sincere?
>
> Does he believe his own pretense?
>
> Or is he an outright swindler?
>
> Is the audience hoodwinked? Or are they just pretending to believe?
>
> And what role does spirit possession play?[24]

When the assumption that masks must be hiding something goes unchallenged, writers find it essential to ascertain the motive governing the deception.

Dogon Masks: Machines for Movement

Frobenius wrote with regret in 1898 that there had not yet been a scholarly study of masks of an Indigenous people (*Naturvolkes*).[25] Indeed, the first monograph devoted to a single African masquerade tradition and the first book written from field research would have to wait forty years, until the publication in 1938 of *Masques dogons* by Marcel Griaule. Having conducted intermittent field research in a number of Dogon communities in Mali between 1931 and 1938, Griaule saw himself as an advocate for Africa,[26] and his publications on Dogon culture helped to make them one of the most famous peoples on the continent for those interested in African art, including many African artists and intellectuals.[27] Furthermore, the colorful masquerades helped burgeon a small tourist industry after World War II that became important to the Malian economy for several decades until 2012, when rebel armed groups backed by jihadists attacked Dogon cultural sites as well as Sufi Muslim shrines.[28] Even after the expulsion of the rebels, Islamist pressure currently precludes masquerade performances, although they may well spring back as has happened in other parts of Africa, adapted to changed cultural mores.[29]

With startling originality, Griaule described the mask as a "m a c h i n e f o r m o v e m e n t" (*appareil de mouvement*) and argued that the sculpture could not be separated from the dance in masquerade.[30] He identified more than eighty different masks and illustrated a variety of songs, headpieces, and accessories. To this day, the text is unique in providing diagrams of some of the dance steps based on film footage (fig. 14). Griaule also observed that the masquerades had changed over time due to improvisation on the part of dancers and sculptors as well as the regular invention of new masks.[31]

Despite the flood of empirical detail, Griaule was strikingly tentative about interpreting the masks. He divided them into the following six categories: mammals, birds, reptiles, things, representations of Dogon people, and representations of foreigners.[32] It is clear that he asked his sources over and over again, "What does it represent?" (meaning: What does it illustrate?). Griaule never considered that the forms might be composites or products of the imagination. For example, he proffers the Kanaga mask,

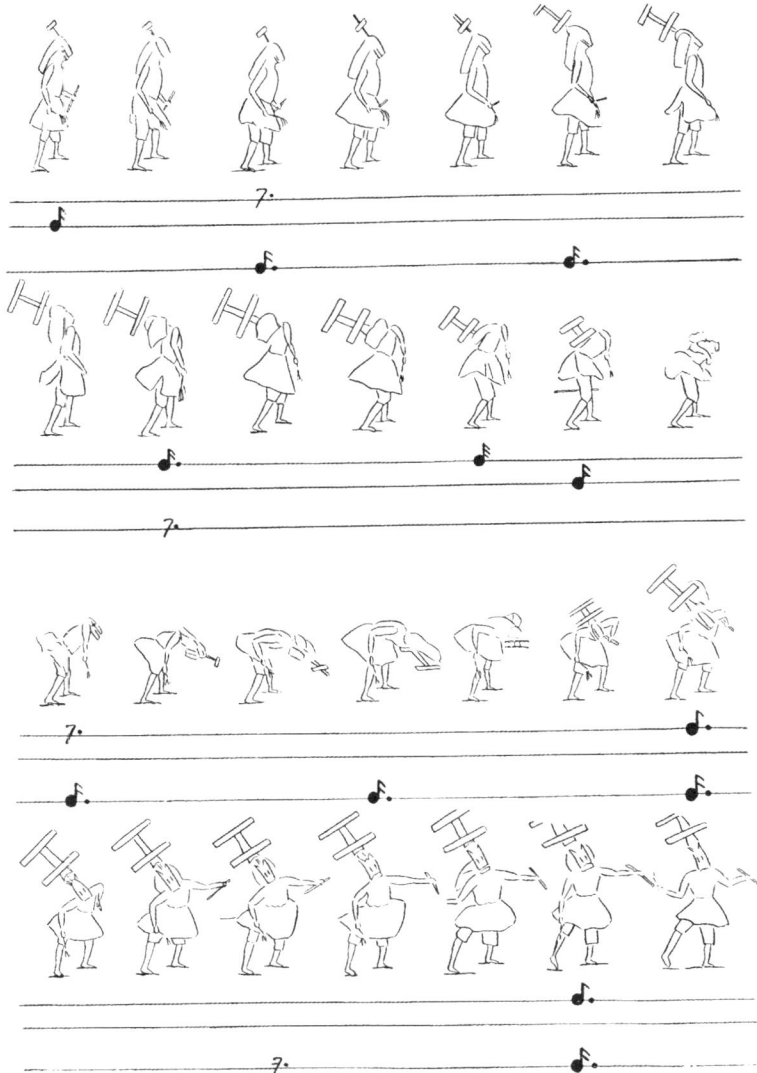

Fig. 14 **Dance *gona* of Kanaga masker to the rhythm *kili boy* (interval ¹⁄₁₈ sec.).**
From Marcel Griaule, *Masques dogons* (1938; Institut d'ethnologie, 1983), 729 (fig. 244).

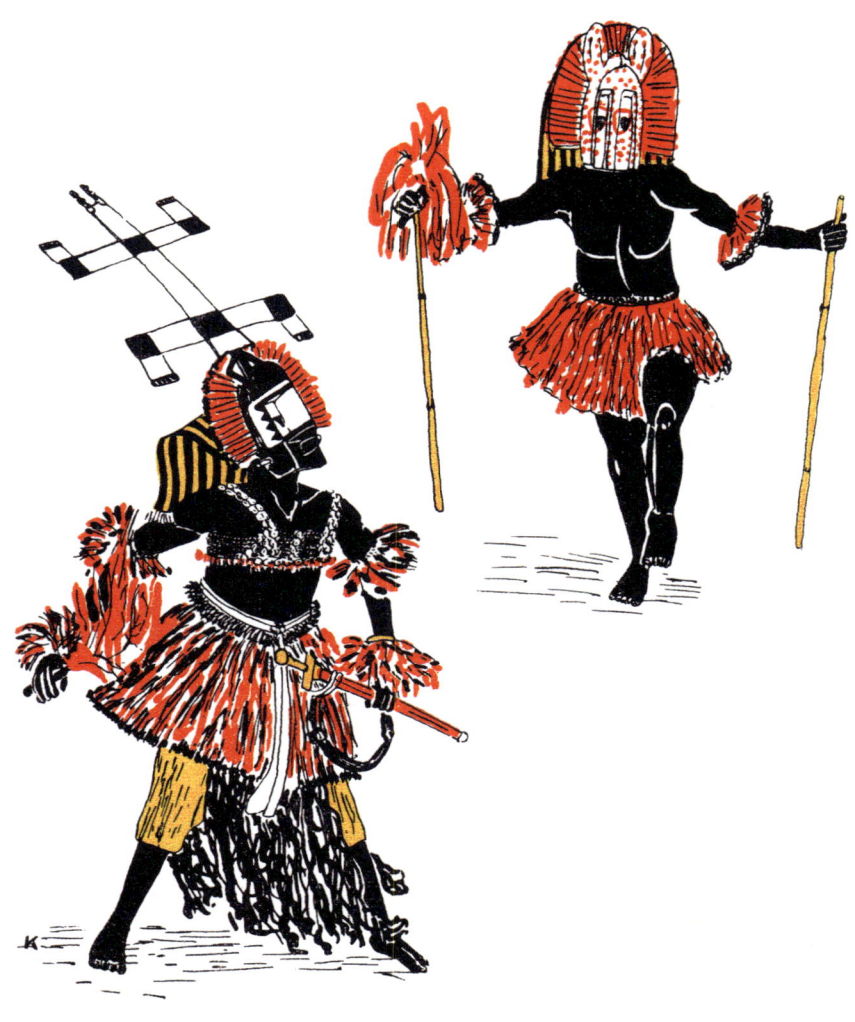

Fig. 15 **Dogon masks Kanaga (left) and the Hare.**
Note the partially exposed torso and legs of these two
popular masks.
Sangha, Mali.
From Marcel Griaule, *Masques dogons* (1938; Institut
d'ethnologie, 1983), 471 (fig. 110).

which once danced by the dozen at Dogon ceremonies, as a depiction of a raptor with a black forehead and a white stomach. This suggestion may explain the beak and tubular tongue, but does little justice to its long ears, the dramatic spiraling dance, or the distinctive superstructure (fig. 15).[33]

Interestingly enough, even if Griaule could not make grand claims on what the masks "represent" to Dogon spectators, he was able to generate a persuasive and even uplifting interpretation of the masquerade as ritual. Like Frobenius, he believed that the masks were rooted in a will to survive in the face of death.[34] After the passing of a certain number of men, masks danced in the early morning on the rooves of the deceased's houses in order to mark the individuals' passing from the ranks of the living to the dead.[35] According to Griaule, the village was imperiled by the souls of the dead, who were reluctant to undertake their lonely voyage into the other world. The "end of mourning" (*dama*) celebration honored the dead but also frightened them into leaving.[36] After the chaos introduced by death, the masquerade helped to restore society to equilibrium, to harmony.

In 1946, following a famous series of conversations with the hunter Ogotemmêli, Griaule and his colleague Germaine Dieterlen came to believe that knowledge was carefully regulated in Dogon society: There was "front-speech," open to children and strangers, and "clear speech," which coordinated every aspect of society with an integrated series of myths on the creation of the world. Everything from the layout of a village to the course of stars in the sky, they alleged, could be explained and ordered by Dogon creation stories. Their belief forced a reappraisal of Dogon masquerading because it relegated Griaule's book to the level of public knowledge rather than wisdom acquired by only a handful of initiates.[37] Eventually, in a later publication, Dieterlen argued that the oldest masks hid cryptic references to the myths of creation.[38] For the educated elite men of Dogon society, the spiraling dance of the Kanaga mask "represents the movement imposed upon the universe" by God.[39]

And yet, Dogon people may simply not recognize this arcane cosmogony published by Griaule and Dieterlen after World War II.[40] That was the contention of Walter E. A. Van Beek, a Dutch anthropologist who has spent many months of research working in Dogon country beginning in 1978. Where Dieterlen claimed that Dogon masks were inspired by creation myths, Van Beek insisted that the "crucial element" lay in the "relation between men and women." He was struck by the paradox that so many of the performers wore (false) breasts, hairstyles, jewelry, and skirts of a style worn by young girls, while real women were systematically bullied and kept at a distance (see fig. 2). This is the kind of argument Eric Lott made in regard to blackface. For Van Beek, what the masks attempted to hide—and therefore what they *revealed* to the canny interpreter—was men's envy of women's reproductive abilities.[41]

Given the voluminous literature, it comes as something of a shock to learn that only a minority of Dogon communities have ever masqueraded.[42] Anne Doquet reported this in her 1999 book devoted to *Les masques dogon*, which also supports many of the doubts raised by Van Beek and others concerning the research methods of the Griaule team. In contrast to her predecessors, Doquet stressed the heterogeneity of Dogon practice rather than insisting on its normative structure. No performance is ever identical to another—in this she actually builds on Griaule's earliest description of improvisation in Dogon masquerading.[43]

Doquet is interested more in what the masks reveal than in what they hide even though she appears to draw more from Griaule's field notes than from her own observations or interviews.[44] In his field notes, Griaule documented several conversations with Ogotemmêli. In one exchange, the Dogon elder drew an analogy between the society of masks and "the entire world." When the masqueraders stepped onto the public square, they danced the "step of the world, the system of the world … in color." Taking inspiration from this, Doquet was particularly drawn to the masks deemed inconsequential by others: those representing foreigners and twentieth-century figures such as the police officer, the marabout, the tourist, the ethnographer. "Once [strangers] have appeared in the masked ballet," she writes, "they take their place in the system of the world." The miniaturized world of the masquerade reflected elements appearing as well as disappearing.[45] Although her terms differed, Doquet agreed with Griaule that the masquerade once had been able to restore social harmony by naturalizing change. What she found pathological was that in Sangha—the community serving as the center for ethnographic research—the dancers had once felt compelled to please outsiders by creating an "illusion of permanence" so that the masks could bear *false witness* to a Dogon world untouched by history.[46] In other words, the masks began to conceal what they once revealed.

Government by Mask?

What do masks hide? From the 1950s through the 1980s, the response from the Anglophone literature was that they dissimulate political control to manipulate a gullible public. In 1950, George Harley, a medical missionary with training in anthropology, published a highly influential and well-illustrated text, *Masks as Agents of Social Control in Northeast Liberia*.[47] Although based in a Mano-speaking region in deep forest, Harley also received Dan-speaking traders and was able to purchase 460 masks from both groups between 1930 and 1941.[48] European modernists were particularly attracted to the geometricizing minimalism of sculpture attributed to the Dan in northwest Liberia. The quantity of Harley's collecting from this region, and the resulting publications, sparked the mid-twentieth-century evaluation that Dan masks should be "regarded as the archetypal African mask."[49]

Whereas Griaule appears to have asked, over and over again, what masks represent, Harley made it a practice to inquire about the function of each object presented to him and, by the end, had recorded dozens of uses for masks. One collected bad debts; one sat in front of the house of a man accused of adultery; another "danced" when presenting a new baby to the public (fig. 16). Another accompanied men to war; others patrolled the borders of the boys' initiation camps. Many were entertainers. The list is dizzying in its variety.[50] "In use," Harley concludes, "the gɛ's [masks] exercised all the functions necessary for control of society on the religious, the executive, and the judicial levels."[51]

For his interpretive frame, Harley was inspired by Edward Alsworth Ross, who in 1896 began to publish a series of articles on the subject of "social control" in the *American Journal of Sociology*. Ross was interested in the varied means by which societies "[mold] the individual's feelings and desires to suit the needs of the group," including via the arts of sculpture and painting.[52] He released his study in final form in 1901 as *Social Control: A Survey of the Foundations of Order*, and the text was reprinted at least fifteen times by 1939. The paradigm of social control became a

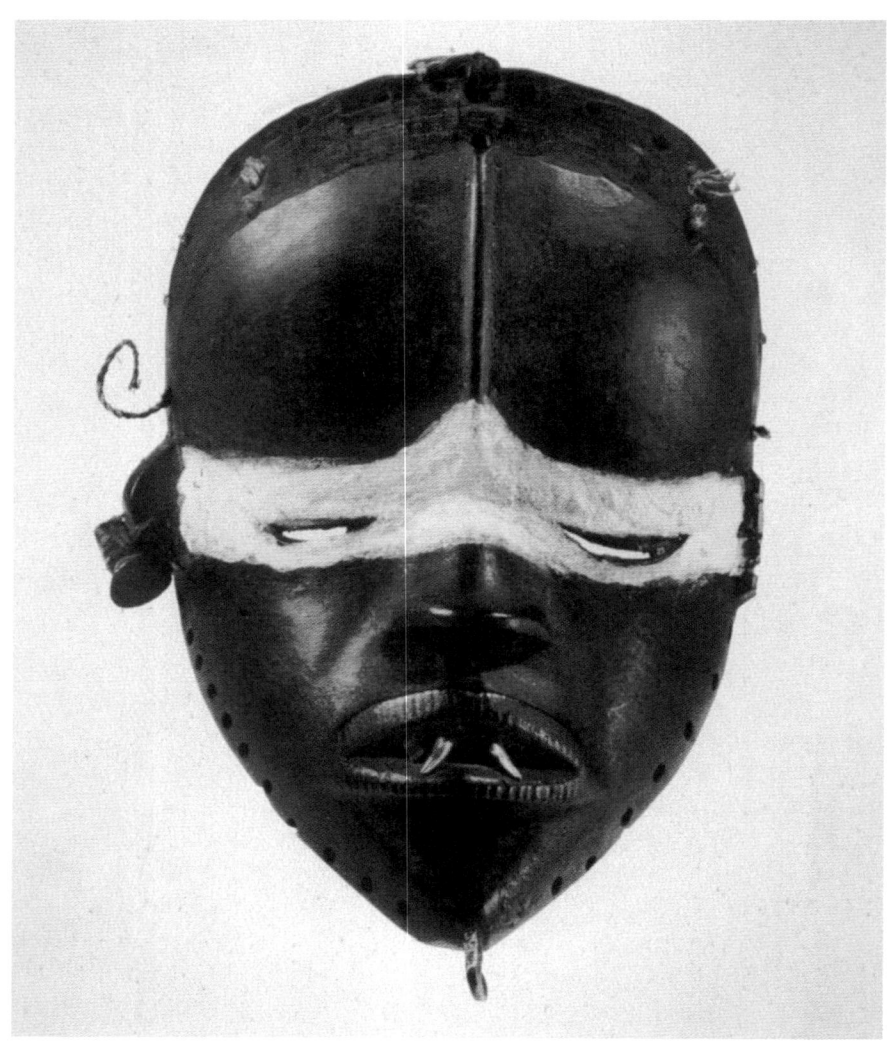

Fig. 16 **Mano mask, collected by George Harley (US American, 1894–1966), artist unrecorded.**
Before 1937, carved wood, black and white pigment, metal, and bone, 8¾ × 6¹¹⁄₁₆ × 3⁵⁄₁₆ in.
The mask accompanied midwives during childbirth.
Cambridge, Peabody Museum of Archaeology and Ethnography, Harvard University.

mainstay of American university courses and sustained three generations of textbooks.[53]

Given how popular the paradigm of social control was in the academy, Harley may well have sought to render African practices *less* exotic by interpreting them through universal sociological principles suitable to the study of American and Liberian artistic practices alike.[54] Harley's most compelling case studies concern masks owned by judges (fig. 17). In his view, these face-to-face communities associated judges with masks in order to displace responsibility onto ancestral spirits for punishments or other actions that might provoke feelings of resentment.[55] However, Harley was conflicted. He recognized that there was duplicity at play and grew uneasy about the idea of the mask "hiding" something. He usually imputed the best intentions to the men he knew but sometimes could not escape a paranoid fear that the masks cloaked a sinister plot for a hereditary clique to control all of Liberia by manipulating gullible villagers through a system of secret but coordinated councils.[56]

Take Zawolo, a Mano chief, judge, and healer. He laid out a mask beside him when he presided over trials in concert with the elder men in his community. When they had reached consensus, "Zawolo would uncover the mask, call it by name, and review the case, telling the mask: 'We have decided so and so. We want to know if you agree with our decision.'" He then threw dice to learn the decision of the ancestors, a decision that was final. Harley the doctor had a good relationship with Zawolo, whom he respected as a "physician, specializing in stomach troubles." Familiarity granted insight: Harley wrote that his friend knew how to throw the dice to get the answer he wanted, as Zawolo was too good-hearted to leave important matters to chance.[57]

Harley was crystal clear that it was men who pulled the strings behind the masks, but the influential art historian Roy Sieber reversed the equation: It was masks who controlled the people. Where Harley had focused on northeast Liberia, Sieber picked up the phrase "social control" in 1962 and helped make it the predominant theory for masquerading across much of Africa for the following two decades. Quoting long passages from Harley's text on judicial masks, Sieber briefly examined practices in three other societies and concluded that "this list of examples could be extended considerably, for nearly every African mask functioned within

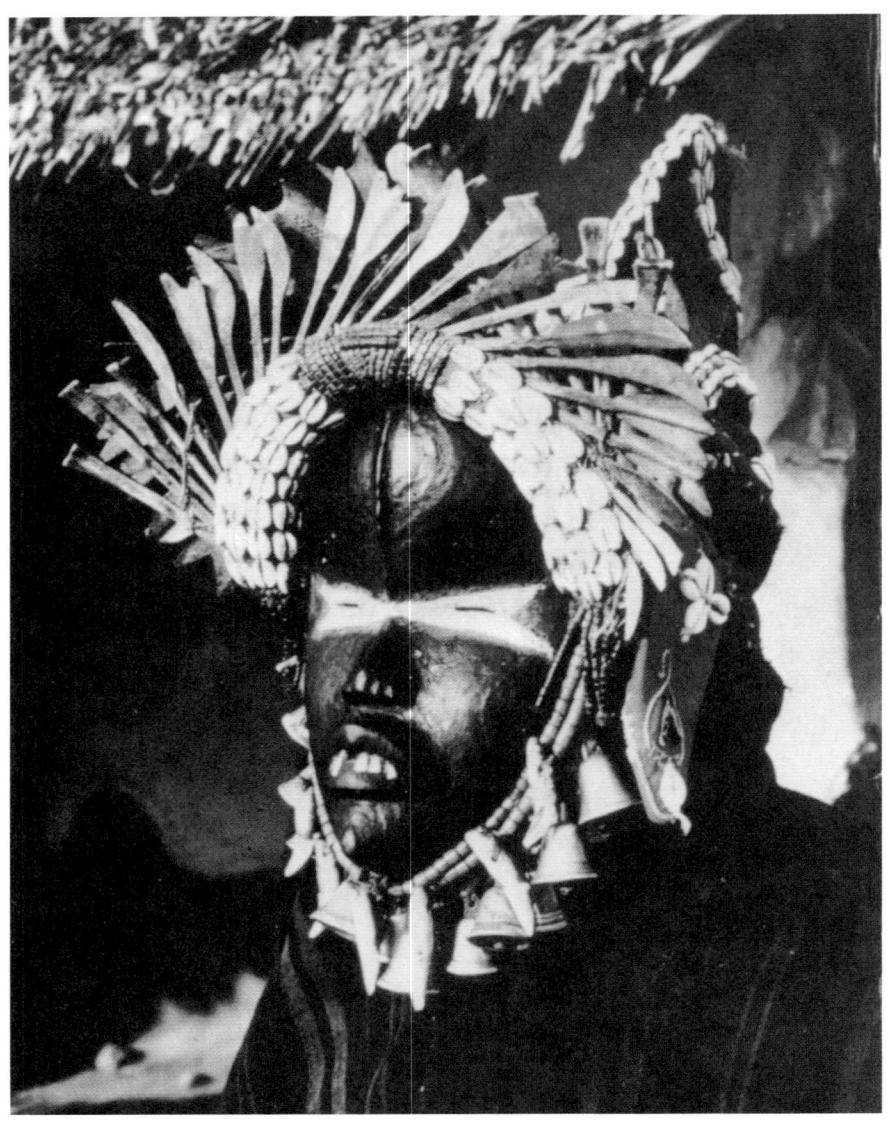

Fig. 17 **Dan peoples.**
Gaa-Wree-Wre, a judge's mask.
Liberia, 1962.
Photo by Robert Farris Thompson.

a value context relating in some degree to the direction or control of human actions."[58] When Sieber recounted Harley's experience with Zawolo, he censored the admission that, thanks to the way the dice were thrown, the chief and judge could rig omens in such a way as to back up the council's decisions. In Sieber's text, thanks to the powers of belief, it is the masks themselves that act even to execute criminals "almost through a form of remote control." Sieber excused the loss of human agency by contextualizing the use of masks in a drive for survival and well-being.[59]

For Anglophone researchers, the model of social control integrated localized fieldwork-based studies into a comparative framework. Nonetheless, after reviewing a literature of 174 case studies, Leon Siroto concluded that the premise of "government by mask" outstripped the evidence and was biased in favor of "what masks should do or what they are wished to do, rather than what they really do."[60] In particular, Siroto rejected any claim that masks were "concerned exclusively with stability."[61] His own field research documented the precolonial history of masks among Kwele peoples (Gabon). In bids for power, individuals and lineages could send a masked champion named "Gon" to represent them at war games. The designated warrior blackened his body with charcoal and wore little else apart from a sculpted headpiece modeled on the skull of an adult male gorilla as he threw spears at all and sundry. Ahead of its time in tracing a long history for a mask of any kind, Siroto's text argued that the social control literature was also flawed by its presentism, which disguised the possibility of masks serving as implements of change in political culture.[62]

Harley's thesis has cast a long shadow on interpretations of masquerading in the region, given that any sociological function can be reconfigured toward social control.[63] Without question, the blockbuster exhibition *African Art in Motion* (1974), with its accompanying catalog, broadcast the most poetic gloss on Harley's interpretation of Dan cultural practices.[64] Basing his analysis on field research conducted in 1967, Robert Farris Thompson praised Dan elders for eschewing "brute authority" to administer "social control through artistic and philosophic means, through a cult of masks."[65] He witnessed the renowned judge Gaa-Wree-Wre preside over a solemn trial with a facepiece composed with "feminine calm of countenance" but also with leopard's teeth to grip the issue at hand (see fig. 17). Gaa-Wree-Wre walked with short steps, bells clanging, swaying its massive skirt, before settling on the earth.[66] Thompson combined visual analysis of face masks and costumes with inspired dance criticism. Defining Dan masks as "motion essays," he contrasted the gravitas of the judge's comportment with, for example, that of Kao Gle, who "[probed] the strength of the social fabric" as he moved through the community with the "syncopic, violent" gestures reminiscent of an enraged chimpanzee.[67] Despite reaching a heretofore unprecedented audience for an African art exhibition, Thompson's methodology of relating the masks to each other, rather than studying them in isolation, and of engaging masked dance as a form of philosophical expression would not be followed up on for decades.[68]

As the Dogon literature shows, if one scholar depicts masks "hiding," those following will often stress what the masks "reveal." Returning to Harley's material in 1986, M. C. Jedrej flipped the terms and argued that the judges' masks exposed far more than they disguised. In his words, they "do not conceal or mask the locus of political authority but, on the contrary, serve to identify precisely those with authority." He makes the point that in three of Harley's examples, the judges laid the mask beside them as an emblem of office. In another case, the judge was dressed by the elders and appeared only in front of the elders. Far from dissimulating who was in control, "ownership of the 'big masks' reinforced and validated the authority of particular chiefs."[69]

Wrestling with the legacy of the social control hypothesis, the ethnomusicologist Daniel Reed works with Dan-speaking people in Côte d'Ivoire and the United States. Even as he has documented a vibrant world of creativity, interpretational diversity, and historical change, he broadly accepts Harley's argument that Ge (the masked figure) served a "historical role as a means of local social control. Ge in performance defines and reinforces Dan patriarchy, for example, providing a deep spiritual rational for male control and domination.… Ge also provides a religious base for local political power."[70] He gave as an example a masquerader crashing into him so that he would learn to do what he was told.[71] By contrast, Monni Adams asked, "Who is controlling whom?" Her research among neighboring Wè in Côte d'Ivoire suggested that *it is the audience* that attempts to "control" dangerous forest spirits through the masks with strategies including (as mentioned above) women seducing acclaimed dancers.[72]

Social control is a unique English-language theory of masquerading drawn from African source material, and as such it periodically reemerges in comparative studies, reaching even from the social sciences into the performing arts. In a disappointing expression of primitivism, the theater giant Richard Schechner hypothesized that "human and animal performances converge," including "on a cultural level where performances are means of social control, providing avenues for the discharge of aggression or providing ways of mobilizing people either to maintain or change a social order."[73] Synthesizing African mask theory with ethology, Schechner interpreted choreographed displays of violence as a means to enforce or transform social hierarchies for political purposes.

Art historians such as Sieber and Thompson attempted to avoid the pejorative tone of the majority of texts relying on the social control hypothesis. Babatunde Lawal contributed to this legacy in his 1996 study of Yoruba Gèlèdé masquerading. Specifically, Lawal attempted to salvage social control by shifting it away from violence and toward an ideal of "social harmony."[74] He situates the arts within the Yoruba concept of Ìfogbóntáayése, using wisdom "to ensure peace and concord on Earth." As Lawal concluded, "since Gèlèdé is primarily concerned with the promotion of social harmony and the avoidance of the use of force to settle human differences and problems, its lessons bear a universal relevance."[75]

Masks sometimes play a role in politics.[76] However important a topic, the role of masks in political culture cannot be forced into one mold. Where social control theorists have been primarily interested in the top-down application of power, a growing body of literature mines masquerade history for responses to political and social dysfunction. I have argued elsewhere that tracing the history of mask inventions can reveal a good deal about the experience of both colonial and postcolonial oppression.[77]

Authors interested in class conflict often turn to Bakhtin's model of the carnivalesque to examine popular culture for evidence of what has been censored by official histories. In a seductive Bakhtinian analysis of the sumptuous masquerade culture of the Oku Kingdom of Cameroon, Nicolas Argenti sought to expose ongoing political violence (see fig. 32). According to his exegesis, the play of pleasure and panic experienced by youths in palace masquerades "reveals to its victims the spectacle of the naked coercion at the heart of palatine hegemony, even as it masks it."[78]

Meanwhile, village masks "reveal what the palace dance obscures and dissimulates.... [They] reveal the connection between the line of masks and the slave caravan that is obfuscated in the separate palace performances."[79] Similar to Lott on blackface, Argenti is the theorist who unveils what the practitioners themselves have repressed: Oku performers "unmask" the trauma of slavery and colonial forced labor and its impact on the present—despite the blockage of "cognitive memories" of past horrors.[80] Notwithstanding the shift away from engaging Harley directly, the dialectical struggle between masks hiding or revealing important truths persists. To evaluate such interpretations, it is germane to ask whether the mask exists as a metaphor for deceit in the relevant African languages.

Chapter 3
Masks Transform?

The Psychology of the Performer

A third option to the long-lived propositions that masks either disguise or expose hidden truths began to gain traction around 1900. By midcentury, no less a luminary than Mircea Eliade proclaimed, "Whether ritual, funerary, or for any spectacle, the mask is an instrument of ecstasy. He who wears one is no longer himself…. He becomes 'other,' even when the mask is his own portrait."[1] According to Eliade, the performer experiences a transformation because he (and it almost always was a he) became a stranger *to himself* as well as to the spectators. In 1988, the historian of religion Henry Pernet was the first to question the obsessive interest of theorists in the psychology of the performer, a seismic shift that he attributed to the impact of psychoanalysis and the popular literature on totemism.[2]

Alas, what may have appeared to be a fresh perspective turns out to have a long, and even sinister, genealogy. During the Middle Ages, for ten centuries, the hierarchy of the Catholic Church opposed masquerades, although it was never able to eradicate them from folk culture (fig. 18).[3] Clerics condemned masks because men had been created in the image of God (Genesis 1:26) and therefore had no business imitating anything else. According to the medievalist Jean-Claude Schmitt, the Church may have considered it perverse for men to disguise themselves as women or animals, but it outright feared masks because they could "induce a real transformation of the subject: *transformatio, transmutatio, transfiguratio.*" It would be the violation of one's very self, modeled on the very

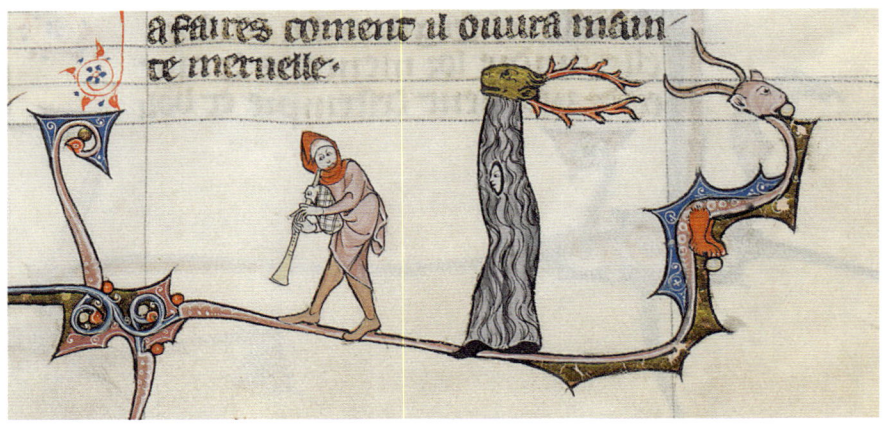

Fig. 18　**Detail of marginalia from a medieval French manuscript showing a bagpipe player leading a stag's mask.**
To counter the hostility of the Church, the artist is careful to depict the performer peeping out, thus showing that "concealment has no place in the meaning of the mask" (Jean-Claude Schmitt, "Les masques, le diable, les morts," in *Le corps, les rites, les rêves, le temps* [Gallimard, 2001], 224). From Robert de Boron, *L'Estoire de Merlin,* thirteenth century, Ms. Fr 95, folio 261r, v°. Paris, Bibliothèque nationale de France.

worst: the devil was the "Mask par excellence, the Great Deceiver"—and his minions, both demons and sorcerers, could make use of his powers of transformation to wreak havoc.[4]

Although the pejorative view of masks remains deeply ingrained, it is confounding to observe that the dread of transformation vanishes—poof!—in the twentieth century. In fact, European modernists became enchanted by the possibility of transformation or metamorphosis, which may have been made possible by the dwindling fear of witchcraft in the second half of the nineteenth century.[5] In 1902, Émile Durkheim and Marcel Mauss argued that stories about metamorphoses were found around the world and, for the least-evolved peoples, they speculated that "the individual himself loses his personality." Here the social scientists drew on the ethnographies of Walter Baldwin Spencer and Francis James

Gillen among the Arrernte (Arunta) of Australia and Karl von den Steinen among the Bororo of Brazil, pointing to a collapsing of the "exterior soul" and the individual's "totem": "He and his 'fellow-animal' together compose a single personality.... The Bororo sincerely imagines himself to be a parrot."[6] Note the emphasis on sincerity. By appropriating von den Steinen's famous formulation about the Bororo, Durkheim and Mauss were able to argue that transformation is predicated upon extinction of human personality. The authenticity of that metamorphosis is guaranteed by the genuineness of belief.

Believing or not believing that masks were spirits became one of the criteria authors developed for distinguishing between a "modern" and "primitive" subjectivity.[7] Lucien Lévy-Bruhl, the notorious philosopher of the "primitive mind," weighed in, nuancing the discussion somewhat differently. Writing in 1910 and pulling from many of the same sources as Durkheim and Mauss, Lévy-Bruhl interpreted the relationship of man to tiger as one of "mystic participation" and believed that "ecstasy" was achieved when "the fusion between subject and object has become complete."[8] Theories like this, seeking to explain totemism and "prelogical mentality," were transferred almost instantaneously to masquerade. Carl Einstein picked them up in *Negerplastik* (1915), writing that the masquerader loses all sense of self when he "dances ecstatically for the tribe, and he transforms himself through the mask into the tribe and the god."[9] Such confusion is the mark of a "primitive," whereas "for us" masks are tools of "deception, pretense"—or so reads Eckart von Sydow's influential book, *Die Kunst der Naturvölker und der Vorzeit* (1923). For "primitives," the image does not play the role of a symbol, nor a representation: "The mask is the spirit."[10] Returning to the subject in 1931, Lévy-Bruhl echoed von Sydow, emphasizing the realness of transformation in order to disentangle masks from deceit: "To put on a mask is not, as for us, a simple disguise under which the individual remains what he is. *It is to submit to a real transformation.*"[11] Pernet warned his readers that numerous intellectuals have taken up Lévy-Bruhl's "hypothesis" of "actual transformation" (often without knowing the source) and that the position is "hardly conceivable other than in terms of the existence of a 'mentality' different from ours."[12]

Twentieth-century philosophers, dramatists, cultural critics, art historians, and social scientists relied on their beliefs in the power of other

people's beliefs,[13] increasingly turning to the phenomenon of possession—the penetration of the body by spirit—to guarantee the authenticity
of the mask in Africa. Georges Buraud was a pivotal figure who reinter-
preted Lévy-Bruhl's model of "mystic participation" through a Freudian
understanding of the unconscious and instinctual drives.[14] His treatise *Les
masques* (1948) won the Prix des Critiques, and its literary (some might say
florid) style captured a distinguished readership, including André Breton
and Gaston Bachelard. From his armchair, Buraud imagined the masquerader undergoing a thorough metamorphosis:

> He no longer knows himself, a monstrous cry escapes his throat, the
> cry of a beast or a god, a superhuman outcry, a pure emanation of
> battle force, of creative passion, of boundless magic power by which
> he believes himself—by which he is, in this moment—possessed.[15]

Buraud's masculinist vision of creative rapture transfixed dramatists such
as Jacques Copeau and Jean-Louis Barrault, who advocated that actors
could profit from masks to transform themselves fundamentally and truth-
fully into their roles.[16] In a paroxysm of theatrical primitivism, Barrault
sought inspiration in Afro-Brazilian Candomblé to restage the *Oresteia*
in 1955, seeking to release instinctual energies to renew his art, parroting
Buraud: "Beneath the mask one is no longer oneself."[17] All this rendered
the Marxist critic Roland Barthes apoplectic, and in 1958 he lampooned
the "myth" that the best actors were "possessed" by their roles, experiencing a deep psychological metamorphosis. Working within the logic of
primitivism, he could accept that archaic Greek actors might have sought
transcendence but rejected the idea that *modern* actors, working in a "desa-
cralized society," could ever experience anything similar. Those actors who
seemed to believe that they could were complicit in a capitalist mystifica-
tion that justified paying them less than a living wage.[18]

Barthes's reservations aside, Buraud captured the attention of
Roger Caillois and Mircea Eliade, two influential cultural theorists with
an interest in ethnography who would popularize the transformation
hypothesis. In 1958, Caillois cited Buraud's monstrous-possession passage
to postulate that putting on a mask triggers possession during which the
"wearer is temporarily exalted and made to believe that he is undergoing

some decisive transformation" (in his own eyes as well as in the eyes of others).[19] Or, Caillois would have us believe, at least masks have this effect in Africa under the influence of the "hypnotic beat of the tom-tom."[20] Under these conditions, according to Caillois's theory of mimicry, "simulation results in a possession that is not simulated."[21] The loss of self is dangerous but has the potential to transform the individual and his society through the release of creative energy. Inspired by Lévy-Bruhl and Buraud, Eliade advocated for a universalizing interpretation of the mask. Even in secular performances, "the mask is an instrument of ecstasy. He who wears one is no longer himself."[22] The explosive popularity of Caillois and Eliade in the 1960s ensured that the frenzied possession of the masquerader became fact for many.

Interestingly enough, although Buraud, Caillois, and others were supposedly inspired in part by African practices, the transformation hypothesis only began to appear regularly in Africanist literature in the mid-1980s,[23] popularized by Herbert Cole's modest classroom exhibition catalog, *I Am Not Myself*. Cole writes that speakers of English suggest that "by means of mask and costume a spirit is represented. This is not the African attitude.... The masker, the wearer who is now 'ridden' or imbued by the spirit, also believes in his own new and altered state. His personal character and behavior are modified, fused with those of the spirit he creates and becomes. Human individuality is lifted from him. He is not himself."[24] Cole's insistence on the masquerader's belief in his own metamorphosis betrays a nagging anxiety that masks may lie. Cole invokes possession to guarantee the mask's truthfulness. The photograph on the cover of the catalog made his interpretation graphic by illustrating a close-up of a masquerader with white-rimmed, staring eyes and dilated pupils against a black background.[25] By the late 1980s, the field had reached such a fever pitch that Edward Lifschitz recommended getting rid of the term *masking* altogether and speaking only of "spirit manifestation."[26]

As Pernet wrote, there are so many well-documented alternatives to the transformation hypothesis that it is puzzling to put it forward as the only possible interpretation of the lived experience of the performer.[27] In DR Congo, interlocutors such as Khoshi Mahumbu, Malenge Mundugu Mukhokho, and Masuwa Léon all pushed me to acknowledge dancers as the inventors of masks. The dancers I subsequently interviewed unanimously explained that they were seeking fame and emphasized their role in generating a new "idea" but also in supervising a collaborative process during which a master sculptor, drummers, and sometimes singers joined together to achieve their vision.[28] These men were singularly uninterested in discussing the experience of wearing a face mask. When pressed, they complained that it was stifling hot, hard to see, hard to breathe, easy to develop headaches—in short, oppressive. Those who felt discomfort with face coverings during the COVID-19 pandemic of 2020–21 will understand immediately what they meant. I have never heard a Pende performer say that he enjoyed wearing a mask or felt "free," even when he sought renown and adulation. Sometimes if the character has a fearsome persona, performers would report experiencing anxiety. Among the Eastern Pende, where the religious context for masquerade was still strong in the late 1980s, possession was the last thing that organizers wished to have happen during masquerades, and they stopped it cold on the two occasions when an audience member began to show signs of susceptibility.

It is the equation of African masquerade with spirit possession that has lent credibility to the transformation hypothesis.[29] For this reason, despite the risk of rendering African masquerade exotic, the subject cannot be avoided.

Transformation and Spirit Possession: Let's Get Literal

By stressing belief, researchers fell into a quandary first posed by Leo Frobenius: Do Africans really believe that the masks are spirits? And if so, why? Is there any way to make their belief comprehensible to outsiders?[30] In 1988, Sidney L. Kasfir proclaimed that masquerade and spirit possession in Africa were the same thing: a "vehicle for the process of transformation."[31] However, only a few researchers with requisite skills have probed the issue, with contradictory results. Writing about Bobo funerary masks in Burkina Faso, Lisa Homann found that her field associates were more concerned with individual agency: They "have never used the language of 'manifestation,' nor have they given me the impression that daytime masks 'manifest,' via transformation, any divinity."[32] Jordan A. Fenton conducted an in-depth investigation on this topic in Calabar, Nigeria, by interviewing the masqueraders themselves. Each insisted,

"I know myself," rejecting any suggestion that they were possessed or transformed by their ancestors.[33]

Conversely, when Kenji Yoshida investigated this question with regard to Chewa conceptions in Eastern Zambia, he came to the conclusion that "masking, spirit possession and sorcery are all, in some sense, considered as means of transformation of humans into animals."[34] He was struck by the fact that the same term, *u-sanduka,* was applied in all three contexts to mark "any change of visible state" associated with metamorphosis.[35] However, Yoshida also identified some important phenomenological distinctions. According to his Chewa interlocutors, the spirit medium (*mgwetsa*) loses consciousness and hosts an animal inside herself even as she remains human in appearance. By contrast, the Nyau masker remains fully conscious and "human inside" even if animal-like in appearance. Only the sorcerer is presumed to fuse inside heart and outside appearance, with unknown repercussions for his state of consciousness.[36] Yoshida comes closest to supporting Sidney Kasfir's position, and yet his in-depth analysis of the different states of consciousness experienced by maskers and mediums or sorcerers adds complexity and nuance that goes well beyond Kasfir's all-encompassing model.

When von Sydow, Lévy-Bruhl, and other early theorists asserted that for Africans "the mask is the spirit of the dead," they were relying on the reports of (often unidentified) travelers with imperfect language skills. And yet, this statement has become the single most common form of evidence offered by scholars in support of the transformation hypothesis. First, a warning is justified when attempting a study of "masks" in an intercultural space: English has more words than any other language on Earth. French comes second and German is a distant third. Any comparative study of "masks" relies on hosts of translators to make interpretations about what exactly is being said. Among the Pende in DR Congo, where I have been researching since the late 1980s, it is not unusual for someone to answer the question "What is a mask?" (*mbuya, ye'itshi?*) by saying "*Mbuya, hamba,*" which some might translate as "the mask is the spirit of the dead." However, it is important to note that the verb "to be" is dropped, which opens a host of interpretive possibilities. The mask *is* the spirit of the dead. It *represents* a spirit of the dead. It *embodies* a spirit of the dead. Or, as I concluded after two years' study, it is a *tool* for contacting the dead.[37]

At its simplest, the term *mbuya* can denote wooden facepieces that cover the faces of the dancers. It also applies to carvings that sit on top of the head or slant down the forehead so that the performer can see and breathe more freely (see fig. 1). More commonly, though, in speech *mbuya* refers to the entire persona created including the dance, music, song, costume, and any headpiece. Movement is an essential part of developing a persona. This is why the sculptor Gistshiola Léon upbraided my obtuseness one day, insisting, "You can't just invent a [face] mask, you need a dance!" The term also extends very naturally to what some would call "puppets" in the West: whirling barrels and large models of people or animals activated by visible performers who pull strings to move various body parts.

To make matters even more complicated, the answer to the question "What is a mask?" (*mbuya, ye'itshi?*) will also depend on who's asking, who's answering, and whoever else may be in earshot. For example, in Zambia, Elisabeth L. Cameron asked a Lunda woman named Maria in private to define the term *makishi*. "She said, 'It is a man wearing a costume trying to cheat us.'" When Cameron looked surprised, Maria laughed, insisting, "[the men] try to trick us." Later, Cameron was inspired to ask Maria the same question in front of a man. Maria responded "with a straight face that it was the spirit of the dead [*makishi*] come back from the grave."[38] A public secret "can be defined *as that which is generally known, but cannot be articulated.*"[39] Maria saying one thing in private and another in public replays a dynamic often noted in masquerade studies.

An example of the public secret in the United States centers on Santa Claus. When I was growing up, no newscaster pronounced, "There is no Santa Claus! He doesn't exist! He's a man in a red suit!" Instead, broadcasters regularly announced in December that children would be able to meet Santa Claus at a given shopping mall and convey to him their hopes for Christmas gifts. Many children learned the truth from other children. I recall the name of the girl who told me on the playground, where she was standing, what she was wearing. I remember the stab of loss and still resent her for it. A friend remembers tackling her older sister and beating her mercilessly when she told her about Santa Claus, in the hopes of making her recant. The anthropologist Michael Taussig, on the other hand, became the tattletale. He also has a vivid memory of the moment when he was hospitalized as a child—"like pulling a rip cord, like a flash of lightning"—when he overheard a nurse identify Santa Claus as a doctor on the ward, provoking Taussig to "[bellow] for all to hear: 'Hey kids! It's not Santa Claus! It's Doctor Jones!'" He credited his painful recollection of the resulting brouhaha as the spark for his own adult interest in the public secret.[40] Following lectures to the public, some audience members have taken umbrage at my comparing a secular, even "trivial," pastime to a "ritual," but even a secular practice can produce intense memories, as demonstrated by my own and Taussig's experiences with Santa Claus and by the opening story about the little girl discovering that Saint Nikolaus had her father's hands.

The equation with spirit possession is a second reason for the tenacity of the transformation hypothesis in the African literature.[41] In a foundational text of ethnomusicology, Gilbert Rouget defined trance as "an altered, transitory state of consciousness" having both "psycho-physiological" and cultural dimensions.[42] Rouget distinguishes three types of what he calls mystic trance. In the first, "possession in the strict sense of the word," the subject loses a sense of self and acts with the person-ality and capabilities of a controlling force, whether "god, spirit, genius, or ancestor."[43] In his influential text *I Am Not Myself* (discussed above), Herbert Cole invokes the conditions outlined by Rouget for possession and insists on the alienation of the masked performer's identity.[44] In Rouget's second category of trance, the dominating force "coexists in some way with the subject but nevertheless controls him and causes him to act and speak in its name." The third category is described as "communion" and "does not involve embodiment of any kind."[45] Some scholars accept a narrow list of cross-cultural universals in trance experience, including the "loss of sense of self, cessation of inner language, and an extraordinary ability to withstand fatigue."[46] Increasingly, scholars accept that there is a spectrum of trance experience extending beyond shamanic or possession rituals to include the "trance of the performer who feels herself to be one with the music she plays; the mild trance of the listener whose whole atten-tion becomes focused on the music."[47]

There are substantiated cases of African masks associated with Rouget's "possession in the strict sense of the word," but they are far less common than Cole hypothesized. The Kalabari are one of the most cited groups. In 1963, Robin Horton documented that Ekine society masquerades were associated with one or more water spirits. These spirit entities received invocations and offerings on the evening before staging a "play" and were usually said to be "walking with" the dancers. However, the spirits' proximity to the dancer could lead to a state "where people say that they have actually possessed their dancers."[48] When interviewed in 2006 and 2008, Horton provided some clarifications. Having conducted decades of field research in the delta of Nigeria, he explained that possession was not welcome and that Kalabari would only go so far as to say that "the spirit climbed on top of the dancer" for certain masks, maybe six out of thirty or more, and only occasionally. It was presumed to happen regularly for no more than one or two. When I asked what it means to say that "a spirit climbed on him," Horton explained that "the dancer feels a force greater than his own." The same vocabulary is used for spirit mediums. When the spirit "enters the head" (or leg) of the masquerader, spectators are warned to be prudent because possessed dancers are prone to violence and they cannot be held accountable for their actions. Horton himself had a near miss when the mask Agiri threw a wooden spear at him.[49] Possession is not a goal for performers, although it occurs in a small percentage of the corpus.[50]

A similar ambivalence exists in Calabar (the capital of Cross River State, Nigeria). Arguing that innovations represent an "expressive currency" with commercial relevance, Jordan A. Fenton documented the addition of skulls or other skeletal remains on Nnabo society masks. The performers are known for "mystical bravado" because, following sacrificial offerings, "the skulls are 'gingered' or encouraged to haunt the performer." It is the performer's challenge to "channel the threatening forces into a greater performance." However, as Edem Nyong Etim observed in 2009, "sometimes you can dance it and it carries you off." On the rare occasions when Fenton witnessed Nnabo performers buckling under the pressure, they fell or "unleashed havoc onto the audience," with the result that their confreres hustled them out of sight to recover. Fenton admits that he cannot say for sure whether such events are choreographed or the result of exhaustion, but he does know that *they permanently damage the reputation of the performer.*[51] The possibility of possession increases the stakes for the performer but is neither common nor particularly welcome.

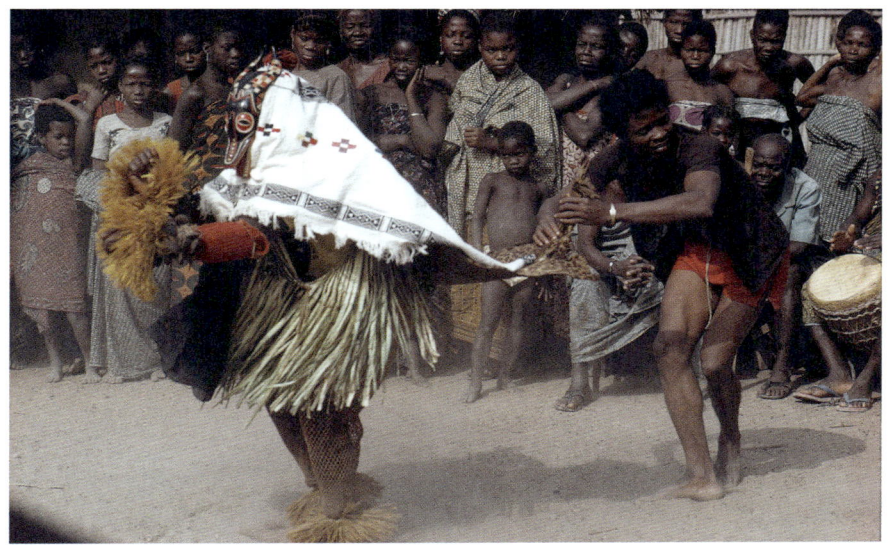

Fig. 19 **Guro mask Zamble performing in Tibeita,**
Côte d'Ivoire, 1975.
Photo by Eberhard Fischer.

The most searching study to date of trance in African masked dance concludes that "trances associated with masks are rare and difficult to categorize." Inspired by Rouget, Anne-Marie Bouttiaux considers trance associated with masks—when it occurs—to belong to an "intermediate" position on a spectrum. There may be an understanding that a spirit makes use of the body of a performer, but the relationship entails neither the loss of consciousness and amnesia associated with classic possession trances nor the sense of an out-of-body voyage common to shamanic rituals.[52] Drawing on her own in-depth research with dancers in Côte d'Ivoire (1994–2002, 2009), Bouttiaux explains that Northern Guro associate a handful of masks out of a large corpus with spiritual entities convoked when sacrifices are made on dedicated altars, which facilitates the transfer of their "powers … to masks during performances."[53] This possibility renders performance dangerous and the dancer larger than life because he runs "considerable risks by measuring himself against supernatural forces for the very panache and beauty of the gesture."[54] One of most famous is Zamble (fig. 19). Performers for Zamble undergo lengthy preparations. They follow a demanding regime of fasting, celibacy, and intense physical training designed to improve speed, precision, stamina, and flexibility.[55] They definitely do not lose consciousness—"they have to be there"—but many do report feeling lightheaded (disembodied) as they seek to move with a speed and suppleness that hardly seems humanly possible.[56]

On videotape footage, Zamble appears almost to levitate, as the performer holds his body immobile while executing chains of blistering, quick, alternating footsteps, causing the audience to explode, clapping, cheering, and crisscrossing the dance floor, the transfer of energy from performer to spectator being too intense for anyone to stand still. One might presume that the experience of Zamble's dancers conforms to Rouget's second category of mystic trance during which the spirit inspires the devotee to exceptional prowess. But on the contrary, it is *the dancer* who lends his sculpted and well-trained body to the spirit.[57] Zamble dancers are identified and may even flash their faces at the audience.[58] During the intense, athletic competitions for which the Guro are famous, "the *individual* is judged and not the spiritual entity that inhabits his body." When different performers dance the same mask, it is their technique that is compared.[59]

It is dangerous to assume that the relatively rare cases of trance comprise the purest, most authentic, most important cases of masking and that all others represent a debased practice. Most societies employ masks for different purposes. As dynamic as Zamble is, Guro have other categories of masks that also arouse intense emotions. The artists' associations sponsor performers who seek "lasting fame."[60] As of 2009, the most celebrated Guro mask was Gyela lu Zauli (Daughter of Zauli), which attracted a national audience for its appearances (fig. 20).[61] Although masks like Gyela lu Zauli are not typically associated with trance or supernatural beings, the performers' flair and technical virtuosity inspire a "cult of personality" such that they carry amulets to protect themselves from jealous competitors.[62]

Claims about transformation are entangled in affirmations of faith. I follow Carlos Fausto in "setting aside the 'problem of belief.'" Belief is too easily confused with doctrine articulated and policed by Christian

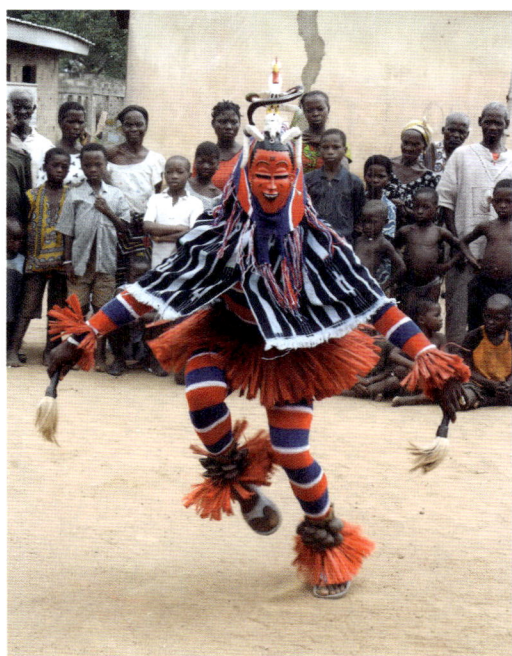

Fig. 20 **Zamble bi Gyè Nestor dancing the Guro mask Gyela lu Zauli.**
Manfla, Côte d'Ivoire, 2009.
Photo by Zoro bi Irié.

and Muslim institutions that not only list what should be believed but also have theories on how to make people believe.[63] Even rituals intended to promote belief wrestle with skepticism and doubt.[64] They encourage reflexivity, defined by Carlo Severi "as a way for ritual action to pose the problem of the definition of its own meaning and effectiveness within the context of ritual communication."[65] By setting aside questions about belief, the viewer is invited to see the *body in the mask,* and this process may provoke reflection on the nature and efficacy of masquerade's ritual propositions. At the very least, it permits viewers to perceive the role of individuals in galvanizing audiences through their creativity, raw talent, and physical prowess.[66]

According to Richard Schechner, a "sliding scale of involvement" is built into many rituals so that spectators have opportunities to lose focus as they muse about an image or gesture and reflect on what they have just experienced. Seeking ideas to reform avant-garde theater, Schechner came to appreciate how "through selective inattention spectators cocreate the work with the performer.... In a real way the spectators become artists."[67] There is even a physical dimension. An audience member's shifting focus will stimulate eye movements, which render the experience psychologically dynamic. African masquerades invite collaboration by periodically breaking the illusion so that viewers become conscious of human appendages or agency. Another strategy is to make use of an episodic organization of the event, which encourages the crowd to change position in order to follow the action. Historically, in the late nineteenth century and throughout the twentieth century, very few African masquerades were structured as narratives to be consumed from a seated position.

Most of the time, scholars bypass the tainted genealogy of totemism to engage transformation as a metaphor for creative change, whether political, sociocultural, artistic, or psychological.[68] After a review of the West African literature, Elizabeth Tonkin concludes that "empirically too not all Masks are ancestors or spirits to their audiences. We should look rather to the feature that I think they all ultimately share: they all entail a transformation."[69] In her view, the central paradox of masquerading is that "two images are combined to make a new single being."[70] Drawing on Marcel Mauss (rather than Caillois and Eliade), Tonkin does not deny the consciousness of the performer, instead framing masquerade as "metaphors-in-action" that embody philosophical propositions on personhood and power.[71] Ultimately, she agrees with George Lakoff and Mark Johnson (discussed in chapter 1) that we think through metaphors, which can effect transformational social change.[72]

A lingering problem for transformation theory is that even as a metaphor it overinscribes permanence. It rips one moment out of an ongoing process of exchange between performers and spectators. If Tonkin argues that in masking, two become one, I would say not for long! Tonkin accepts that the paradoxical content of masquerade practice, the contradictions that it presents, are essential to its interpretation. The paradoxes that she highlights trigger strong feelings, all the more so because they are embodied. However, writing in 1979, she operates under a strict separation of cognitive and emotional domains that is no longer justifiable.

Chapter 4
How Do Masks Make You Feel?

A beautiful mask, a beautiful poem, is one which produces in the
public the emotion aimed at: sadness, joy, hilarity, terror.

—Léopold Sédar Senghor, 1956[1]

As it turns out, African masqueraders have something in common with
German philosophers: an interest in aesthetic emotions, which are the feelings that arise while viewing or listening to a work of art. For their part, US
Americans often convey their expectations that music should process and
negotiate the emotions. Some genres are named after particular melan-
cholic textures, like the blues. Military marches are associated with feelings
of patriotism. The exercise industry harnesses music to help the health-
conscious feel peppy and able to do more than they ever thought possible.
Classical opera is still in part dedicated to the processing of death. And,
moving beyond music, both artists and scientists are asking which emotions are associated with the visual arts.[2]

Igbo artists in Nigeria have invested time and skill in producing
beauty so that, as the artist and art historian Chike Aniakor wrote, an
"art object becomes in the eyes of Igbo a thing of wonder *olua di ebube,*
even amazement or literally instils in one, fear mixed with wonder *olua
di egwu.*"[3] Herein lies the challenge. Aniakor associated a single aesthetic
judgment—beauty—with an entire range of emotions: marvel, astonishment, fear mixed with wonder. Beauty in many West and Central African
languages is associated conceptually with goodness, efficacy, and the

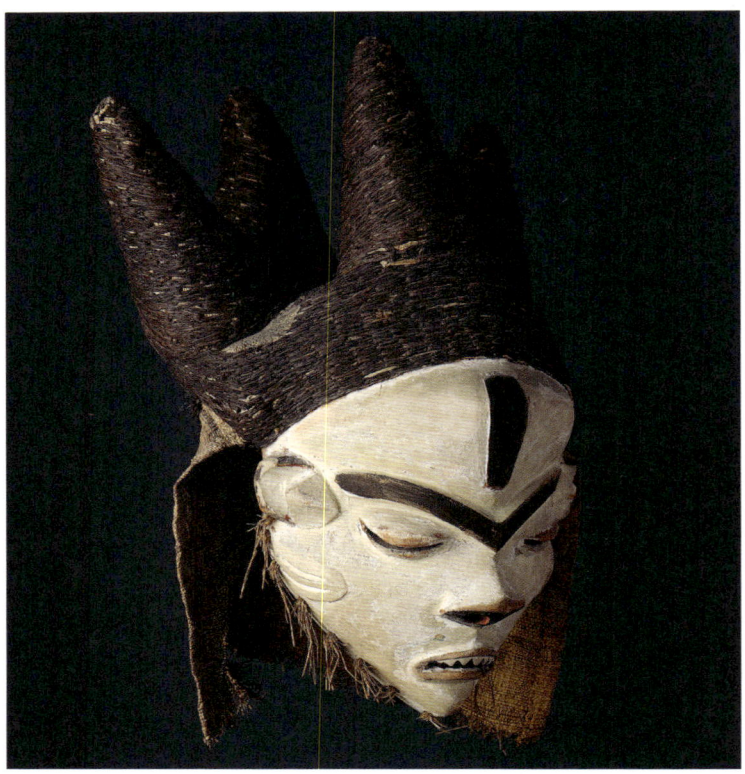

Fig. 21 **Attributed to the Central Pende artist Maluba (d. ca. 1935).**
Pulugunzu mask.
Nioka-Munene, DR Congo, ca. 1930.
The William Rubin Collection. Courtesy of Phyllis Hattis Rubin. Photo © Visko
Hatfield.

"promise of happiness."[4] When speaking of a person, beauty has ethical, metaphysical, and metamoral connotations.[5] There are traces of the conflation of physical and spiritual beauty in English—for example, when an individual is deemed "beautiful" for a loving and generous nature. However, when speaking of a *thing,* "beauty" signifies first and foremost in Bantu languages that something is well made and pleasing to the eye, and—for a mask—that the mode of representation conveys the persona of the character.

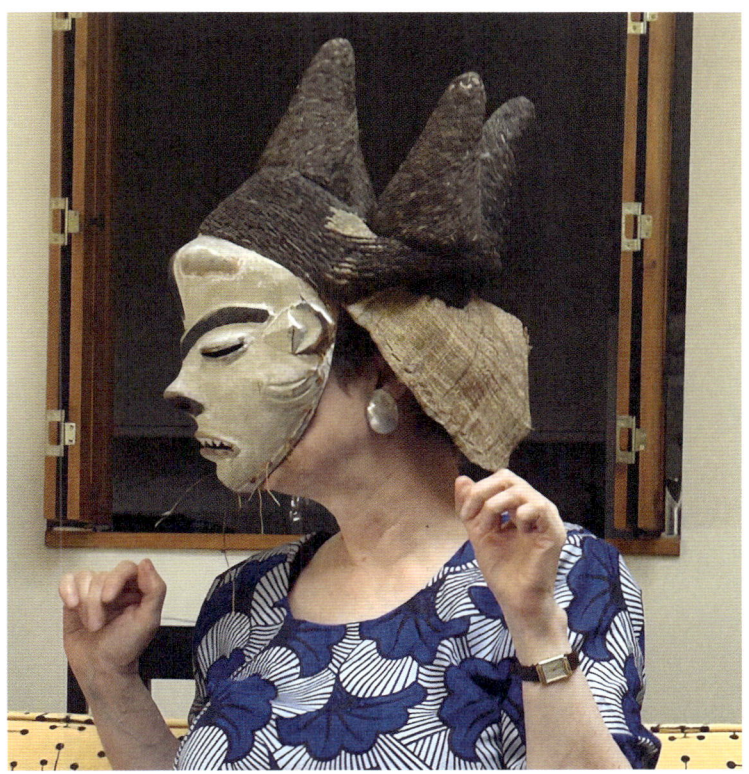

Fig. 22 **Author wearing Pulugunzu.**
A face mask arousing fear in one context can become
whimsical in another, depending on the mode of
presentation.

Consider a white-faced Central Pende mask named Pulugunzu pos-
sibly carved by the artist Maluba, circa 1930 (fig. 21).[6] The face is symmet-
rical and the forms harmonious. A sculptor works by periodically holding
the mask against his own face. In contrast to the object that Lorna Simpson
depicted in her photographic composition (see fig. 10), this example is
smooth on the inside. It fits like a glove over the face, yet the wearer can
breathe easily; the eye slits are spaced with skill to ensure that the performer retains stereoscopic vision of the dance terrain (fig. 22). A sculptor

needs to be pushed by the commission of an exacting, experienced dancer to achieve this level of precision in carving the inside of the mask. Dancers will sell off headpieces no matter how lovely if they are uncomfortable.

According to Pende theories of physiognomy, the masculine gender of the mask is unmistakable. Whereas the female face ideally is oval in silhouette, with a flat forehead and soft, rounded cheeks, the sculptor has made the face of Pulugunzu oversize and distinctly peanut-shaped: in full frontal view, the forehead bulges, the cheekbones are angular, and the chin is pointed. The masculine gaze, said to be more aggressive, is represented by upper eyelids protruding into space. In the hands of a skilled sculptor, the upper eyelids of a female mask will curve down over the eye, whereas those on the male face should thrust out into space. In this instance, the upper eyelids push out into space, *yet the edges also curve under.* Much of a sculptor's reputation rests on skill in handling the eyes. The artist gives a masterful interpretation of the chief's face, situated ideally between men and women, definitely masculine but imbued with perceived feminine traits of nurturing and patience.[7] The recognition of the chief's face is confirmed by the coiffure, depicting a wigged hat once popular for older men but adjusted with rounded horns to complement the softer portrayal of chiefs.

Is this mask beautiful? (*Mbuya, yabonga?*) Oh, yes. It is exceedingly well made and gives an insightful interpretation of its subject. But what if the question for the viewer were changed to ask,

"How does it make you feel?"

To answer, the mode of presentation is critical (see figs. 21, 22). During his performance, Pulugunzu was dressed elegantly, as a chief, and carried two fly whisks; however, he was glimpsed from a distance as he appeared on the fringe of the community, as twilight approached. Because the great majority of Pende masks have red faces, the luminous white visage was out of the ordinary and hard to interpret in the gloaming. The crowd inched forward, hoping to see more clearly, despite the menace of racing drum rhythms, when <u>suddenly</u> Pulugunzu's assistants began to blow a mysterious white powder in the spectators' direction so that they stampeded backward. According to Nzanda Gahondo of

Nioka-Munene (initiated 1916–19), the white face of Pulugunzu was both beautiful and frightening.[8] He never forgot it.

A corpus of ominous apparitions was invented between the 1910s and 1930s, when colonial power was imposed with great brutality in Pende-speaking regions of DR Congo. These apparitions, extremely varied in form, are called *mbuya jia mafuzo,* "masks [accompanied by] something blown," and were associated with mystery and danger.[9] In particular, the *mafuzo* masks expressed a negative image of chieftaincy. Once depicted as a nurturer and a peacemaker with a feminized face, the chief metamorphosed into an agent of the state, associated with the imposition of forced labor and myriad new laws under threat of whipping and imprisonment. In its performance context, Maluba's rendition of Pulugunzu held in tension the image of what the chief should be with what he had become. And the onlookers fled.

Whereas the *mafuzo* masks once made their audiences withdraw or even bolt, other masks make them bend over with laughter or trill with delight, with pleasure, with thankfulness. I was chatting with a colleague, Kassim Kone, and told him that many of my interlocutors among Pende dancers and sculptors classify their masks by the emotions that they arouse. He cut me off out of excitement: "Yes! It's the same with Bamana [in Mali]!

The function of masks is to trigger the emotions.

That's how they relate to 'art'—[how] they're utilitarian."[10] While many authors have opined that African art is "functional," envisioning figurated combs or stools, Kone turns this formulation on its head. Masking is an art because it excels at what he considers to be the function of all art: the stirring of emotional response. The shared interest in the inner life of the audience was unexpected because Bamana live at least three thousand miles from the Pende, farther even than New York to Los Angeles, and they are also quite different culturally in many respects.

Kone's insights resonate with those of Léopold Sédar Senghor.[11] Although he may never have seen a masquerade outside of a secular, political context, Senghor understood that "a beautiful mask, a beautiful poem, is one which produces in the public the emotion aimed at: sadness, joy, hilarity, terror."[12] Based on Congolese testimony and the wider literature, I would adjust Senghor's list. There appear to be four primary emotions that serve as the goals for masked dances: joy, hilarity, fear, and surprise. Sadness garners little mention, although it has a place, to be discussed. Surprise is essential.

Emotions in/through Culture

A "revolution" has taken place in emotion studies, according to many experimental psychologists, neuroscientists, anthropologists, and historians.[13] The apotheosis of rationality and the concomitant fear of the senses that took hold in the seventeenth century are finally losing their grip so that the study of affect and emotions has become an urgent and intellectually justified subject of inquiry. Mounting waves of scholars from diverse disciplines are challenging the proposition that emotions are universal, physical responses localized in specific regions of the brain. In fact, neuroscience has not been able to identify a "consistent bodily fingerprint for even a single emotion."[14] Over twenty years of well-publicized psychology experiments built around the interpretation of facial diagrams and photographs have been discredited for failing to correct for cultural bias and the unconscious coaching of subjects. In the aggregate, such experiments have failed to prove that there are biologically based emotions that can be dependably recognized across cultures or even within a given culture.[15]

Although there is no unanimity on how to define "emotion" in the midst of a paradigm shift,[16] an influential approach integrates mind, body, and culture. Encapsulating this view, the psychologist Lisa Feldman Barrett roundly rejects the notion that emotion is a "brute reflex, at odds with rationality."[17] Instead, emotion is the interpretive process whereby individuals "make our physical sensations meaningful" through emotional categories learned through culture.[18] Some still endeavor to locate emotional centers in the brain, but the intertwining of cognition and feeling and the essential role of culture in shaping our perceptions of our bodily experience are positions that are generally accepted. The historian Robert Boddice is militant about the need to expand emotion beyond a "neurobiological narrative": "Meaning always has to be made, and it is always made in context, in culture, and in society."[19]

The new valuing of the emotions and the senses in science and social science has paralleled developments in the arts and history of art. Rejecting the paradigm of medium specificity, an ever-increasing number of contemporary artists are exploring multimedia, multisensory installations. A friend lured me to one such event by saying that she had seldom before experienced "joy" at a contemporary art exhibition. In a world premiere at The Shed in New York in 2019, the visual artist Gerhard Richter collaborated with the composers Arvo Pärt and Steve Reich and the filmmaker Corinna Belz. In the first act, spectators mingled, standing in a white cube adorned with textiles and vertical strips of textured wallpaper. When the music began, the lighting shifted to spotlight the wallpaper strips so that the colors seemed to jump off of the wall. <u>Suddenly</u> the realization hit that the singers were moving among the crowd, dressed like anybody else, and that their voices were continually modulated by proximity and distance. The tenors chanted rhythmically while soprano voices floated overtop. Despite the absence of dancing and audience participation, the event reminded me of a Pende masquerade. We were standing, adjusting our positions for different views, affected bodily as performers approached and withdrew, immersed through music in a dominant mood but pricked by surprise with the introduction of <u>sudden</u> changes.

For centuries, tracing back at least to Aristotle, there were said to be five senses: sight, hearing, touch, taste, and smell. However, neurologists today propose between nine and twenty-one—and the number seems to be growing. In his proposal to study "African Art and the Senses," Henry Drewal lists seven that he considers relevant, including "motion" and extrasensory perception. With the idea of motion, Drewal folds together two senses now recognized by neurologists: balance centered on the inner ear and proprioception, the awareness of the body localized in space. For extrasensory perception, Drewal has little to say beyond the fact that it is "related to synesthesia—the simultaneous body-mind interplay of multiple senses." Advocating "sensiotics," as he calls it, Drewal challenges scholars to integrate sensory response into their analysis of works of art.

In a powerful description of a Yoruba warrior mask in action, Drewal conjures up six of the senses on his list: vision, hearing, touch, taste, smell, and proprioception. The mask's "performative power or *ase,* resides not only in its striking colors and assemblage of power packets attached to its costume, but other multi-sensorial elements as well—the powerful chorus of praise songs that energize it; the kinetic energy of its dance amplified by the aggressive … demeanor of its attendants … the gritty taste of dust kicked up in the chaos; the pulsing beat of drums; the heavy thud of the masker's combat boots; and especially the pervasive, overpowering stench that emanates from the animal sacrificial offerings on its blood-soaked tunic!" Drewal recognizes the oscillating focus of spectators who might notice the power packets and wonder what is in them, feel the vibration of the masker's stamps, feel the drum rhythms coursing through their body, taste the dust, and smell the blood as the performer draws near.[20]

Increasingly, the literature on the senses and the emotions is "colliding"[21] as psychologists increasingly argue that "emotions" are what we make of our physical sensations. In the domain of the arts, multi-sensorial compositions seem to be particularly effective strategies for choreographing intense emotional experiences, which explains why African masquerades, predicated upon music, dance, and visual display, have such power to move their audiences. It is still the role of culture to help individuals make meaning from what the body captures through its various organs.

Aesthetic Emotions in Africa

In a blistering critique of the 1960 Musée Guimet exhibition *Le masque,* André Breton, a contemporary of Senghor, published photos of himself and surrealist colleagues in masked performance. He was invoking the gamut of emotions missing from museum displays and texts. Breton complained that the scholarly method, "which presupposes detachment and frigidity, constitutes a priori an insurmountable obstacle to knowledge" of masks.[22] In particular, he regretted the suppression of experiential knowledge in ethnographic commentaries. Breton was absolutely correct that twentieth-century scholars were wary of addressing the emotions released by African masks, which were of key interest to a Burkinabé videographer who sells CDs to participants to remember the occasion (fig. 23). Nonetheless, plenty of parenthetical remarks on the subject may be found buried deep in field reports.

The most dramatic of these digressions appears in *Masques dogons.* After 788 pages of deadening description, Marcel Griaule stops to reflect on aesthetic emotions.[23] The anthropologist opens his surprising excursus by observing that, "in order to develop, art needs to provoke a reaction from its viewers."[24] He contemplates the emotions "released" by the setting, by the myths, and by the "rich ensemble" of masks evoking the cosmos in all its diversity. For him, the "sign of art" lies in its ability to rise above individual experience to arouse "collective emotion":

> The opera [i.e., masquerade] performed in a public space is felt to some degree as a therapy applied for the benefit of society. But little by little the form emerges from the background, the theatrical element wins the day. From being attentive to the smooth perfor- mance of the rite, the crowd becomes attentive to the spectacle itself: they see the colors and the forms, they hear the songs, they follow the rhythms of the instruments and of the dancers.[25]

Because funerals were a primary site for masquerades, Griaule concluded that "aesthetic emotion and the expansion of death are intimately tied together."[26] He is here referring to a myth recounting that it was the desire for beauty that brought death into the world. Griaule and his team made the Dogon world-famous in the mid-twentieth century, but so far as I know, no one has ever engaged this more poetic element of his research.

The challenge in analyzing the emotional content of a work of art or a performance is that it is embedded in both individual experience and cul- tural expectations. Rather than reporting what people said, Griaule mused over what he had observed. Noticing how people respond is certainly a good beginning, but one must be attentive to how people interpret their experiences in order to avoid jumping to conclusions. Many years later, in 2013, Polly Richards interviewed Dogon drawn from a range of subject posi- tions for a short film called *Mask Stories.*[27] Most of Richards's interlocutors reflect not on what masks represent but on what they have experienced as spectators. A stonemason says, "Even a grown man feels something, if he suddenly sees a mask." Usually, the interviewees speak about their qualms, their uneasiness, their fears, how they were coached as children: "You have to look. It won't come and touch us." One woman reflects on the happiness

Fig. 23 **Supporters Matenin Sanou and Fiso Sanou (on either side) praising a dancing *Lèrènya* mask as videographer Ali Zouré (far right) captures their emotional reactions in memory of the funeral celebration.**
Sya district, Bobo-Dioulasso, Burkina Faso, 22 April 2018.
Photo by Lisa Homann.

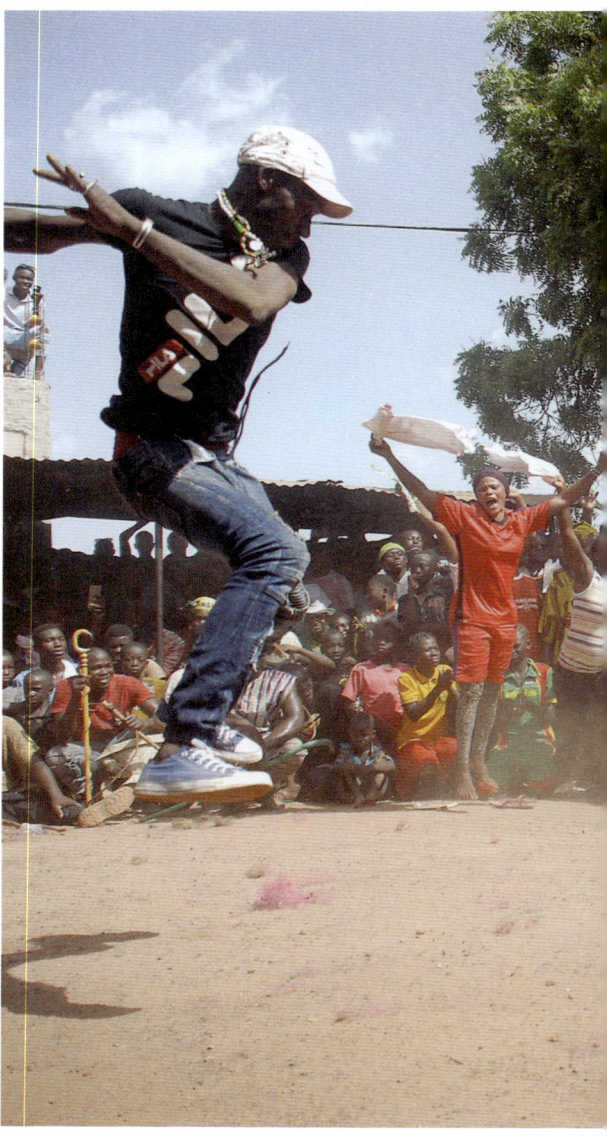

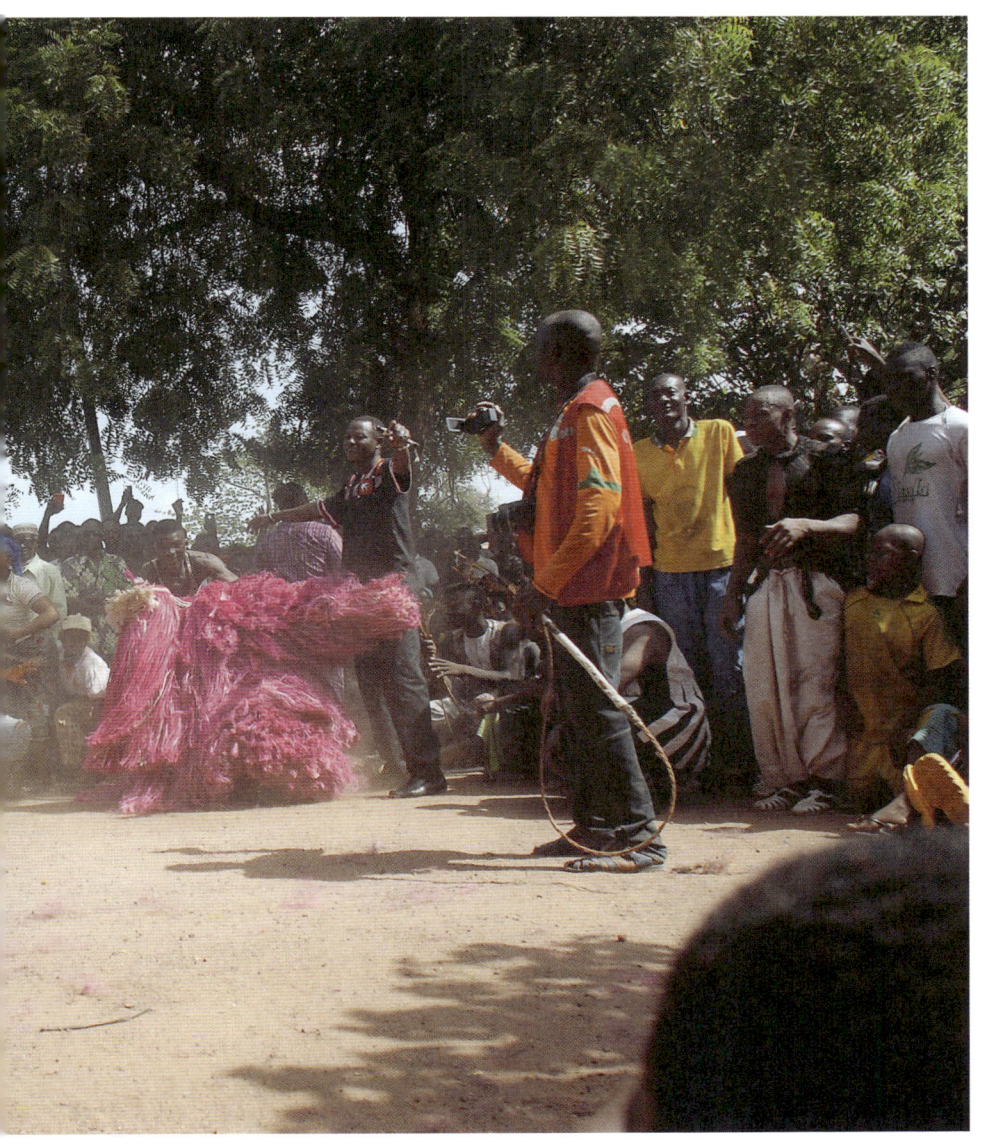

she derived from viewing the beauty and skill of certain dancers. Breton would have been pleased.

Particular spectra of feelings tend to dominate discrete domains. Connoisseurs of classical German music are likely to cultivate different sensations than do enthusiasts of French impressionist painting. In the study of aesthetic emotions in philosophy—initiated by Immanuel Kant—some of the more widely published aesthetic instances are sublimity (including wonder, awe, and astonishment), delight, joy, melancholy, and humor.[28]

Unfortunately, the cultural training and subjective investments needed to make such judgments are seldom addressed. From fieldwork, I remember a Canadian missionary in the late 1980s who invited a group of Congolese women to her house on Christmas Day in order to share a recording of George Frideric Handel's *Messiah*. She was hurt when they grimaced and plugged up their ears to block out what they experienced as an assault of screeching noise. In contrast, the film *Kinshasa Symphony* documents a Congolese pilot's efforts a generation later with a handful of devotees to master and share their love for Ludwig van Beethoven's Ninth Symphony in the capital city.[29] Whatever doubts many Congolese in the orchestra's social circle expressed about the value of European classical music, the amateur musicians' love and dedication convey the German directors' conviction that great music is universal.

The intertwining of marvel, surprise, and danger is a leitmotiv in the limited literature on aesthetic emotion in African visual culture. As discussed above, Chike Aniakor identifies a suite of emotions, even warring emotions, such as "fear mixed with wonder" associated with works of art.[30] The implication seems to be that skill so far out of the ordinary can sometimes trouble viewers.

Few people picked up on Aniakor's insights until the anthropologist Wyatt MacGaffey conceded that aesthetic emotion was important to the original makers and audience of Central African power objects, one of the best known of African art genres.[31] Previously, if anyone had attributed any emotion at all to the contemplation of power objects ("fetishes"), it was terror.[32] However, after immersing himself in early twentieth-century commentaries penned by young Kongo Christian converts in their native language (Kikongo), MacGaffey realized that that sophistication in carving and assemblage was designed to provoke feelings of "*ngitukulu,* 'astonish-ment,' in the mind of the beholder, suggesting the presence of something extraordinary."[33] *Ngitukulu* derives from *–yitukwa,* "to be surprised; to come upon <u>suddenly</u>."[34] Significantly, surprise is almost always configured in the passive voice as something received rather than as a feeling imposed on someone else.[35] The signification can be neutral or joyous, as when one names a child Diangitukwa—"it's a surprise!"—to celebrate a "quasi-miraculous" birth of a child to parents who had despaired of having one. According to Fu-Kiau Bunseki, *yitukwa* means "to be surprised, impressed, astonished, or 'taken out of oneself,' and the term refers to intense experi-ences such as the shock one feels when a loved one dies <u>suddenly</u> without illness, or is <u>suddenly</u> healed when all was thought lost."[36]

In Bantu languages such as Kikongo, conceptual categories are not usually subject to a binary logic of being wholly good or wholly bad (as they are too often in English). Instead, they slide along a spectrum. Depending on context, the experience of "astonishment" can be pleasurable or joyous (as in the birth of a child) or full of grief. Strong works of art also stimulate the interplay of multiple sensations, which may conflict or layer one upon the other. The renowned Kongo sculptures full of nails (*mbau* or *minkisi nkondi*), MacGaffey wrote, were "impressive, causing 'astonishment' (*ngitukulu*), but above all frightening (*nkadulu a nsisi*)." It was their visual complexity that made them effective judicial tools.[37]

The social scientist William P. Murphy was inspired by MacGaffey to explore the "aesthetics of power" among Mende in Sierra Leone. Murphy was intrigued by the flexibility in the application of the term *kabânde,* which might be used both to praise dance performance—particularly masked dance—and to comment upon mysterious political success. *Kabânde*'s first meaning is wonder, but it can also communicate feelings of awe and astonishment,[38] which led Murphy to put the concept into dialogue with the sublime as constituted by Immanuel Kant and Edmund Burke, "in which power is constituted by the relation between awe-inspiring effects and their source in hidden, mysterious power, including divine or supernatural forces."[39] Struck by the "conceptual similarities between Mende wonder and the European sublime," Murphy concluded that "wonder rather than beauty" might offer a fruitful line of inquiry in the study of African art and politics.[40]

Aniakor's and MacGaffey's publications have prompted scholars to ask different questions of masquerade as well as figurative sculpture. Ute Röschenthaler found that Aniakor's argument resonated with her own conclusions drawn from research in southeast Nigeria and southwest Cameroon. Ejagham masked performers used various strategies to confound and mystify viewers—for example, projecting voices, the source for which cannot be localized; or mounting masks as high as palm trees while viewers were distracted:[41] "They show only as much of their powers as necessary (so that they cannot be copied) to make things happen, making people surprised, amazed, cheer and shiver."[42] Wonder quickly mutated into surprise, admiration, or uncanniness but was nonetheless deeply memorable.

Röschenthaler aside, "terror" has been until recently the emotion drawing the most attention from researchers of African masquerades. Based on research conducted between 1984 and 1992, Laurel Birch de Aguilar argues that Nyau masks among the Chewa of Malawi are "invested with a sense of dread," or *opysa,* such that "the very word 'Nyau' makes some people catch their breath and step back. People have said it causes the skin to tighten and the hairs to stand up."[43] Because the most important context for Nyau performances is in funerary rituals, "the sight of the masked dancers is a memory of death and dying, of losing someone known to them."[44] Birch de Aguilar's focus on a single emotion differentiates her from Griaule, who perceived Dogon spectators as becoming absorbed in the artistry of events despite the masks' associations with funerals.

From 1994 to 1996, another researcher in Malawi, Peter Probst, explored the contradictions of Nyau performance in the Chewa community of Kalumba. On the one hand, Probst agrees with Birch de Aguilar that initiations to Nyau were always organized within the context of a funeral ceremony and that the "forms of the mask were intended to be dreadful and fearsome (*oeipa*)."[45] On the other hand, he observes that Nyau performances included a great deal of ribald entertainment and were expected to arouse "astonishment, wonder, and excitement."[46] People in Kalumba often described their "feelings upon encountering nyau masks" as *zizwa,* a Chichewa term signifying "amazement or astonishment"; however, an undercurrent of danger is embedded in the term due to its etymological kinship with the word *zizi,* "feeling both cold and fear." Probst believes that dancers exploit this orientation by [suddenly] bursting on the scene while spectators are distracted so that women and children "scatter wildly."[47]

Historically, social scientists were likely more comfortable commenting on fear than on other emotive reactions because they could relate it more easily to an analysis of power and "social control." Daniel B. Reed is a rare voice who perceived joy in masked performances in the Dan region of Côte d'Ivoire. Whereas George Harley and M. C. Jedrej debated the political uses of masks, Reed discovered their multifaceted emotional life in the mid-1990s through his study of music. As he explains it, *genu* are "spirit intermediaries between people and God," some of whom choose to manifest themselves through a masked performer and through a particular sonic texture.[48] Sacred *genu* supervise emotionally charged situations such as initiations, healing ceremonies, and investigations for sorcery. Each sacred *ge* interacts with the human realm through three groups of spirits: "the *yinannu* of manifestation of joy, who inspire the *ge* to dance; the *yinannu* who enable a *ge* to read someone's destiny; and the *yinannu* of war, who enable a *ge* to defend themselves and attack others in a mystical sense."[49]

Almost in passing, Reed acknowledges that warrior *ge* maintained the social order by serving as "traditional versions of police and army officers," but his most eloquent testimony is about the contagious impact of joy.[50] First, the drummers entice the *yinannu* of joy to arrive; they then inspire the performer to dance with suprahuman skill, and the combination of music and dance communicates a sense of exultation to the audience. Reed quotes one performer:

> The face of the mask is resting in the sacred house over there, but … it is the drum which wakes up the mask … when the drum resounds in my presence … the mask which is over there [in the house] acts within me. When it acts on me, on the spot, I do the dance steps of the mask…. So [it's] the joy that animates you, the joy that animates you by the sound of the drum…. It's the drum that builds the joy of the mask…. It's the sound of the drum that gives the power to the mask.[51]

The various *yinannu* have surely descended if someone is moved to dance, roused to war, or gifted with insight. From what Reed describes, it seems that people are pushed by their feelings into action. Feelings are motivators.

Reed's scholarship demonstrates the value of asking: How do various African constituencies interpret the physical sensations that they experience during masquerades, and what emotional categories do they create to communicate their experiences? Whatever theological or ontological definitions may pertain, masquerades arouse intense emotions, including fear, wonder, astonishment, hilarity, and joy. Their sensiotics, as Drewal would say, are complex, layered, and potentially conflicting.

Kassim Kone eloquently conveys the ambivalence of aesthetic emotions surrounding Komo masks (which are also power objects). In Bamana language (Mali), they raise "goosebumps—a physical expression of fear and awe."[52] Officers of the initiation society have been quite successful in limiting outsider access to Komo performances over the years. Nonetheless, the masks live vividly in the imaginations of even those who have never seen them. They appear at night, and the uninitiated are obliged to stay indoors with their doors closed and the lights off. This "unseeing audience" includes visitors from other communities, foreigners, and most if not all women and children.[53] Individual objects have their own names; on a given night it might be announced that Obscurity will be performing, or the King of Clawed Beasts, or Killer of Its Own Master.[54] The images raised from the accompanying songs are contradictory. One will refer to Komo as a crocodile and another as a hyena or as "big bird from the thicket." A thick sonic texture is created from the clatter of bells punctuated by blasts of horns that mimic the trumpeting of a charging elephant and the sounds of old men moaning, a motif that is exceptionally disturbing in a society that upholds the virtue of stoicism. No one expects to hear elders give voice to their suffering, and it sends "chills down the spine."[55]

The newly initiated experience sheer horror when witnessing their first performance. The headpiece rests on top of the head and allows the dancer to breathe more easily. By the light of a flickering wood fire, the initiates witness an athletic performance by the masker, who wears a thick cape of vulture feathers and who either spits phosphorescent fire or screeches on a mirliton (fig. 24). The headpieces are individualized in

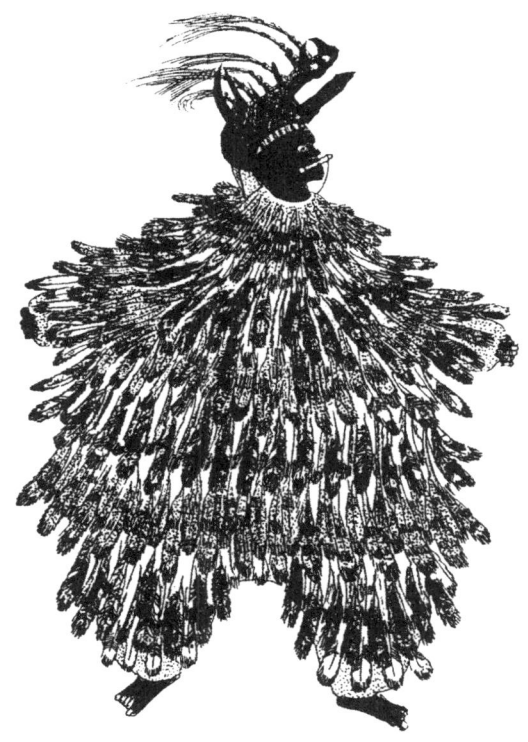

Fig. 24 **Masque wara.**
A Minyanka performer of the wara mask for a Komo fraternity in Mali.
From Philippe Jespers, "La puissance du masque: De l'audible au
visible," in *Puissances de la voix: Corps sentant, corde sensible,* ed. Sémir
Badir and Herman Parret (Presses universitaires de Limoges, 2001), 60.

form, especially in the accumulation of horns, quills, and bundles full of
medicated earth. Even those present do not know what is in the attached
bundles; they speak to great pharmaceutical knowledge that can be
directed to various purposes. With several performances, the horror felt
by the initiate develops into awe—awe at the energy released and the skills
of the performer, the sculptor, and others involved in the production of
the headpiece.

Eventually, with age and experience, the response matures into an appreciation of beauty. Many consider Komo headpieces to be beautiful because they are also efficacious power objects. Kone compares the craquelure of the surface, built up through multiple libations and offerings over a period of years, to the deep fissures on the face of an aged individual who should be both respected and feared. And for their part, elders judge the headpieces as beautiful because they associate them with the healing of individuals or family groups. Paradoxically, these "terrorizing sculptures" are fierce guardians of widows and orphans. Nonetheless, even for elders, a sense of anxiety can return willy-nilly. No one can completely escape their conditioning, those years spent huddled in the dark, listening to moans and mirlitons.

In the performance setting, emotions comingle and reflect the subject position of the onlooker. Komo is an extreme case, but Kone reinforces his point through analogy to the masks of Ntomo (a Bamana boys' puberty initiation): "They trigger emotions according to one's subject position: old, young, circumcised, uncircumcised. Depending on this position, [participants] may feel fear, joy, nostalgia. Those newly initiated savor their position of authority ... *it's their turn.*"[56] The intensity and range of emotions differs, but the principle is the same.

Since the 1980s, clinical psychologists have designed "emotion wheels," illustrated and widely circulated on the internet, to help patients articulate a broad spectrum of emotional response. In the center, they propose that there are at least six primary emotions: joy, love, fear, anger, sadness, and surprise.[57] However, a single emotion concept such as joy refracts into a subspectrum of happiness, cheerfulness, or enthusiasm, manifesting itself in delight, in optimism, or in thankfulness. Fear may surface as anxiety, panic, terror, or horror.

In the introduction to this chapter, recall that Senghor identified four predominant emotions associated with masks in African aesthetics: sadness, joy, hilarity, terror (setting aside love and anger).[58] Drawing on African testimonies offered by spectators and performers, I would adjust this list to highlight four basic emotions that serve as the goals for masked dances: joy, hilarity, fear, and surprise. In the scholarly literature, instances of surprise dominate, characterized as astonishment, amazement, wonder, and awe. Whether in a ritual or secular setting, masked performances in West and Central Africa arouse rather than express (or portray) emotions.[59]

Ritual vs. Secular Masquerade: Case Studies from DR Congo

The Economy of Feeling in a Ritual Masquerade (Eastern Pende)

Perhaps unexpectedly, the question posed at the beginning of this chapter, "How does it make you feel?," was first applied to the study of "ritual masquerades," such as those Griaule described for Dogon peoples, or Kone for Bamana, or Reed for Dan-speaking peoples. Ritual masquerades are popularly understood to be situated within an indigenous African religious context and to mandate a series of actions carried out according to a strict and unchanging protocol.[60] Among the Eastern Pende in the 1980s, it was true that holding a masquerade necessitated the renewal of altars, the cleansing of community fires, the soothing of divisive quarrels. Scholarly silence about aesthetic emotions in secular masquerades probably results from anxiety about changes in masquerade practices across the continent due to religious, social, and economic change (as noted for Dogon peoples). The pace of change leads both African and Western audiences to fret sometimes: Has the creation of "new" masquerades diminished their importance and rendered their interpretation moot?[61] The following section uses a case study set among a single ethnic group to demonstrate that despite significant and ongoing change, the cultivation of aesthetic emotions remains of utmost importance to masquerade practice.[62]

First of all, what is a mask? In public, in the late 1980s, I asked this question of a range of Eastern Pende interlocutors: "*Mbuya, ye'itshi?*" Everyone responded, "*Mbuya, nvumbi*" ("Mask, spirit of the dead"). Everyone—100 percent. However, when I posed the same question to the same men and women one-on-one, I received that answer only from individuals who had been tracked through mission schools. The majority of adults would respond, "*Mbuya, hamba*" ("The mask is a hamba"). But what's a *hamba?* The great majority demurred, recommending that I speak to "the experts"—that is, chiefs and ritual specialists. It took two years of immersive learning before I felt comfortable translating *hamba* as "tools for contacting the dead."[63]

At that time, there was still a sizable community among the Eastern Pende who had grown up in or were still practicing Pende religion, which was predicated on a cycle of reincarnation. God created the world but gave responsibility for the health and well-being of junior family members to their elders.[64] Periodically, the living needed to contact the dead (or, more precisely, their elders among the dead). Masks are specifically danced *hamba,* which are used to reunite the living and the dead in a safe space in order to allow the living to thank the dead for good harvests, hunts, and the birth of children, and to urge them to continue to care for their younger relatives.[65]

To do their job, the masks operate within an economy of feeling. Eastern Pende dance community masks (*mbuya jia kifutshi*) for two reasons, summarized by Nzomba, a longtime research associate: "(1) to be in communion with the dead in order to obtain blessings and happiness; (2) entertainment."[66] Cultivating happiness is a central goal of the events, and the communitarian values of entertainment and laughing together should not be underestimated. The emotional palette for happiness will include thankfulness, joy, bliss, and love.

The film composer Deniz Hughes coined the metaphor "emotional palette" to describe the "combustion of conflicting emotions" that distinguishes fine art. Hughes was inspired while closely examining a painting of water lilies by Claude Monet to discover that what appeared purple from a distance was composed of a myriad of colors including strokes of white, black, and red. Transferring this metaphor to film, Hughes notes, for example, how film characters may be simultaneously happy and sad, confident and doubtful, and how there may be passages of contrary emotions "suspended" in a work—such as sorrow or an appreciation of beauty—that encourage the viewer to detach and reflect. Musing on the mix of emotions masked dancers might feel, she predicts pride (in their skill and in their masculinity), anxiety, relief (if they succeed), or embarrassment (if they fail). Hughes recognizes that ambitious performers stake out an identity during their performances, but she is also familiar with those who go on "automatic" as they surrender to the choreography that has become ingrained through muscle memory.[67]

When I showed Hughes video footage of various African masked dancers, she asked who was responsible for the intent or meaning of an event. After some reflection, I realized that it is the Eastern Pende chief and his close advisers who determine when a dance of masks (*ulumbu wa mbuya*) is desirable. To guarantee that as many as people as possible experience the feelings that constitute happiness, the organizers make sure that certain masks appear, and they do their best to secure talented dancers and an accomplished lead drummer.[68] It may also be necessary to resolve any outstanding disputes in the community, and many masquerades will be postponed or canceled outright should there be a death in the community.

Grief is not welcome.

No one has the option of staying indoors to nurse their individual anguish or heartache. In fact, once the masquerade begins, it is against the law to remain in one's house, even though the masquerade can last two to seven days. Joining with others in this ritual expressing gratitude and joy is conceived as a kind of psychological therapy. The import of emotional experience became clear during one consequential day for my research when everything went wrong (29 February 1988).[69]

Chief Kingange had organized a two-day masquerade to offer thanks for the bounty of the harvest season. He was counting on a neighbor to lend him several masks, as he had for years. One of the masks was the character Mabombolo, also known as Kindombolo. Unexpectedly, the neighbor refused at the last minute, unleashing a huge brouhaha. How could they mount a performance without Mabombolo?

The dramatic reaction to the neighbor's refusal to make the loan was surprising, because no one had ever mentioned that Mabombolo was necessary. If anything, people spoke dismissively of the character. First, he is the "policeman" whose job it is to keep the dance floor clear. He carries a whip and chases members of the crowd who press in on the dance arena (*bula dia ulumbu*). Knowing that they might be struck if they infringe on the rules, women and noninitiates are wary and keep an eye on Mabombolo. He is skillful at blending into the background so he can take people by surprise. He is a joker (*muenya sau*) with good comic timing who engages in all sorts of outrageous antics: He might steal a baby or squeeze the breast of one of the female-gendered masks. He constantly blurs the line between stage and audience. Mabombolo amuses people and, importantly, *makes them laugh out loud.* The crisis raised by Mabombolo's absence revealed that although joy may be the goal of the masquerade, surprise and hilarity are essential.

At Kingange they decided to persevere without Mabombolo. However, the day began badly when the first dancer was run off the floor within five minutes, criticized by all and sundry. People milled about, unable to focus on a second dancer who was struggling to compensate, when <u>suddenly</u> a roar of laughter rang out from behind. Turning, we saw a huge pile of leaves with the face of a horned initiation mask bicycling up to the stage. The surprise and incongruity of it—and the release of tension— delighted the crowd. The switch in headpieces made for a clever substitution because initiation masks also have mischievous personalities.

Mabombolo worked hard to animate the crowd, but otherwise the day was deadly boring. It seemed as though most of the performers were merely going through the motions. I had invited Chief Nzambi (Kibunda a Kilonda), a good friend, to accompany me, seeking to benefit from his shrewd skills of analysis. Minutes before the day ended, when I had begun to wonder why I had devoted years of my life to this kind of research, Nzambi stood up, called for a pair of fly whisks, and began to perform the Lukongo—the signature dance of Kipoko, the most important Eastern Pende mask—without costume or headpiece. It was as if an electric switch had been flipped. <u>Suddenly</u>, as my photos from that day show, members of the audience began to grin and clap along with the music. In praise, young men and old stuffed gifts of money into Nzambi's pockets. A number of women crowded onto the dance floor, rattling dishes as if they were musical instruments. Some circled Nzambi, trailing a textile, as they ululated in praise. Even though his performance lasted only a few minutes, the excitement was contagious, and people left content.

When Nzambi sat down, I asked him, "Why did you do that? You were the one who told me a chief should never dance after his inauguration for fear of looking like someone who could not share the limelight with others?" His response drew attention to the importance of emotions: "I know, I know. But I felt sorry for you. You had come all the way from America to see masquerades and the day had lost its joy because the lead performer got drunk and failed to perform his duties properly." Earlier that week, some men in the community had returned from the diamond mines with Scotch whisky and they poured it out liberally for the dancer over lunch. Whisky has a far higher percentage of alcohol than local beverages such as palm wine. As a consequence, the dancer staggered drunk onto the terrain and neglected to throw roundhouse kicks over the altar in the center of the arena. The semicircular kicks composed a danced prayer asking the dead to continue to protect the community. This was when I learned—after fourteen months in the field—that the dead must be formally invited to attend the event organized in their honor. Since the Kipoko dancer had not consecrated the event to the dead, they had not come to dance among the living.

It was precisely the lackluster quality of the event that day that led Nzambi to diagnose that something had gone wrong. His superb execution of Kipoko's dance reminded everyone why they were there and that *they also had a responsibility to make the event a success*. The women showed their thanks to the ancestors for the past year's harvests by throwing down millet, crashing open manioc tubers, and circling around him with goods that they had purchased with funds deriving from the previous year's harvest. A young mother even danced around him, sweetly touching her baby's feet to the ground periodically in time with the rhythm to acknowledge the indelible link between health and agricultural abundance. The gestures manifesting joy and warmth demonstrated to Nzambi that the dead had accepted the invitation and joined the celebration. Those not tuned in to masquerade as religious practice still experienced the event as a success because of the good feeling generated in the community.

Mabombolo provokes short flashes of fear (*woma*) when he charges audience members or appears out of nowhere, but it is the mask Pumbu whose signature song is "Are You Afraid?" (*Udi nu woma ba?*). Historically, only a handful of paramount chiefs have enjoyed the right to commission Pumbu, and this mask's relatively rare appearance testifies to the prestige of the chief's clan and, sometimes, to the gravity of the occasion.[70] Pumbu appears as the closing act for a multiday masquerade; once he appears, he must kill something before he can be retired for the night.

Dressed in the chief's own best clothes, Pumbu appeared brusquely from an unexpected direction, armed with a machete, bow and arrow, and throwing stick. He flashed his blade from side to side while advancing inexorably in the quintessential assassin's dance (*kuhala kua ungunza*), a stylized walk with a progressive stutter-step. One or two young men restrained Pumbu with thick ropes of the type used to set traps for wild boar. A chorus of twenty to thirty young men bearing whips accompanied him while singing war songs (fig. 25). Ideally, Pumbu circulates through the community to collect gestures of tribute from subordinate chiefs: once raffia cloth, axes, or arrows, and maybe money or a chicken today. The chorus accompanying him must also be paid to bring out the drum of war.

On the closing day of Kingange's masquerade described above, Pumbu appeared near twilight, causing the other masks to disappear. Two well-built young men pulled theatrically with all their might on thick ropes tied around Pumbu's waist. They fought to restrain him, sometimes stumbling or being dragged along as the masquerader pushed forward. I captured the scene in my field notes:

Suddenly, the mask cut one of the ropes and the crowd groans: MMM MM MM. There's palpable fear and flight in every direction. The stampeding crowd is crying,

Pumbu yatomboka! (Pumbu has become dangerous!)
Málébá! (Pardon!)
Tuabuba! (Have mercy! Please don't hurt us.)

Pumbu cut the second cord. Looking for a chicken, he threatens the drummers and even gestures his blade in the direction of the chief, who shouts: "No! Stop! Stop!"

Since the domestic animals had also fled in the pandemonium, Pumbu quietly withdrew from the empty square to oversee the final rituals.[71]

The reception of Pumbu is a telling example of how a single mask can affect people in different subject positions quite differently, as Kassim Kone described for Komo. For the cohort accompanying Pumbu, "*it's their turn.*" The volume and gusto of their singing, the smiles in their voices, and the way they threw themselves bodily into the steps left no doubt about their pleasure in assuming adult status (see fig. 25). Women had long since disappeared, although some peeped out from their houses. Amid the rout,

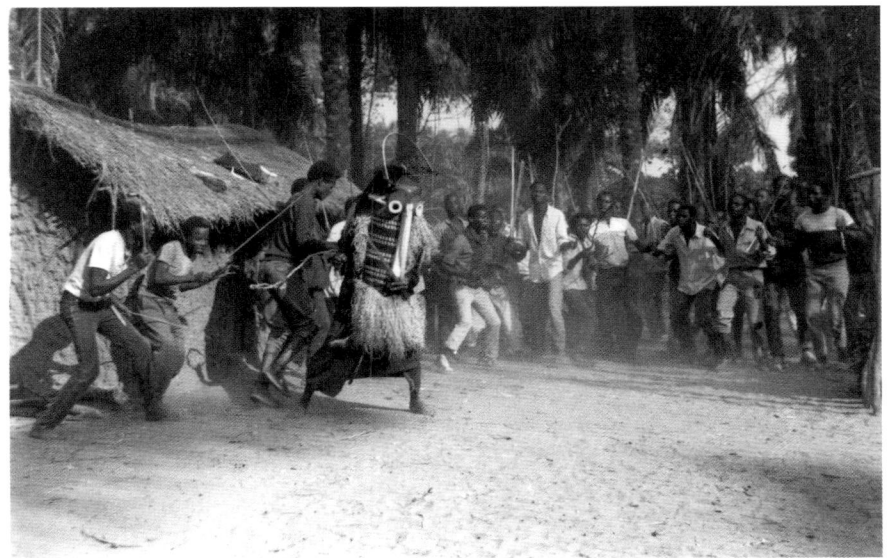

Fig. 25 **Eastern Pende Pumbu, accompanied by the age grade drafted in times of war, who sing "Are you scared?"**
Only the highest chiefs have the right to Pumbu. In this case, the mask associated with war danced to petition the dead to heal the community's beloved Chief Kombo-Kiboto (Mukanzo a Kilumbu).
Ndjindji, DR Congo, 1987.
Photo by Z. S. Strother.

my photos show that some of the boys ran with grins on their faces. I was not acquainted with Kingange's dancer, but Chief Kombo's dancer liked to brag that only he had the audacity (*unduyi*) to dance Pumbu. Nonetheless, confidants told me that he sweat bullets when he dressed, unnerved to wear a headpiece that normally was stored in the chief's ritual house, the portal of the dead. Others complained of nightmares after performing as Pumbu. One woman who became confused and knelt before Pumbu to be healed fainted and experienced a seizure. The elders were relieved that no one was harmed. The day was marked in memory by emotional intensity in all registers.

How Do Masks Make You Feel? 85

The emotional palette of the masquerade (*ulumbu wa mbuya,* "dance of masks") deepens further with one's relationship with the dancers. Nzomba Dugo Kakema writes that even though sadness (*kikenene*) is not an emotion that one seeks during a masquerade, "it can manifest itself" in certain persons when a performance makes them recall a defunct friend or family member who loved to dance a particular mask. He believes that surprise (*kukema*) or marvel (*kudihula*) is felt most often when one sees, for the first time, a dancer execute the steps and the changes in rhythm with unexpected skill and knowledge.[72] Interestingly, both of Nzomba's examples are predicated on knowledge of the dancer's identity. As argued in the introduction, the ability of individuals to name performers *increases,* rather than diminishes, the complexity and profundity of the event for audience members.

Eastern Pende organizers worked hard to center ritual masquerades around a dominant emotion (in this case, joy). However, following the event through time reveals, to quote Hughes again, a "combustion of conflicting emotions" open to individual interpretation—that is, *when the day is a success.*

The Economy of Feeling in a Secularized Masquerade (Central Pende)

The Central Pende region was celebrated as one of the most intense masking cultures of DR Congo in the twentieth century, although it has not been acknowledged in the literature that these performances were overwhelmingly secular in nature. During the Pende Rebellion in 1931, desperate people had put their faith in the dead to protect them against Belgian machine guns. The crushing defeat left them feeling bitterly betrayed, and most Kwilu and Central Pende abandoned the practice of local religion. Many times, when I tried to ask about the *hamba* in 1989, excited elders would shout "*Mambu! Mambu!*" ("It's a lie! It's a lie!") Nonetheless, a number of Central Pende communities continued to be enthusiastic masqueraders through the 1980s.[73] During the colonial period, the booming drums and crowds united in song and dance bolstered a sense of ethnic pride in face of the colonial state.[74] The masked dances were gradually transformed into secular rituals reminiscent of an idealized US American Thanksgiving.

Why dance the masks? The most common answer I have received from Central Pende organizers and performers has been "to make the community rejoice" (*gusuanguluisa dimbo*). The same potent verb is used to translate the Psalms or Christian hymns into Kipende: *Musuanguluge!* ("Rejoice!"). Dancing the masks "beautifies the village" (*gubongesa dimbo*) and strengthens it (*gukolesa dimbo*). When asked for more information about how the masks beautified the community, enthusiasts at Nioka-Kakese began to speak about joy (*manzangi* or *gusuanguluga* or *kiese*). Those who spoke French rejected the translation of *bonheur* as happiness with connotations of well-being, contentment, prosperity. No, they said. It is something stronger.

"Joy seizes you."

The goal of the dance in building good feeling is taken so seriously that masquerades cannot be scheduled if there are quarrels in the village. "The dance must begin on the inside, in the heart." It's a chicken-and-egg situation: "When we are seized by joy, we dance the masks" (*Kumbi ditukuata manzangi, tukenyi mbuya*), but the dance itself should trigger delight.[75]

Masquerades should strengthen the community (*gukolesa dimbo*) because, as the retired dancer Muhenge Mutala (initiated ca. 1921) explained, they make "rejoice the bodies that are shivering."[76] The cold, the ill, the feverish, the aging curl up around themselves, their posture signaling psychological withdrawal, an inward focus on their aches and pains. According to Muhenge, dance warms the body and the heart. It drives out the chill of incipient death.[77] It stimulates the weak and ill so that they feel stronger and interested in others as well as themselves. For both Central and Eastern Pende, one of the greatest compliments on a performance is granted when an older man or woman forgets their frailty, warmed by enthusiasm to dance one-on-one with a masked dancer, and regains for a short time the lissome potential of youth. On these occasions, the roar of exaltation is deafening. Everyone shares in the moment of triumph when dance puts death at a distance.[78]

Central Pende created dozens of community masks in the twentieth century.[79] When I tried to compile lists by interviewing sculptors, dancers, chiefs, and connoisseurs, my interlocutors would first categorize them according to their dominant aesthetic emotions. The masks of joy (*mbuya jia kiese*) make women ululate with delight (*mbuya jia miyéyé; mbuya jia miyelele*).[80] The masks that joke (*mbuya jia ilelesa*) make people laugh out loud. And then there are the masks that make people flee or shout "Have pity!" (*Tuabuba!*).[81] As with Pulugunzu (see fig. 21), no outsider would ever be able to predict the emotional palette associated with a mask by how it looked, although they might well learn to do so by the sonic texture associated with it.[82]

Pende masking categories, instead, are what social scientists call goal-oriented concepts. There are various strategies for arousing emotions, which themselves encompass a spectrum of responses. To begin with, beauty (*ginango*) is one of the surest means to arouse pleasure and happiness. Masks representing young women are automatically classed as "masks of joy" (*mbuya jia kiese*) by Central Pende. Ideally, the rendering of the face and coiffure and the perfect fitting and styling of the costume are all important, but what is probably the most important feature is the letter-perfect rendition of a woman's dance style … by a man.

Other mask types are not so easy to recognize. Muyombo used to be one of the canonical masks of joy. And yet, the mask's appearance likely comes across as more strange than beautiful to outsiders because it includes a facepiece resting on top of the head, a large hat of feathers, a hoop covered by cords and furs, and tufts of raffia on the upper arms (fig. 26; see fig. 1). Muyombo should always wear the most expensive of foot rattles, whose cheerful tinkling is keyed to the timbre of the human voice. In my experience, famed performers were punctilious in creating and maintaining clean and perfectly fitted costumes incorporating the best of materials. The small things mattered, like always using fresh feathers. For much of the twentieth century, the dance attracted some of the most gifted dancers and demanded a precision in matching steps to complicated drum sequences that aroused pure pleasure in spectators. When presented with Muyombo's facepiece, interlocutors categorized it as a mask of joy as they remembered the feelings aroused by individual, outstanding performances.

The *goal of beauty* is to make women cry with joy—to ululate, or cry *yéyé*. With only a little cultural training, these cries make happiness contagious. Matala, the modern young man, is also classed as a *mbuya ya kiese*. As for the female mask, the form of the face conforms to gendered canons

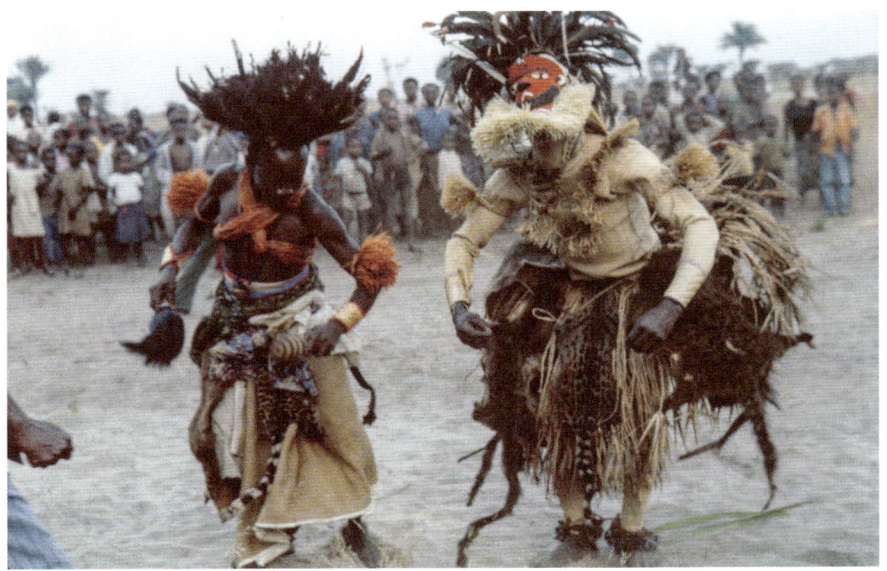

Fig. 26 **Masuwa Léon performing the Central Pende mask Muyombo.**
A retired dancer for this mask is inspired to join him, forgetting his arthritis and regaining some of the flexibility of youth.
Nioka-Munene, DR Congo, 1989.
Photo by Z. S. Strother.

of physical beauty. However, as for Muyombo, the performance itself serves as a criterion to judge beauty. Dancers of Matala should have a good sense of theater, catching the audience by surprise with quick changes of step. They need to be both athletic and flexible, so much so that the wife of one performer scoffed when her husband announced his plans to dance: "*Wanema!*" ("You're too heavy!")—meaning slow and stiff. In both Bandundu and Kasaï provinces, the young women's and men's masks may also engage in light comedies. Gambanda may primp before a mirror or mimic women's chores preparing food. Matala strikes vainglorious poses. These antics usually make people smile with amusement rather than laugh out loud. Such gestures enhance beauty.

Some of the masks that make people laugh out loud are ugly, literally. The crowd greets Tundu with cries of "*Wabola!*" ("You're ugly!").

Originally, the performer appeared with a raffia cloth drawn over the face. Over the course of the twentieth century, sculptors began to compete to make the most lumpy and asymmetrical visage that they could create. Eastern Pende mark their clown (Kindombolo) with the scars of smallpox. The clowns wear foot rattles that sound funny—*kerchunk kerchunk*—and with which performers emphasize <u>sudden</u> lunges. Despite the laughter, these maskers can <u>suddenly</u> rouse a touch of fear, as they carry whips for crowd control. Ironically, though, some of the most renowned masks that really do make people run and shout for pity may be appreciated for their beauty, expressing the charisma of power, even when dangerous (see fig. 25).

In the end, categories of aesthetic emotions are no more strictly defined than any others, but they do indicate how Pende themselves think about masks. Up to the present, I have never found sadness to be a goal, but it has a place. For one thing, there is the nostalgia that Nzomba mentioned in the context of Eastern Pende masquerade. Across West and Central Africa, it is not uncommon for retired dancers to relive the past as they dance one-on-one with the performer (see figs. 19, 26). They may also take the floor to show up what they consider a flawed performance. Everyone understands the dynamic, an intoxicating mix of triumph and loss for the dancer and sympathetic amusement for onlookers.

When I spoke about the perceived denial of sadness at a seminar at the Université de Kinshasa, some colleagues demurred, holding that sadness is *represented* by certain masks, such as Gandumbu (the little widow) for Central Pende.[83] However, they agreed when I stipulated that her performance does not provoke sadness on the part of the audience. Phalanxes of young women joke and shout encouragement to Gandumbu as they coax her away from the precipice of bitterness and remind the community of its responsibility for her care.

After some reflection, Father Didier Mupaya proposed to the group that

s a d n e s s   i s   p r e s e n t   i n   i t s   a b s e n c e ,

a powerful insight given the prohibition against grief during Pende masquerades and the important role of masked dances in concluding many funeral cycles in West Africa.[84] Bringing the meeting to a close, the Pende historian Sikitele

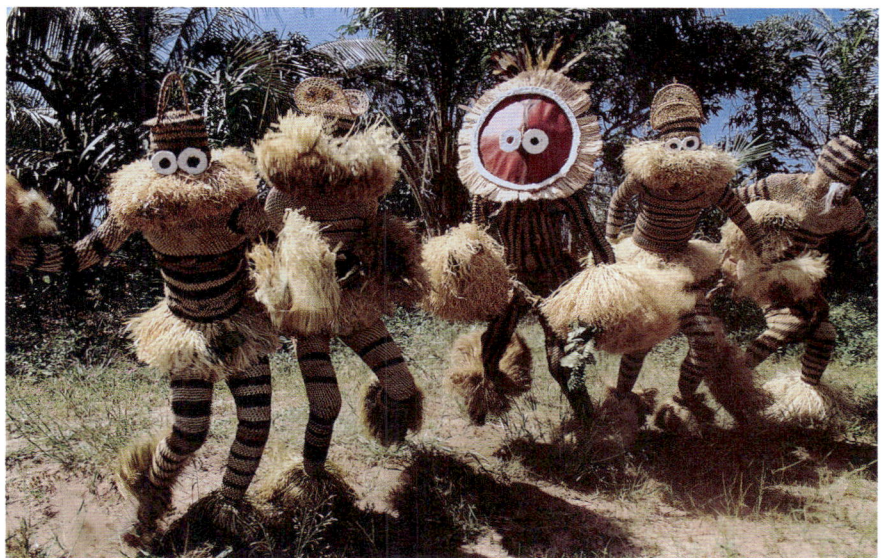

Fig. 27 Kwilu Pende Minganji masqueraders.
Near Gungu, DR Congo, 1970.
Photo by Eliot Elisofon.
Eliot Elisofon Photographic Archives, Smithsonian Institution,
Washington, DC.

Gize gave a moving confirmation to Mupaya's proposal when he cried out, "I was marked by the masks" as he recalled the profound emotion that washed over him during a masquerade organized in his honor in 1966. The Kwilu Pende had known a terrible cycle of suffering, beginning with an invasion by their Chokwe neighbors in the 1880s, followed by the Belgian colonial occupation, which in turn led to a revolt in 1931, and finally ending with the brutal suppression by the postindependence government of the Mulelist rebellion, from 1963 to 1965. And yet, when Sikitele returned home from the safety of boarding school, he could not get over the "exuberance" of Minganji maskers (fig. 27) and of the people singing and dancing with them. The masquerade proved a touchstone throughout Sikitele's life, and he was so moved (*tellement ému, tellement émotioné*) that he composed a series of poems in order to process why it had been so meaningful. In "Suffering," Sikitele writes that "I saw, believe it, ghostlike men, dying men, men living in famine…. Believe it! I saw these men, these [same] men … with candid smiles showing their white teeth. In Musanga [one of the chieftaincies ravaged by reprisals] … They have taught me to sing and dance." In "The Message," he concludes: "Instead of pity, have the courage to admire this true courage…. Taste these beautiful smiles / burning with pain."[85] Sikitele went on to become a renowned historian of the Pende revolt and knows better than anyone the atrocities associated with its suppression. And yet, what he often replays in memory is the exhilaration and sometimes the unexpected humor of the Minganji dancing, which allowed him to process sorrow and loss, and which taught him how to be resilient, how to come back to life (*rebondir*), how to confront misery without becoming "stuck in sadness." The speed, power, and whips of the Minganji had terrified Sikitele during his childhood initiation, but their "exuberance" aroused very different aesthetic emotions in the context of social and cultural devastation. After the seminar, we discussed the ongoing and remarkable reinvention of the Minganji by Kwilu Pende in Kinshasa.[86] By setting aside their whips, their "unique capacity to create joy" may be increasingly harnessed to conclude periods of mourning. Sikitele has even witnessed widows inspired to dance with them. Secular or no, the emotional palette of these masks remains powerful.

The audience-participants of masked performances experience a host of feelings, notably happiness, humor, anxiety, and fear. This economy of feelings will be carefully stimulated by the organizers who assemble the dancers, musicians, singers, and sometimes ritual practitioners for social or religious reasons. Personal ambition also plays a role as organizers or performers seek to become renowned (*or to make a living*) by developing a fan base in search of certain kinds of experiences.[87] And individuals in the audience may explore some of the more private emotions, such as sadness, grief, or nostalgia, when they remember how a deceased friend or family member loved to dance a particular mask. There is one emotional category, however, in the kaleidoscope of aesthetic emotions associated with masquerade that demands to be discussed in depth: surprise.

Chapter 5
Masks and the Uncanny

Surprise: The Ultimate Masquerade Emotion

Surprise is one of the primary aesthetic emotions embedded in masquerade, and just maybe the most important. The adverb <u>suddenly</u> (and some of its synonyms) have been underlined throughout the text to signal how often masked performance is associated with abrupt, unexpected changes of perception. The spectator's astonishment helps ignite the "combustion of conflicting emotions" that make the event memorable.[1] Nonetheless, surprise is never a goal unto itself unless it is extended in time to take the form of marvel or awe. Most often, surprise serves as an ancillary emotion heightening the arousal of all the other aesthetic emotions. Building on Edmund Burke and a deep history of German philosophy, the literary critic Karl Heinz Bohrer argues that marking of suddenness in narratives is constitutive of the aesthetics of terror.[2] Without a doubt, masquerades exploit surprise as an intensification agent of anxiety and fear. Is it time to run or not? When the Pende Pumbu masker abruptly cut the cord restraining him, people and animals were routed before him (see fig. 25). Interestingly, everyone knew that Pumbu would eventually cut the cord—but when? Prolonging the uncertainty heightened the emotional investment of audience members and the "ever-present threat of <u>sudden</u> destructive acts" creates the right ambiance for many masks.[3]

Besides being instrumental for sharpening sensations of anxiety and fear, surprise is also an ancillary emotion intensifying the expression of the other primary masquerading emotions of humor and even happiness. A pile of leaves pedaling a bicycle is incongruous, but its unexpected arrival during a tense moment induces laughter. One of the songs for Muyombo, a Central Pende "mask of beauty," urges the performer to dazzle the crowd: "Make us cry 'wow'!" (see fig. 26).[4] I have seen people smile recalling particular performances in the past. In its heyday, Muyombo attracted some of the finest performers, and onlookers took deep pleasure in replaying flash-bulb memories of the dancer's out-of-the-ordinary grace and skill.

The marking of suddenness in a narrative is a "sign of discontinuity" that points to "whatever resists aesthetic integration."[5] Although this perspective tilts the discussion toward the negative, or at least the perverse, it can be enjoyable to be caught in a paradox. Despite a dominant mood, the spectators' attention and engagement will oscillate during a masquerade performance as they themselves jostle to see and when, for example, their appreciation of a letter-perfect rendition of a contemporary women's dance is pierced by the <u>sudden</u> recognition of oversize men's hands. The thicker the resistance to cognitive consolidation, the more likely it is that the event will be replayed over and over in memory. If surprise is essential to masquerade, its most powerful instance may be found in the quality of feeling called "uncanny."

Why Do Masks Trouble Us?

An avid collector of masks, André Breton regretted that the "learned glosses" of scholars dodged the most important question of all: Why do they trouble us?[6] A friend mused over the same question when she told me about a birthday party organized as a masquerade ball. All the men were instructed to come in tuxedos and to wear domino masks. The women had a wider range of costumes. In principle, although Cari knew many or even the majority of the guests, she had to work at recognizing people from their height and physique. She found the men menacing in their anonymity. She also found it hard work to dissimulate her own identity, to take care to modulate her voice and body language. Some took pleasure in the exercise, but Cari found it disturbing—although something she liked to think about, especially as her husband loathed and resented it. She had thought the party would be fun but instead found it "weird, disconcerting, overwhelming."[7] Nothing should be more familiar to us than the human body, so the mask's ability to render it strange, to create noise in its interpretation, can provoke a visceral reaction whether in entertainment or ritual contexts. The *troubling* aspect of the uncanny differentiates it on the spectrum of aesthetic emotions from experiences of wonder or awe.

While invoking the idea of the uncanny, I hasten to explain that I am not interested in imposing a psychoanalytic reading cross-culturally, as if building on Sigmund Freud's argument that the experience of the uncanny is rooted in a "return of the repressed." Instead, I am returning to certain of Freud's sources who were attempting to identify an "aesthetic category," in the sense of a quality of feeling, of "lurking unease" that lay within the sublime.[8] In 1906, the psychologist Ernst Jentsch identified an intriguing ambivalence between the German terms *heimlich* (homey), with its domestic connotations of all that is comfortable, quiet, and cozy, and *unheimlich* (usually translated as "uncanny" in English and as a "worrisome strangeness" [*l'inquiétante étrangété*] in French). Jentsch analyzed the loss of orientation and feelings of insecurity or anxiety, which arise from the (unexpected) introduction of new or foreign elements into the old and familiar.[9] The "lurking unease" provoked when the familiar mutates into the unfamiliar is central to much masquerade experience.

Beginning with Otto Rank in 1914, many theorists have remarked on the importance of doubling for triggering experiences of the uncanny because it highlights the difficulties in distinguishing between reality and representation. Face masks are powerful tools for invoking a sense of the uncanny because they literally layer one face over another. Here Sarah Kofman's observation is well taken: "the double does not double a presence, but rather supplements it, allowing one to read, as in a mirror, originary 'difference.'"[10] In other words, the outer face does not obliterate knowledge of an inner face but supplements its signifying capacity with uncertainty about the relationship of inner to outer and self to other. Although European and American writers tend to think of masks playing the former tension (between inner and outer), many examples in this volume illustrate that African masquerade artists often double the face top to bottom (see figs. 1, 4, 8, 24).

Comparing masked to unmasked dance in West Africa, Simon Ottenberg concludes that the "aim of the performer seems not to be to express emotion by his behavior but by his actions to arouse emotions in the viewers." Both groups of performers, he found, could stimulate "feelings of pleasure, humor, and admiration of skill," but maskers could also provoke fear, anxiety, and awe. Persuaded by Freudian psychoanalysis, Ottenberg argues that the blank, expressionless faces of the maskers could provoke "stronger" emotions because they allowed viewers to project infantile fantasies and repressed memories onto the performer.[11]

Nevertheless, as I have been insisting, the mask exists in a breathing, moving body unless it is a thing on the wall. Europeanists writing on double consciousness tend to privilege the psychology of the performer, as when Terry Castle discerns that the "pleasure of [eighteenth-century urban] masquerade attended on the experience of doubleness, the alienation of inner from outer, a fantasy of two bodies, simultaneously and thrilling present, self and other together, the two-in-one."[12] By contrast, Monni Adams found evidence that the audience for Bo masquerades in Côte d'Ivoire experienced "a kind of double consciousness, shifting from one to another perception," sometimes acutely aware of the performer as an individual and sometimes "accepting of the *gla* as a forest spirit."[13] Whether we think of the masker as having two bodies, or two personae, there is a dramatic tension, meaning that the relationship between the two is never resolved for onlookers.

"Audiences relish the artifice behind theater."[14] This was the most important lesson that the award-winning theater director Julie Taymor learned during four years of study in Indonesia (1975–79). When she allows the audience's attention to move back and forth between actor and illusion, the dramatist engages spectators as creative partners who "experience the art from several perspectives at once."[15] In the stage spectacle *The Lion King,* Taymor rarely covered the faces of performers but routinely doubled them through a dazzling variety of puppetry and masking effects. She sometimes wondered whether the audience could become "too conscious of the artifice, too aware of the technique.... But whenever one of the actors began to master the form, I felt the tremendous emotion that a puppet or mask can communicate. I watched Scar [the villain] and knew that a human being alone could not achieve the same visual power without the mask" (fig. 28).[16] Taymor attributes the impact of this type of theater to the "magic" of watching something inanimate "come alive, the duality moves us."[17] We are used to taking for granted that we can distinguish a thing from a living being, that we know how people in our social circle

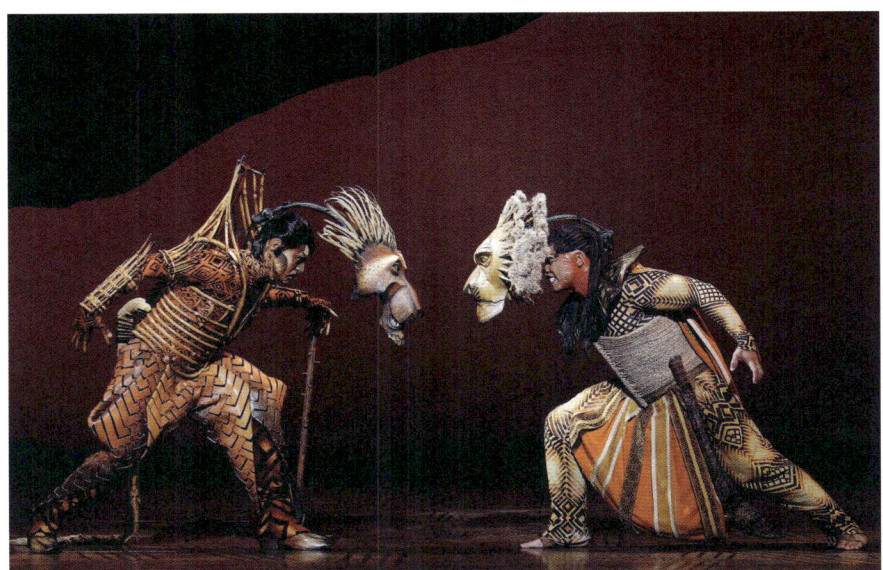

Fig. 28 **Left to right: Scar (J. Anthony Crane) challenging Mufasa (Dionne Randolph).**
From the national tour of Disney's *The Lion King*, produced by Julie Taymor.
Photo by Joan Marcus.

behave. What Carlos Fausto called the "cognitive instability" created by masks[18] is a powerful stimulus for emotional response.

Instances of surprise are crucial in engaging the audience. John Rudlin—like Dario Fo, another theorist of *Commedia dell'Arte*—counsels actors that

> "a real mask should never be hung on a wall, unless its working days are over, since its gaze will be diminished by unanimated familiarity." [19]

Rudlin raises a critical issue for masquerading: how to keep the mask, intended as a tool for estrangement, from being neutralized by overfamiliarity. Probably the most common technique is to shroud the mask in long periods of invisibility. Indeed, it is not uncommon in

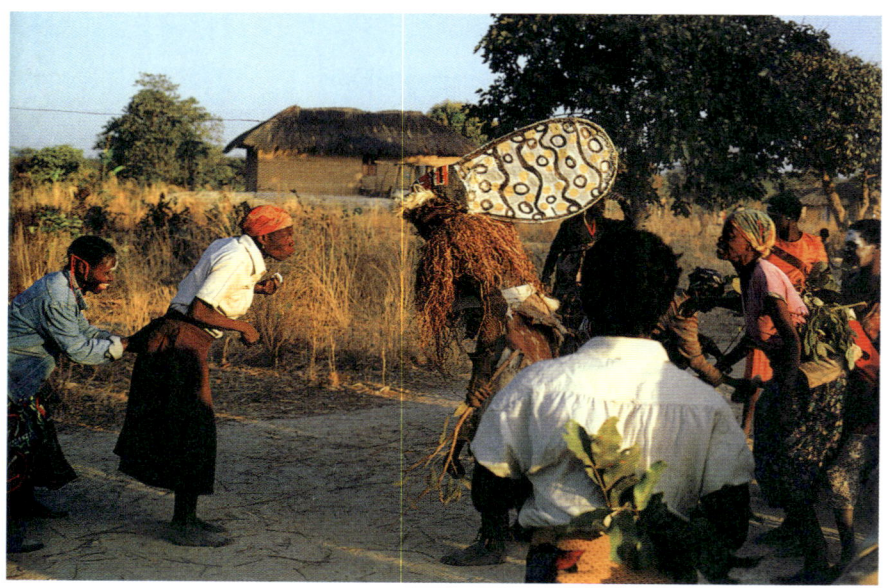

Fig. 29 **Women taunting and "playing" with masked figures during the men's initiation (*mukanda*).**
Reserve village, Kabompo District, Zambia, 1992.
Photo by Elisabeth L. Cameron.

Africa for masks to appear for no more than a couple of minutes at any one event.

An alternative means of maintaining aura around masks is to make them unpredictable, especially if they perform for long periods.[20] Elisabeth Cameron recorded fascinating evidence for this strategy in Zambia. In a society where only men masquerade, she notes that women not only privately identified the performers but also interacted very differently with masqueraders depending on their kinship relationships, whether the dancer was a brother, paternal cousin, or lover (fig. 29). From time to time, for fear that the women had domesticated the mask, the men in the community would hire an outsider to come dance who would not be inhibited by such relationships. If the woman did not figure out quickly enough that

Chapter 5

a substitution had taken place, she risked being struck by a switch, punished for approaching too closely.[21]

Think about this woman's experience. She knows who the performer is. Or does she? There's the moment of doubt. And then she realizes that he is *probably* not who she thought. He is both lover and not-lover, both brother and not-brother. And this woman's experience, observed by the other women, reintroduces doubts for them too. Surely there can be no better example of the "sliding of coziness into dread."[22] Nonetheless, as Siona Wilson wrote me, there is "no specific moment of stable and certain uncanniness, but rather a necessary oscillation between the familiar and the unfamiliar."[23] This is why the men had to bring in the stranger: to create doubts. It is important that masks never be taken for granted. However, even if there can never be a guaranteed trigger for the uncanny, mask cultures often work very hard to predispose their audiences to be receptive to the experience. To analyze this conditioning process, I turn again to my immersive learning experience among the Eastern Pende of DR Congo.

Don't Touch! No, Touch!
How to Neutralize the Uncanny

Turning the tables on one hundred years of theorizing on masks, the iconoclast Michael Taussig has concluded that "everything seems to hinge not on the mask but on *unmasking*."[24] It is important to observe that Taussig continues to work within the European paradigm of masking as a "theater" of truth and deceit; however, his seductive twist is the proposition that acts of sacrilege revitalize the sacred.[25] Taussig drew inspiration from Martin Gusinde's 260-page narrative of the initiation that he had commissioned into a men's society among the decimated Selk'nam population of Isla Grande (Tierra del Fuego) in 1923.[26] Taussig does not discuss the haunting photos that Gusinde coauthored with Selk'nam, who struck some intimidating postures despite their need to be still for the camera. Their mask practice combined individualized full-body painting to enhance the physique with cloth head coverings, sometimes pulled so tightly that the features of the face appear squashed and blurred (fig. 30).

There has never been a better example of masking holding in tension two personae through the vehicle of the human figure. It would have been

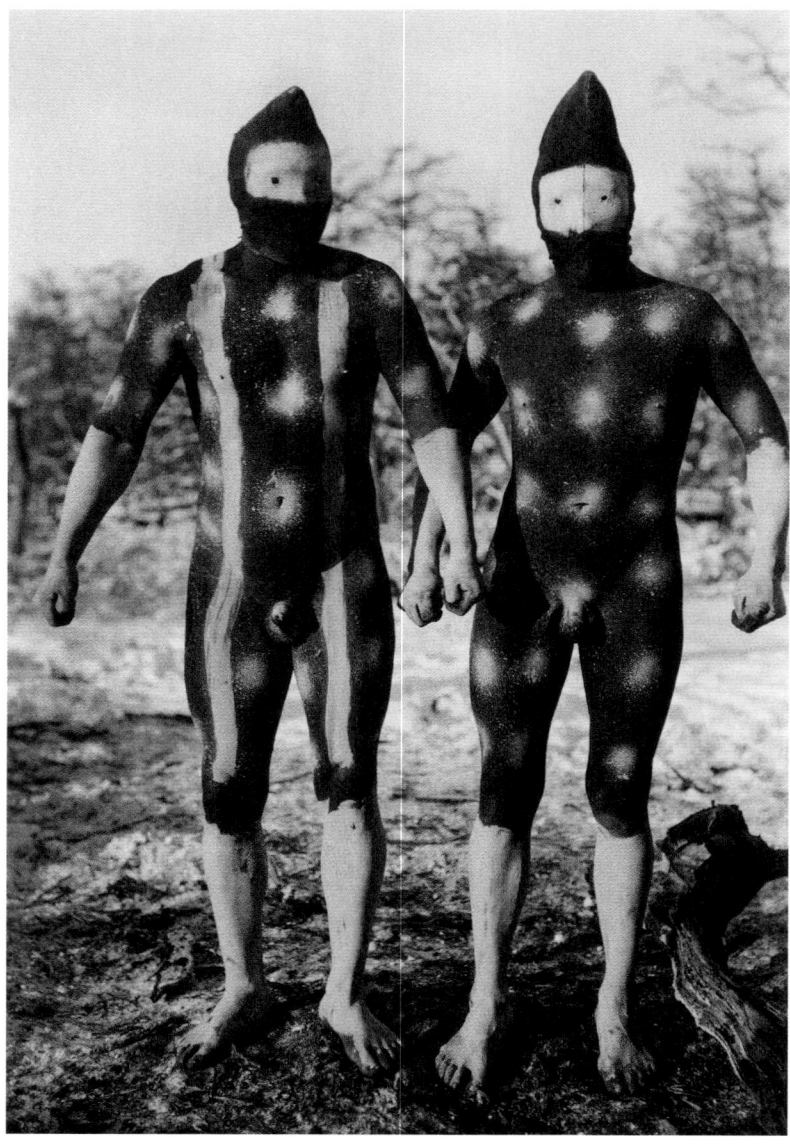

Fig. 30 **Selk'nam Hain ceremony, 1923.**
Tierra del Fuego, Chile.
Photo by Martin Gusinde.

impossible for someone to go unrecognized in small Selk'nam communities, especially as the artful body painting drew attention to the individuality of each human form. And yet, as outlined in the introduction, masks are brilliant at shifting signifying capacity away from the face to the body. In this case, even as the limbs and torso became hypervisualized, the dissolving of the facial features delivered a warning that the initiate could not depend on expected relational norms. Even the still photo causes the viewer's eyes to flicker involuntarily between head and body, pondering the significance of the clenched fists. The body in movement would have upped the ante as onlookers sought frantically for clues to intentionality. Gusinde reported that induction into the men's society culminated when the initiate was ordered, "Touch it!" The boys began by lightly stroking the shoulder and chest of the masked figure, building the courage to "grab" and "raise" the head covering.[27] Taussig looks past the masked body to argue that the "apocalyptic moment of unmasking" transforms the deceived into deceiver who passes on the secret and thereby "consecrates that which it so spectacularly destroys, namely the illusion regarding contrived spiritual performance."[28]

But I ask,
            "why so much emphasis on the sense
of touch?"
            I was able to document from start to finish two Eastern Pende boys' initiations (*mukanda*) in DR Congo in 1987 and 1988, which hold intriguing parallels to what Taussig extrapolates from Gusinde's experience among Selk'nam. However, my Pende interloctors did not conceive of the apocalyptic moment as a visual or metaphorical "unmasking" even though the initiates were obliged to rip the headpiece off a masker. Instead, the ritual was framed as a *tactile experience* designed to inoculate initiates against the uncanny effects of masking.[29]

Before delving into the initiation proper, it is helpful to place masks in a wider social context. To begin, it is a common misperception that African children learn about masks only through a formal initiation process. Children encounter masks throughout life and may even play at mask-making themselves.[30] In addition to having opportunities to participate in community masquerades, Eastern Pende children will encounter *mukanda* maskers who burst forth daily over a period of several months from the tall grass into the village. These maskers carry switches cut from branches, which can draw blood. But there are many rules about whom they may strike. The main targets are adolescents (girls and uninitiated boys) and the mothers of initiates. Furthermore, it is forbidden to hit all strangers. *This means that the victims know their persecutors.* Pende masquerading exploits an intimate relationship between the masker and audience.

People in Pendeland usually hear the masks before they see them. Masqueraders are required to carry rattles. Moreover, as creatures of the bush, their costumes incorporate masses of raffia threads, which rustle noisily. As a result, even the masker's shuffling walk creates a distinctive sound that once learned is never forgotten. Since it is difficult to take anyone unawares, masks must resort to cunning. They like to hide behind buildings or shrubs to ambush their prey, but it is rare for them to be able to surprise their targets.

In 1987, I was walking by myself along a savanna path. The skies were blue and I could see palm trees ahead, indicating that I was close to home. I heard a slight rattle, and—<u>suddenly</u>—the sunny landscape was tinged with menace. I recognized the sound of a *mukanda* masker and knew that they never traveled alone. Standing stock-still, I surveilled my surroundings but could only see tall grass swaying in the breeze. A privileged trigger for the uncanny is when the sense of vision is in conflict with the other senses. My eyes told me that I was alone, safe, but my ears said otherwise.

When individuals meet masks, they will need to process quickly who might be stalking them, looking for clues in the masqueraders' relative size, body language, and exposed hands and feet. Can they figure out if it is a friend or brother who will only tease? Or is it the local bully, who would risk breaking the rules? Is it a stranger, who may charge but who will always veer off without contact? Or is it a son, who misses his mother and is taking this opportunity to show off for her, hoping that she will guess who he is? For both mother and son, this is a poignant moment. I have seen mothers simultaneously smiling and teary-eyed after such encounters. While it reassures her to see her son healthy and mischievous, she cannot help feeling a little sad that she may not touch him or address him by name. The experience of proximity and separation drives home the reality that her son has moved beyond her domain into the realm of men.

Additional rules ensure a raucous atmosphere reminiscent of tag, a game where would-be victims taunt the masqueraders before they dash to safety. In Pendeland, small children cannot be struck but they *are* chased, and they are terrified of the masqueraders, who often figure in their nightmares. Masks may never travel at night. Masqueraders may never enter houses, so sprinting women and children often slam doors in their faces. Frustrated, the maskers will kick the doors as hard as they can. Inside, the inhabitants watch with bated breath as the door jumps on its hinges, <u>suddenly</u> anxious that it might not hold. Whether one believes in Freudian analysis or not, it is these intense childhood experiences with masks that sediment in the body certain instinctive reactions in masks. I was startled to realize when caught on the path that only a few weeks of experience was needed to condition an intense Pavlovian reaction on my part to the mask.

In Chief Kende Kakele (Katshivi Koji)'s *mukanda* camp, the opening ritual began when the first nine boys who had clamored to be initiated were brought to a site in the bush where they could see three masqueraders leaping, lunging, pirouetting, and stamping up a cloud of dust. Boys who had run from masks all their lives were told, to their horror, to pull off the headpiece of the masquerader marked by a shiny green leaf skirt. The dancers were all tall, well-built young men, and the boys' average age was twelve. Finally, Luya Chombe, the fourteen-year-old son of a hunter, broke ranks and wrestled with the target, but he simply was not big enough and received terrible blows on the back (fig. 31). Finally, Luya's father, Sh'a Lamba, could no longer stand it. He launched himself on the masquerader and was the one who actually pulled off the headpiece. Outraged, the young men running the initiation started to brawl with the fathers. Technically, Sh'a Lamba broke the rules, but this kind of thing happens all the time, and it is one of the ways adolescents bond with their fathers.

When things settled down, the more timid boys were obliged to pull a leaf from the costume and receive a symbolic blow. In the end, the experience was designed to increase the boys' self-confidence because each of them had wrestled with his worst fear and emerged triumphant. He had touched the mask! Boys continued to join the camp over a period of several months, and each individual without fail had to experience his own personal ritual during which he was ordered to tear off the headpiece or a piece of the costume and receive a small blow in punishment.

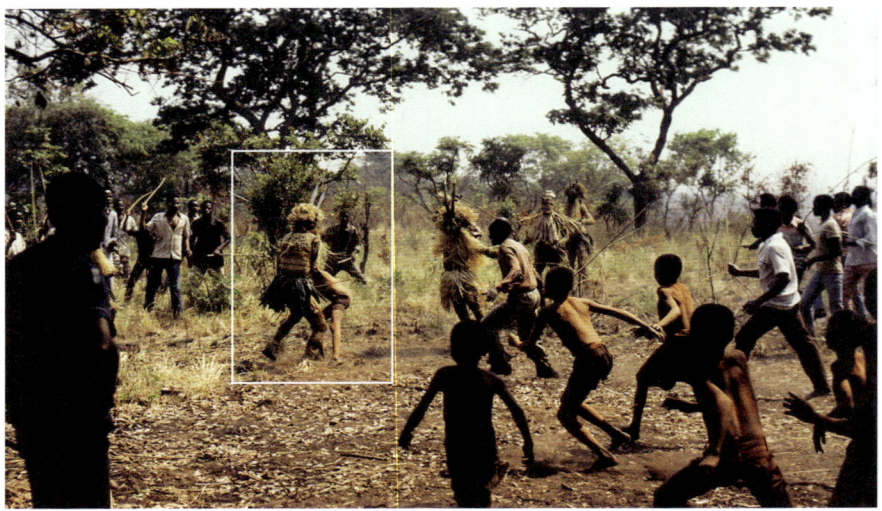

Fig. 31 *"Kukuata mbuya!,"* signifying "Touch/Seize/ Take possession of the Mask!," the opening ritual to the Eastern Pende boys' initiation (*mukanda*).
Luya's father charges up to help his son rip off the headpiece from the masker with the green skirt. A bodyguard with whip raised will catch the boy before his father can intervene.
Ndjindji, DR Congo, 11 July 1987.
Photo by Z. S. Strother.

Is this the unmasking highlighted by Michael Taussig? In my field notes, I kept referring to it as such—after all, the headpiece was ripped off the body of the dancer. However, I always knew better. It is difficult in Kipende to talk about removing the face covering because mask (*mbuya*) always signifies the package of face covering (if there is one), costume, and dance. Nor does it work as a metaphor—in Kipende there is no "unmasking" of some hidden truth. Instead, the ritual is called *kukuata kua mbuya. Kukuata* is a common verb in West Bantu languages signifying "to touch, to take, to lay hands on, to take possession of, to hold on to, to engage in hand-to-hand combat." What is important here is taking possession by strength of arm. Boys go voluntarily to *mukanda,* and it shows that they are ready to be men if they are able to wrestle with and take possession of the masks. After the ritual, in the company of other initiates, the youngsters may name performers, but the most important result of the experience is not to reveal a secret of some sort; it is to shatter the emotional grip of the masks.

Touch is the enemy of the uncanny.

Laying hands on the masker brings the initiate close and reconciles vision with all the other senses.

Rising interest in the interrelationship of the senses and the emotions has led to a reassessment of tactile experience, long denigrated by aesthetes such as Friedrich Schiller as "a mark of savagery."[31] And yet, it is good to remember that many European philosophers, notably Johan Gottfried Herder, considered vision to be untrustworthy, a source of illusion, whereas the sense of touch could establish truth itself.[32] The initiations choreograph just such a conflict of perception in which the hands tame the flights of imagination inspired by what the boys saw, heard, or smelled, through tangible experience of flesh, wood, and fiber.

A Delicious Shiveriness

For those not privileged to touch, confronting the moving, breathing body of the mask introduces ambiguity into the perception of space. Tony Vidler has emphasized that European literature is dominated by a spatial experience of the uncanny where the "home" becomes estranged and increasingly threatening.[33] Vidler's emphasis on the spatial experience of the uncanny is particularly relevant here.

Masks are matchless in their ability to transform the most banal of public spaces into an oneiric world outside of time, where rules no longer apply. Bring in roaming masks and suddenly the village square, a clearing in the bush, or a soccer field becomes a sacral space, strange in its newfound unfamiliarity. I would argue that it is the special ability of maskers to destabilize domestic spaces that accounts for their widespread use in initiation rituals.[34]

During community masquerades, the organizers rip public space out of the real world in order to suggest an invisible world to which the living often can be oblivious. As one man reprimanded some young graduates who were horsing around during the refurbishment of an altar, "You're joking, but you don't realize that all the dead are here, even all of the deceased [former chiefs]." When everything had been prepared correctly, when disputes in the community were settled, when the dead were invited as they should be, when the audience participated with a full heart, the moment would come when older practitioners reported being able to sense the invisible dead dancing alongside. On one such occasion, Kin'a Ndusu, radiant, tugged at my sleeve and asked:

"Do you feel them? They're here."

Confused, I asked: "Who?" *Nvumbi,* she answered: the dead. Here the masks most definitely *did not* represent the dead, they *did not* embody the dead (although that is what you tell children), but they created an ambiance in which the sensitive viewer experienced the eerie sensation of invisible beings manifesting in the sunshine of the village square. Unexpectedly, such an encounter, carefully structured both temporally and spatially, produced not dread but joy. The conflicting emotions intensify the experience.

Freud articulated his theory of the uncanny through a reading of Ernst Theodor Wilhelm Hoffmann's story "The Sandman" (1817), where the word *uncanny* never appears. However, Hoffmann did offer his own insightful interpretation in another story called "The Uncanny Guest" (1819). On an autumn night, a merry party is gathered around a tea table when a "shiver <u>suddenly</u> passed through them." Their senses were out of sync; they could see the blazing fire and smell the steaming punch, and yet they felt chilled. As they analyze the sensation that they shared, they savor it as a "delicious shiveriness" but are thankful that its duration is brief.[35]

In the story, the barrister Dagobert discovers something important about the experience of the uncanny and the family of related aesthetic feelings, such as wonder or awe. Nothing can be guaranteed to produce these sensations, but certain conditions render the subject more receptive (or predisposed, as Hoffmann words it). Above all, the subject must be in a position of safety. That is why the "home" looms so large in German terminology. And yet, one only experiences safety when danger looms. Think of the game of tag—how the ability to run to home base emboldens children to experience risk as pleasure. It is only from a position of safety that one may embrace one's own powerlessness and inconsequentiality in the face

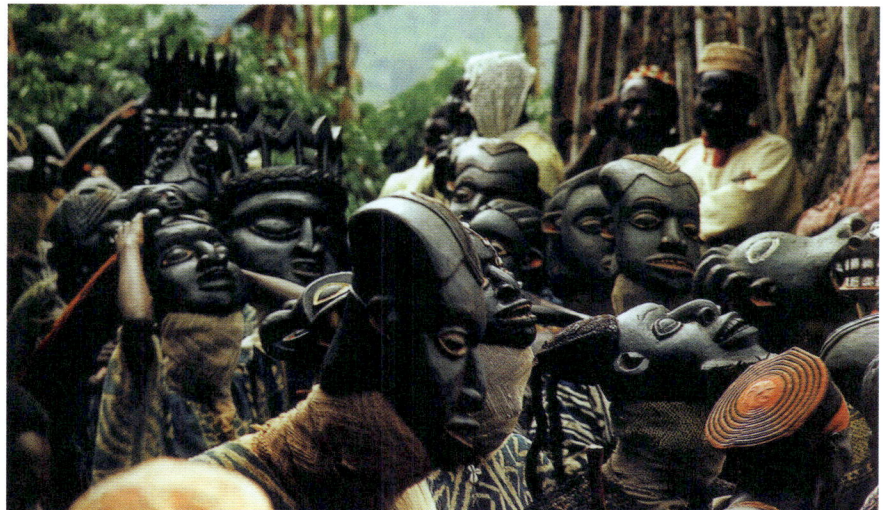

Fig. 32 **Memorial celebration in Mboh.**
Oku, Cameroon, 1976.
Photo by Hans-Joachim Koloss.
Berlin, Ethnologisches Museum, Staatliche Museen zu Berlin.

of nature or the supernatural. But it is a fragile, fleeting sensation, always on the cusp of fear.[36] Dagobert hypothesizes that "pleasurable" sensations may even act as lures leading to encounters that trigger "a horror which makes the hair stand on end."[37] As Hoffmann situates them, wonder and awe sit on an emotional spectrum bleeding into terror.

The hostess of the party disagrees with Dagobert's universalizing interpretation, favoring nurture over nature. She argues that such feelings emerge from a regression into childhood, a memory of what they had felt as children listening to ghost stories in the night. In the end, the group agrees that the "shudder of awe" is experienced as an "echo ... [of] strings" first sounded in childhood.[38] The resonance is why the familiar sensation feels like a memory that cannot quite be recalled.

Through stylistic exposition, another aspect of the uncanny emerges. Hoffmann writes that his characters felt "as if one were <u>suddenly</u> casting a glance, with one's eyes open, into some strange, mystic dreamworld."[39] Wonder and the uncanny are triggered by the experience of "suddenness."

In essence, the experience of wonder or uncanniness is itself the experience of a rapid shift in worldview.

There is a palette of aesthetic emotions including surprise, wonder, awe, and uncanniness that share a certain kinship. These are all rooted in an oscillation of the familiar and the unfamiliar, entail a radical change of views, offer the thrill of risk from a position of safety, and also somehow stir childhood memories. The difference is that the uncanny, as almost every writer has recognized including both Hoffmann and Freud, is associated with real peril. The child with Saint Nikolaus, the women in Zambia, the passersby on the path who hear a telltale rattle—all learn that there is no safe vantage point. Sooner or later, everyone is exposed.

Nicolas Argenti wrote of the "alluring danger" in Oku (Cameroon) of lineage masquerades.[40] As he describes a memorial service: "It is into this packed and teeming environment that the masquerade … <u>suddenly</u> bursts forth, producing a breathtaking explosion of sound and movement" (fig. 32).[41] Although he found that these performances were eagerly anticipated, even scheduled, Oku people described their aesthetic effect as one of surprise. Argenti's interlocutors exclaimed, "My mouth dried," a phrase accounting for "the loss for words which results from amazement or wonder"; it "also points to the lack of saliva that accompanies fear." Argenti concluded that dry mouth points to the "sensation of the presence of the unknown." The surprise invoked emerges from "proximity to the unfathomable."[42] Dry mouth is a "compound of fear and attraction." Oku people speaking Cameroonian English say, "We don [sic] see wonders today!"[43]

Freud and the philosophers emphasize the frightening aspect of the uncanny. Freud speaks of "what arouses dread and horror."[44] But the artists are well aware of its pleasures, which Hoffmann described so eloquently as a "delicious shiveriness." Under strictly controlled circumstances, the <u>sudden</u> brush with the incomprehensible produces joy, although the management of fear has been fundamentally constitutive for Pende and Oku masquerade experience.

The four primary emotions serving as goals for masked dance—joy, hilarity, fear, and surprise—are all intensified by the cognitive dissonance, those flashes of recognition of the body in the mask, which shake audience-participants from their confidence in mastery of the world.

Notes

INTRODUCTION

1   Hans Belting, "Towards an Anthropology of the Image," in *Anthropologies of Art,* ed. Mariët Westermann (Sterling and Francine Clark Art Institute, 2005), 47.

2   Vicki Bruce and Andy Young, *In the Eye of the Beholder: The Science of Face Perception* (Oxford University Press, 1998), 250–53.

3   Dario Fo, *The Tricks of the Trade* (Routledge, 1991), 27, 29. Originally published in Italian as *Manuale minimo dell'attore* (Einaudi, 1987).

4   The US American playwright Eugene O'Neill lampooned actors who treated their bodies as "bored spectators that have been dragged off to the theatre when they would have much preferred a quiet evening in the upholstered chair at home." Eugene O'Neill, "Memoranda on Masks" [1932], in *Playwrights on Playwriting: The Meaning and Making of Modern Drama from Ibsen to Ionesco,* ed. Toby Cole (Hill and Wang, 1960), 70. For an overview of twentieth-century dramatists' views on masks, see David Wiles, *Mask and Performance in Greek Tragedy: From Ancient Festival to Modern Experimentation* (Cambridge University Press, 2007), 67–101, 113, 115–16. Jacques Lecoq was particularly influential as an advocate for the value of training actors with masks; see, for example, Richard Schechner, "Julie Taymor: From Jacques Lecoq to 'The Lion King': An Interview," *The Drama Review* 43, no. 3 (1999): 36–41.

5   Julie Taymor, personal communication with author, 21 September 2022.

6   Richard Schechner, *Performance Theory* (1988; rev. and expanded ed., Routledge, 2003), 22n10.

7   Kim Richter, email to author, 15 October 2008 (my emphasis).

8   Germaine Dieterlen, "Symbolisme du masque en Afrique occidentale," in *Le masque,* exh. cat. (Musée Guimet, 1960), 50.

9   In fact, one of the earliest sketches from Dogon country, from Leo Frobenius's expedition to the Bandiagara Cliff in September 1908, shows rabbit maskers dancing energetically with bare chests, arms, and legs; see Leo Frobenius, *Auf dem Wege nach Atlantis,* ed. Herman Frobenius (Vita Deutsches Verlagshaus, 1911), 233.

10   Guy Le Moal, *Les Bobo: Nature et fonction des masques* (1980; Musée royal de l'Afrique central, 1999), 168. Unless otherwise indicated, all translations are mine.

11   See also Le Moal, *Les Bobo,* 166, plates 11, 18, 19, 20, 24, 30. For the reasons given, I must dispute Van Beek and Leyten's insistence that the "African definition" of the mask presumes an "invisible dancer." Walter E. A. Van Beek and Harrie M. Leyten, *Masquerades in African Society: Gender, Power, and Identity* (James Currey, 2023), 49.

12   Roland Barthes, *Camera Lucida* (Hill and Wang, 1980), 26–27.

13   Robert Farris Thompson, *African Art in Motion: Icon and Act in the Collection of Katherine Coryton White,* exh. cat. (University of California Press, 1974), 275.

14   Monni Adams, "Agency and Control in Masked Festivals Among the Bo People, Southwestern Côte d'Ivoire," *Zeitschrift für ethnologie* 130, no. 2 (2005): 195–221; and Monni Adams, "'It Opens Your Mouth!': Forest Spirit Identities in Public Display and Private Discussion; Masking and Rhetoric in Canton Boo, Southwestern Côte d'Ivoire," *Archiv für Völkerkunde* 56 (2006): 1–30. Adams's field research was conducted from 1983 to 1985 and 1988 to 1990.

15   Adams, "Agency and Control," 203. *Gela* will appear elsewhere in this text, but readers will find that the spelling for similar terms among neighboring Wè and Dan communities will be rendered differently in English, depending on the scholar's training and regional differences in pronunciation. Commonly, one finds the following patterns of transcriptions: *gela* (pl. *gla*) among Wè in Côte d'Ivoire; *ge* or *gué* among Dan in Côte d'Ivoire (pl. *genu*); and *gɛ* (pl. *genu*) among Dan in Liberia. I thank Yann Petit for his clarifications; email to author, 28 December 2024.

16   Adams, "Agency and Control," 201.

17   Adams, "Agency and Control," 217.

18   Georges Buraud, *Les masques* (Seuil, 1948), 7. Reissued in 2014 by Musée du Quai Branly.

19   Adams, "Agency and Control," 203–9.

20   Adams, "'It Opens Your Mouth!,'" 10.

21   Carlos Fausto, "Le masque de l'animiste: Chimères et poupées russes en Amérique indigène," *Gradhiva,* no. 13 (2011): 52, 55.

22   Leo Frobenius, *Und Africa sprach … ,* vol. 2 (Vita, 1913), 40.

23   I thank Professor Weise for sharing her remarkable film, *Masquerade* (2000).

24   Chinua Achebe, "The Igbo World and Its Art" (1988), in *Hopes and Impediments* (Doubleday, 1989), 65. In Nigerian English (as in Achebe's text), "masquerade" refers to the conceptual package of face mask (if there is one), costume, and performer (in action).

25   Anne-Marie Bouttiaux, "La danse des hommes, la jubilation des esprits: Masques guro de la région de Zuenoula, Côte d'Ivoire" (PhD diss., Université Libre de Bruxelles, 2000); Anne-Marie Bouttiaux, "Porteur de Zamble en pays Guro: Les enjeux de la célébrité," *Art'in, revue d'arts plastiques et darts du spectacle (Université de Valenciennes)* 1, no. 1 (2001): 77–85; Patrick McNaughton, *A Bird Dance near Saturday City: Sidi Ballo and the Art of West African Masquerade* (Indiana University Press, 2008); and Jordan A. Fenton, *Masquerade and Money in Urban Nigeria: The Case of Calabar* (University of Rochester Press, 2022).

26   Elisabeth L. Cameron, "Women = Masks: Initiation Arts in North-Western Province, Zambia," *African Arts* 31, no. 2 (1998): 58; Peter M. Weil, "Women's Masks and the Power of Gender in Mande History," *African Arts* 31, no. 2 (1998): 28–37, 88–90, 94–95; and Amanda B. Carlson, "In the Spirit and in the Flesh: Women, Masquerades, and the Cross River," *African Arts* 52, no. 1 (2019): 46–61. Cameron argues that instead of asking "Why don't women wear masks?," we should ask why women rarely wear "wood face masks," which leads to the "real question": "Why is it that women usually do not carve or work in hard materials [such as wood]?" ("Women = Masks," 58). Gagliardi

emphasizes that women play an active role in the audience for masks, even when they do not see them; Susan Elizabeth Gagliardi, "Seeing the Unseeing Audience: Women and West African Power Association Masquerades," *Africa* 88, no. 4 (2018): 744–67.

27   Ute M. Röschenthaler, "Honoring Ejagham Women," *African Arts* 31, no. 2 (1998): 49; Ute Röschenthaler, *Purchasing Culture: The Dissemination of Associations in the Cross River Region of Cameroon and Nigeria* (Africa World Press, 2011), 427–28; and Ute Röschenthaler, email to author, 19 March 2018. For authors wrestling with how to categorize women's masks, see also Monni Adams, "Women and Masks Among the Western Wè of the Ivory Coast," *African Arts* 19, no. 2 (1986): 46, 54–55; Cameron, "Women = Masks"; and Nicholas Argenti, *The Intestines of the State: Youth, Violence, and Belated Histories in the Cameroon Grassfields* (University of Chicago Press, 2007), 189, 208–10.

28   Röschenthaler, "Honoring Ejagham Women," 38. See also Ute M. Röschenthaler, *Die Kunst der Frauen: Zur Komplementarität von Nacktheit und Maskierung bei den Ejagham im Südwesten Kameruns* (Verlag für Wissenschaft und Bildung, 1993).

29   Röschenthaler, "Honoring Ejagham Women," 48–49.

30   Röschenthaler, *Purchasing Culture,* 428.

31   Röschenthaler, "Honoring Ejagham Women," 49. Although some believe that the women conceal themselves through darkness, their voices can be recognized as they sing or intone proverbs. As observed for male dancers, the prohibition against voicing the names of performers is more important than the act of disguise. On the acoustic experience of night performance, with its strong emotional impact, see Edward Lifschitz, "Hearing Is Believing: Acoustic Aspects of Masking in Africa," in *West African Masks and Cultural Systems,* ed. Sidney L. Kasfir (Musée royal de l'Afrique central, 1988), 221–29; Philip M. Peek, "The Sounds of Silence: Cross-World Communication and the Auditory Arts in African Societies," *American Ethnologist* 21, no. 3 (1994): 484–86; Philippe Jespers, "La puissance du masque: De l'audible au visible," in *Puissances de la voix: Corps sentant, corde sensible,* ed. Sémir Badir and Herman Parret (Presses universitaires de Limoges, 2001), 51–70; Argenti, *Intestines of the State,* 208–10; Gagliardi, "Seeing the Unseeing Audience"; and Fenton, *Masquerade and Money,* 113–49.

32   Fausto, "Le masque de l'animiste," 55.

33   The time depth and currency of such affiliations are open to debate given the investment of colonial regimes in mapping (or even creating) ethnicity. Terence Ranger, *The Invention of Tribalism in Zimbabwe* (Mambo Press, 1985); and Leroy Vail, ed., *The Creation of Tribalism in Southern Africa* (University of California Press, 1989). Nonetheless, the historian Sandra Green warns that the literature on colonial ethnicity formation can be overgeneralizing, stating that "ethnic identities did, indeed, exist in precolonial Africa, that these identities were as subject to change during this period as in the colonial period, and that such changes necessarily involved not only the powerful but also the marginalized." Sandra E. Green, *Gender, Ethnicity, and Social Change on the Upper Slave Coast: A History of the Anlo-Ewe* (Heinemann, 1996), 15.

34   Peter Probst, "Picture Dance: Reflections on *Nyau* Image and Experience," *Iwalewa Forum* 1/2000, 24.

35 Léopold Sédar Senghor, "The Lessons of Leo Frobenius," in *Leo Frobenius on African History, Art and Culture: An Anthology,* ed. Eike Haberland, trans. Patricia Crampton (M. Wiener, 2007), viii–ix. Originally published in 1973 as *Leo Frobenius on African History, Art and Culture: An Anthology*. It is conceivable that Africanists have been leery of addressing emotionality in the arts due to the notoriety of Senghor's aphorism, "Emotion is Negro, as reason is Greek" (Manthia Diawara, "The African Public Intellectual: The Negritude of Léopold Sédar Senghor," in *Dak'Art. Afrique: Miroir?,* exh. cat. [Biennale de l'Art African Contemporain, 2008], 200, 205n1). Soyinka famously quipped that Senghor had substituted the Cartesian "I think, therefore I am" with "I feel, therefore I am" (Wole Soyinka, *Myth, Literature and the African World* [Cambridge University Press, 1976], 135), and it is disturbing when Senghor cites approvingly archracist Arthur de Gobineau for describing Blacks as "the being[s] most energetically affected by artistic emotion" (Léopold Sédar Senghor, "The Spirit of Civilization, or the Laws of African Negro Culture," *Présence africaine,* no. 8–10 [June–November 1956], 52). In Senghor's defense, Diagne has argued that the poet's alexandrine ("L'émotion est nègre, comme la raison héllène"), penned in the late 1930s, should be understood as making a philosophical "analogy: Hellenic art is to analytic reason what African art is to emotion." In other words, Senghor was arguing that art is a form of knowledge. Souleymane Bachir Diagne, "Négritude," *The Stanford Encyclopedia of Philosophy,* ed. Edward N. Zalta (Summer 2018), https://plato.stanford.edu/archives/sum2018/entries/negritude. With the passage of time, Soyinka has also come to forgive the hyperbole of "metaphorical weapons forged in the heat of contestation" (Wole Soyinka, *The Burden of Memory, The Muse of Forgiveness* [Oxford University Press, 1999], 183). In any case, in this text, I am engaging Senghor's sensitivity to the bond between the artist and their public rather than his philosophical project of justifying emotion as a "higher state of consciousness." Léopold Sédar Senghor, "Emotion" [1962], in *Prose and Poetry,* ed. and trans. John Reed and Clive Wake (Heinemann, 1976), 34.

36 Robert Boddice, *A History of Feelings* (Reaktion, 2019), 10. See also Mark M. Smith, *Sensing the Past: Seeing, Hearing, Smelling, Tasting and Touching in History* (University of California Press), 2008.

37 Nick Routley, "A Visual Guide to Human Emotion," 8 April 2021, https://www.visualcapitalist.com/a-visual-guide-to-human-emotion.

38 From the program of a symposium, The Experience and Use of Wonder, held by the Department of the History of Art at the University of Michigan, Ann Arbor, 13 September 2008.

CHAPTER 1

1 Claude Lévi-Strauss, "The Many Faces of Man," *World Theatre* 10, no. 1 (1961): 20.

2 *Webster's New Collegiate Dictionary,* 8th ed. (1977), under "mask." The impact of the COVID-19 epidemic is unclear, with its ugly public health debates concerning the utility of "face coverings," on definitions of the verb "to mask," especially in easily edited online dictionaries. For this reason, I have preferred to consult a well-established, prepandemic print dictionary.

3   Cesare Ripa, *Baroque and Rococo Pictorial Imagery: The 1758–60 Hertel Edition of Ripa's "Iconologia,"* trans. Edward A. Maser (Dover Publications, 1971), item 127.

4   Mikhail Bakhtin, *Rabelais and His World,* trans. Hélène Iswolsky (Indiana University Press, 1984), 40. Originally published in Russian in 1965.

5   I thank Grace Dingledine for recommending this poster to me and for a lively exchange on masks in American popular culture.

6   Louisa May Alcott, *Behind a Mask* [1866], in *Alternative Alcott,* ed. Elaine Showalter (Rutgers University Press, 1988), 106.

7   Alcott, *Behind a Mask,* 102.

8   John Picton, "What's in a Mask?," *African Languages and Cultures* 3, no. 2 (1990): 188–89.

9   In French, the associations of *mascarade* with duplicity, political farces, and shams are so strong that it is always a struggle to find a neutral translation for the Africanist understanding of "masquerade" as a gathering of masqueraders. See *Linguee,* under "mascarade," https://www.linguee.fr/francais-anglais/search?source =auto&query=mascarade. For the problems of translation, see Amanda M. Maples, Jordan A. Fenton, and Lisa Homann, eds., *New African Masquerades: Artistic Innovations and Collaborations,* exh. cat. (New Orleans Museum of Art, 2025).

10   George Lakoff and Mark Johnson, *Metaphors We Live By* (University of Chicago Press, 1980), 7.

11   Lakoff and Johnson, *Metaphors We Live By,* 156.

12   Lakoff and Johnson, *Metaphors We Live By,* 157, 163.

13   Friedrich Nietzsche, *The Birth of Tragedy,* trans. Clifton P. Fadiman (Dover Publications, 1995), 52. Originally published in German as *Die Geburt der Tragödie aus dem Geiste der Musik* (Verlag von E. W. Fritzsch, 1872).

14   I was struck by how common the metaphor of lying masks is while reading texts drawn from my own course syllabi at the University of California, Los Angeles, and Columbia University. Sources: **[Neurotics]** Joan Rivière, "Womanliness as a Masquerade," *International Journal of Psycho-Analysis* 10 (1929); Hervey Cleckley, *The Mask of Sanity: An Attempt to Re-Interpret the So-Called Psychopathic Personality* (Kimpton, 1941); and Frantz Fanon, *Black Skin, White Masks* (Grove Press, 1967) (originally published in French as *Peau noire, Masques blancs* [Seuil, 1952]). **[Capitalists and Colonialists]** David Harvey, *The Condition of Postmodernity: An Enquiry into the Origins of Cultural Change* (Blackwell, 1989), 100; John Berger, *Ways of Seeing* (BBC, 1972), 149; Pierre Bourdieu, *The Logic of Practice,* trans. Richard Nice (Stanford University Press, 1990) (originally published in French as *Le sens pratique* [Minuit, 1980]), 126 (emphasis in original); and Homi Bhabha, "Of Mimicry and Man: The Ambivalence of Colonial Discourse," *October* 28 (Spring 1984): 129. **[Anthropologists and Art Historians]** Johannes Fabian, *Time and the Other: How Anthropology Makes Its Object* (Columbia University Press, 1983), 99 (emphasis in original); and Donald Preziosi, *Rethinking Art History* (Yale University Press, 1989), 52. **[Bad Artists]** Nietzsche, *Birth of Tragedy,* 36; and Rosalind E. Krauss, "Reinventing the Medium," *Critical Inquiry* 25 (Winter 1999): 291–92.

15 Isak Dinesen, quoted in Terry Castle, *Masquerade and Civilization: The Carnivalesque in Eighteenth-Century English Culture and Fiction* (Stanford University Press, 1986), 340.

16 *Batman Begins,* written by Christopher Nolan and David S. Goyer, directed by Christopher Nolan (Warner Bros. Pictures, 2005).

17 *Black Panther,* written by Ryan Coogler, Joe Robert Cole, and Stan Lee, directed by Ryan Coogler (Walt Disney Studios Motion Pictures, 2018).

18 In Castle, *Masquerade and Civilization,* 73.

19 Quotations in Castle, *Masquerade and Civilization,* 340, 73. *Masquerade and Civilization* is one of the most insightful (and delightful) texts ever produced on European masquerade. The author examines eighteenth-century English middle- and upper-class urban practice and profits from a rich literature written by both the players and observers themselves. The book demonstrates by contrast what is missing from most other studies: the voices of the practitioners.

20 David Wiles, *Mask and Performance in Greek Tragedy: From Ancient Festival to Modern Experimentation* (Cambridge University Press, 2007), 68, 80, 94, 123, 188.

21 Dario Fo, *The Tricks of the Trade* (Routledge, 1991), 37. Originally published in Italian as *Manuale minimo dell'attore* (Einaudi, 1987).

22 In Fo, *Tricks of the Trade,* 37.

23 In Wiles, *Mask and Performance,* 109.

24 Edmond Radar, *Invention et métamorphose des signes* (Éditions Klincksieck, 1978), 26; and Julie Taymor, personal communication with author, 21 September 2022.

25 Bakhtin, *Rabelais and His World.*

26 Judith Butler, *Gender Trouble: Feminism and the Subversion of Identity* (Routledge, 1990), 134–41. Although Joan Rivière's essay "Womanliness as a Masquerade" is usually cited as the inspiration for this kind of analysis, Rivière regarded the need to "masquerade" as a pathology—a Freudian reaction formation developed to protect professional women from retribution in an oppressive society (Rivière, "Womanliness as a Masquerade," 1929). It was Bakhtin who authorized the "liberating" potential of masquerade, a view roundly rejected by Achille Mbembe, who argued that the people are not liberated so long as the despot stays in power. Achille Mbembe, "Aesthetics of Vulgarity" [1992], in *On the Postcolony* (University of California Press, 2001), 102–41.

27 Mercer and Julien encapsulated the interest of the 1990s in gender masquerade when they wrote that entertainers such as Little Richard and Prince are said to "'play' with stereotypical codes and conventions to 'theatricalize' and send-up the whole masquerade of masculinity itself. By destabilizing signs of race, gender and sexuality these artists draw critical attention to the cultural constructedness, the artifice, of the sexual roles and identities we inhabit … [and thus] remind us that our pleasures are political and that our politics can be pleasurable." Kobena Mercer and Isaac Julien, "True Confessions," in *Black Male: Representations of Masculinity in Contemporary American Art,* ed. Thelma Golden, exh. cat. (Whitney Museum of American Art, 1994), 200. For a helpful overview of this literature, see Andrew Perchuk and Helaine Posner, *The Masculine Masquerade: Masculinity and Representation* (MIT Press, 1995).

28 The card quotes Wilde's aphorism "One's real life is so often the life one does not lead." Elsewhere, Wilde wrote: "Man is least himself when he talks in his own person. Give him a mask, and he will tell you the truth." Oscar Wilde, "The Critic as Artist," in *Intentions* (1891; Brentano's, 1905), 185.

29 Grace Dingledine, personal communications with author, 2008.

30 Eric Lott, *Love and Theft: Blackface Minstrelsy and the American Working Class* (Oxford University Press, 1993).

31 Ralph Ellison, *Invisible Man* (Random House, 1952).

32 Paul Laurence Dunbar, "We Wear the Mask," in *The Complete Poems of Paul Laurence Dunbar* (Dodd, Mead and Company, 1918), https/www.poetryfoundation.org /poems/44203/we-wear-the-mask. I thank Jordan Mayfield for bringing to my attention that Dunbar's poem likely inspired the Fugees' popular hip-hop song "The Mask" (1996), which conveys the psychic cost of conforming to society's expectations (https: //genius.com/Fugees-the-mask-lyrics).

33 Cheryl I. Harris, "Whiteness as Property," *Harvard Law Review* 106, no. 8 (1993): 1710–14 (quotations 1710–11).

34 Harris, "Whiteness as Property," 1712n5.

35 Fo, *Tricks of the Trade,* 26. Thanks to Yann Petit for introducing me to the Simpson image.

36 See Edward W. Said, *Orientalism* (Pantheon, 1978), for a model of how productive the European academy was in creating methodologies for study of the languages, cultures, and physical environment of colonized peoples.

CHAPTER 2

1 Flora Brandl, "Mask Metaphors in the German Language and Austrian Vernacular," manuscript prepared for the seminar Masquerade: Rhetoric/Theory/Practice, Columbia University, 2020.

2 It may be that a shared Christian heritage (as outlined in the discussion of transformation in chapter 3) is enough to ensure the association of the "mask" with duplicity in German and other Western European literature.

3 Curiously, Bastian does not speak of Africa even though he was himself one of the first to conduct fieldwork along the Loango Coast in the 1870s.

4 "*Bei all der Vielgestaltigkeit buntester Formen, wie sie uns bei den Masken, entgegentritt, liegt als unterste nun jene Wurzel des Schreckens versteckt, des Schreckens und des Abschreckens.*" Adolf Bastian, "Masken und Maskerein," *Zeitschrift für Völkerpsychologie* 14 (1883): 337–38.

5 Bastian, "Masken und Maskerein," 347–55.

6 Bastian, "Masken und Maskerein," 357–58.

7 Bastian, "Masken und Maskerein," 338, 355.

8 Richard Andree, "Die Masken in der Völkerkunde," *Archiv für Anthropologie* 16 (1886): 477. Andree expanded and systematized Bastian's initial categories; see especially Bastian, "Masken und Maskerein," 342–47. Andree is forgotten today, but his magnum opus, *Ethnographische Parallelen und Vergleiche,* 2nd ed. (Veit & Comp., 1889), was an essential resource for innumerable scholars of ethnology and comparative religion, including James Frazer, author of *The Golden Bough.*

As Pernet words it, Andree compiled a "database" on masks organized "into categories that have been constantly taken up" by scholars ever since. Henry Pernet, "Masks," in *The Encyclopedia of Religion,* ed. Mircea Eliade, vol. 9 (Macmillan, 1987), 259. Andree consulted an impressive number of travelogues and early ethnographies in English and German and presented his conclusions in a dedicated article, "Die Masken in der Völkerkunde" (1886), before publishing the full list of examples in the expanded edition of his book (Andree, *Ethnographische Parallelen*).

9   Andree, "Die Masken in der Völkerkunde," 477.

10   Andree, "Die Masken in der Völkerkunde," 478.

11   Andree, "Die Masken in der Völkerkunde," 489.

12   Joseph Roucek, *Social Control* (D. Van Nostrand Co., 1947; repr. 1949; 2nd ed. 1956), 299.

13   Van Beek and Leyten agree that "most African cultures do not have masks at all" and most African countries have no masking traditions. Walter E. A. Van Beek and Harrie M. Leyten, *Masquerades in African Society: Gender, Power, and Identity* (James Currey, 2023), 13. Their map "Distribution of Masking in Africa" is remarkably similar to that of Frobenius, even though they drew heavily on scholarly sources published after 1990 (9–12 [maps 1–4]). Whereas Frobenius speculated about the routes for diffusion across Africa, Van Beek and Leyten examine the ecological and sociological conditions favoring the independent invention of masquerade traditions. They are careful to stipulate that masks were not adopted by every society within the major "masking zones," nor even by every village or town within a given ethnic community (14). Still to be drawn is a map highlighting the masking rituals created in the past fifty years in multiethnic, religiously diverse urban centers such as Freetown, Bobo-Dioulasso, Calabar, and Douala. For more on these dynamic, contemporary practices, see John W. Nunley, *Moving with the Face of the Devil* (University of Illinois Press, 1987); Lisa Homann, "When Muslims Masquerade: *Lo Gue* Performance in Southwestern Burkina Faso" (PhD diss., University of California, Los Angeles, 2011); Lisa Homann, "Alluring Obscurity: Dancing Nocturnal White Masks in Southwestern Burkina Faso," *Res: Anthropology and Aesthetics,* no. 65/66 (2014/2015): 158–78; Lisa Homann, "Controversy and Human Agency in 'Portrait Masks' from the Studio of André Sanou," *Africa* 88, no. 4 (2018): 768–801; Jordan A. Fenton, "Expressive Currencies: Artistic Transactions and Transformations of Warrior-Inspired Masquerades in Calabar," *African Arts* 52, no. 1 (2019): 18–33; Jordan A. Fenton, *Masquerade and Money in Urban Nigeria: The Case of Calabar* (University of Rochester Press, 2022); and Amanda M. Maples, Jordan A. Fenton, and Lisa Homann, eds., *New African Masquerades: Artistic Innovations and Collaborations,* exh. cat. (New Orleans Museum of Art, 2025).

14   Leo Frobenius, "Die Masken und Geheimbünde Afrikas," *Nova Acta: Abhandlungen der Kaiserlichen Leopoldinisch-Carolinischen Deutschen Akademie der Naturforscher* 74, no. 1 (1898): 1–278.

15 Bernhard Streck, "Leo Frobenius," in *Masques,* exh. cat. (Musée Dapper, 1995), 256; and Pernet, "Masks," 260.

16 *"Auszugehen hat diese Studie von der Erkenntniss, dass die afrikanische Maske nicht einem Bestreben, das Menschengesicht naehzubilden, entstanden ist."* Frobenius, "Die Masken," 202; and Leo Frobenius, "Les masques et les sociétés secrètes d'Afrique," trans. Alfred Schwartz, in *Masques* (Musée Dapper, 1995), 309.

17 Frobenius, "Die Masken," 204; and Frobenius, "Les masques," 311.

18 Frobenius, "Les masques," 311. It is annoying to admit that despite some absurd theories—for example, his belief that Atlantis was located in Nigeria—Frobenius sometimes hit the nail on the head, as when he insisted that one needed to examine the "mask-body" in its entirety and not just focus on the headpiece preserved in a museum. Frobenius, "Die Masken," 172; and Frobenius, "Les masques," 279. For an insightful overview of Frobenius's career and contradictions, see Suzanne Marchand, "Leo Frobenius and the Revolt Against the West," *Journal of Contemporary History* 32, no. 2 (1997): 153–70.

19 Max Buchner, in Beatrix Heintze, ed., *Max Buchners Reisen nach Zentralafrika, 1878–1882* (Rüdiger Köppe, 1999), 509.

20 Buchner, in Heintze, *Max Buchners Reisen,* 511: *"ein gutter Theil des Genusses … lag im Vergnügen des Gruselns. Unter fröhlichem Zetergeheul stoben … genau so wie bei unseren Maskeraden die Strassenjungen."* As an adjective, *gruselig* signifies uncanny, weird, eerie, hair-raising, and creepy. See Harold T. Betteridge, ed., *Cassell's German Dictionary* (Macmillan, 1978), 282.

21 Frobenius, "Die Masken," 233; and Frobenius, "Les masques," 336.

22 Frobenius, "Die Masken," 235; and Frobenius, "Les masques," 338.

23 Frobenius, "Die Masken," 236; and Frobenius, "Les masques," 338.

24 Frobenius, "Die Masken," 235–36; and Frobenius, "Les masques," 338. Widely read authors who entertain the same set of questions include Lucien Lévy-Bruhl, *Le surnaturel et la nature dans la mentalité primitive* (1931; Presses universitaires de France, 1963), 130–32; Roger Caillois, *Man, Play and Games,* trans. Meyer Barash (University of Illinois Press, 2001), 92 (originally published in French as *Jeux et les hommes: Le masque et le vertige* [Gallimard, 1958]); Jean-Louis Bédouin, *Les masques* (Presses universitaires de France, 1961), 21; and Michael Taussig, *Defacement: Public Secrecy and the Labor of the Negative* (Stanford University Press, 1999), 122–25.

25 Frobenius, "Die Masken," 264; and Frobenius, "Les masques," 355.

26 Anne Doquet, *Les masques dogon: Ethnologie savante et ethnologie autochtone* (Karthala, 1999), 88–89.

27 Senghor praised Griaule for studying African civilization rather than its customs and regularly illustrated his philosophy of Négritude with references to Dogon philosophy and art, which he disseminated to the general public in talks, essays, and radio addresses, inspiring artists such as Iba Ndiaye and Moustapha Dimé to make study trips to Dogon country. Léopold Sédar Senghor, "Préface," in *Ethnologiques: Hommages à Marcel Griaule,* ed. Solange de Ganay, Annie Lebeuf, and Jean-Paul Lebeuf (Hermann, 1987), vi–vii; Manthia Diawara, "The African Public Intellectual: The Negritude of

Léopold Sédar Senghor," in *Dak'Art. Afrique: Miroir?*, exh. cat. (Biennale de l'Art African Contemporain, 2008), 201–4; Léopold Sédar Senghor, "No. 30 Composantes de l'oeuvre africaine," *Léopold Sédar Senghor: Enregistrements historiques,* ed. Philippe Sainteny (Frémeaux et Associés, 2006); Thomas McEvilley, "An Interview with Moustapha Dimé," in *Fusion: West African Artists at the Venice Biennale,* exh. cat. (Prestel, 1993), 42; and Franz-W. Kaiser and Iba Ndiaye, "Conversation," in *Iba Ndiaye: Painter Between Continents,* ed. Okwui Enwezor and Franz-W. Kaiser (Adam Biro, 2002), 60. Dancers and choreographers such as the Ivoirien Famedji-Koto Tchimou pored over *Masques dogons* to identify African performance fundamentals. Famedji-Koto Tchimou, *Langage de la danse chez les Dogons* (L'Harmattan, 1995). Strangest of all, cultural critics drew on Dogon cosmology to ensure the African authenticity of modernists as different as the photographer Malick Sidibé and the multimedia artist El Anatsui. See Manthia Diawara, "The 1960s in Bamako: Malick Sidibé and James Brown," in *Everything but the Burden: What White People Are Taking from Black Culture,* ed. Greg Tate (Broadway Books, 2003), 178–84; and Olu Oguibe, "Beyond Death and Nothingness," *African Arts* 31, no. 1 (1998): 53–54. African American artists inspired by Dogon sculptures include Kehinde Wiley (https://harn.emuseum.com/objects/12741/dogon-couple) and Robert Pruitt (https://www.metmuseum.org/art/collection/search/705956). For a superb introduction to the visual culture of Dogon peoples as presented in the twentieth century in Europe and the United States, see *ReCollecting Dogon,* https://www.menil.org/read /online-features/recollecting-dogon, curated by the Africanist Paul R. Davis. Davis convincingly describes Dogon peoples as having "one of the most studied, collected, and mythologized visual cultures on the African continent" despite their small and diverse population.

28   D. Keita, M. M. Tessougue, and Y. Fane, "Patrimoine culture Malien sabordé au nom d'un Islam puritain," *Annales de l'Université Ouaga I Pr Joseph KI-ZERBO,* series A, vol. 25 (2018): 1–27.

29   The anthropologist Walter E. A. Van Beek is hopeful that the "masks will reappear," especially as Mali is seeking UNESCO recognition for other aspects of Dogon "immaterial world heritage." If so, there will likely be adjustments for practices deemed sensitive to Islamist sensibilities, such as male-gendered dancers wearing false breasts and women's hairstyles (see fig. 2). Walter E. A. Van Beek, email message to author, 19 July 2024.

30   Marcel Griaule, *Masques dogons* (1938; Institut d'ethnologie, 1983), 799.

31   Griaule, *Masques dogons,* 797, 802–5.

32   Griaule, *Masques dogons,* 399–401.

33   Dieterlen hypothesized that Kanaga represented a water insect, and Van Beek suggested a stork or an antelope. Germaine Dieterlen, "Masks and Mythology Among the Dogon," *African Arts* 12, no. 3 (1989): 87n6; Walter E. A. Van Beek, "Enter the Bush: A Dogon Mask Festival," in *Africa Explores,* ed. Susan Vogel (Center for African Art, 1991), 61; and Van Beek and Leyten, *Masquerades in African Society,* 170.

34 "*L'art des Dogons est une lutte contre la pourriture.*" Griaule, *Masques dogons,* 819. Doquet cautions that the masks had a far greater range of action in the early twentieth century. Doquet, *Les masques dogon,* 149–50.

35 Griaule, *Masques dogons,* plate IA.

36 Griaule, *Masques dogons,* 789, 72, respectively. See also Van Beek and Leyten, *Masquerades in African Society,* 168–74; and Van Beek, "Enter the Bush," 67.

37 Dieterlen, "Masks and Mythology," 34.

38 Dieterlen, "Masks and Mythology," 35.

39 Dieterlen, "Masks and Mythology," 35. See also Marcel Griaule and Germaine Dieterlen, *The Pale Fox,* trans. Stephen C. Infantino (Continuum Foundation, 1986), 194–97, 472. Originally published in French as *Le renard pâle* (Institut d'ethnologie, 1965).

40 Walter E. A. Van Beek, "Dogon Restudied (A Field Evaluation of the Work of Marcel Griaule)," *Current Anthropology* 32, no. 3 (1991): 139–67. Shortly before the publication of Van Beek's restudy, Clifford reviewed concerns in the ethnographic literature about Griaule's methodology and gave a literary critical reading of Griaule as an author in the French colonial mold. James Clifford, "Power and Dialogue in Ethnography: Marcel Griaule's Initiation" [1983], in *The Predicament of Culture: Twentieth-Century Ethnography, Literature and Art* (Harvard University Press, 1988), 55–91.

41 Van Beek, "Enter the Bush," 65–67. My close analysis of Van Beek's argument is not intended ipso facto to undercut it. Many Pende men told me in 1987 and 1988 that the boys' initiation (*mukanda*) compensated men for women's control over childbirth. Some Chewa of Zambia have justified their control over masks in similar terms: "Because women make a secret of birth, we make a secret of death." Kenji Yoshida, "Masks and Transformation Among the Chewa of Eastern Zambia," *Senri Ethnological Studies* (Osaka) 31 (1991): 267.

42 Doquet, *Les masques dogon,* 24. Griaule obfuscates this point, arguing that the Society of Masks is important for "Dogon unity" even if masks do not everywhere enjoy the same importance. Griaule, *Masques dogons,* 773.

43 Doquet, *Les masques dogon,* 152, 178.

44 Doquet's text illustrates how hard it is for scholars to extricate themselves from Griaule's and Dieterlen's interpretations. For example, she writes that the older masks recall the creation of the world and the "rapid circular movement [of Kanaga's dance] recalls the primordial gesture of creation" (*Les masques dogon,* 184). Doquet does not cite the sources for her statements, but they clearly derive from Griaule and Dieterlen, *The Pale Fox;* and Germaine Dieterlen, "Mythologie, histoire et masques," *Journal de la Société des Africanistes* 59, no. 1–2 (1989): 7–38.

45 Doquet, *Les masques dogon,* 178–79.

46 Doquet, *Les masques dogon,* 203–4.

47 On Harley's research methods and collecting practices, see Monni Adams, "Both Sides of the Collecting Encounter: The George W. Harley Collection at the Peabody Museum of Archaeology and Ethnology, Harvard University," *Museum Anthropology* 32, no. 1 (2009): 17–32. Christopher B. Steiner is currently researching

Harley's "involvement in the African art market in Liberia during the 1950s and 1960s" ("Rereading the Missionary Archive: Dr. George W. Harley in and out of the African Art Market," paper presented at the Columbia University Seminar on the Arts of Africa, Oceania, and the Americas, 6 December 2023).

48 Adams, "Both Sides of the Collecting Encounter," 17; and Harley, *Masks as Agents of Social Control in Northeast Liberia* (Peabody Museum of Archaeology and Ethnology, Harvard University, 1950), vi.

49 M. C. Jedrej, "Dan and Mende Masks: A Structural Comparison," *Africa* 56, no. 1 (1986): 71. Notable publications on Dan artists include Eberhard Fischer, *Dan Artists: The Sculptors Tame, Si, Tompieme and Sòn; Their Personalities and Work* (Scheidegger & Spiess, 2014) (originally published in German as "Künstler der Dan," *Baessler Archiv,* n.s. 10, no. 2 [1963]: 161–263); Hans Himmelheber, "Personality and Technique of African Sculptors," in *Technique and Personality,* ed. Margaret Mead (Museum of Primitive Art, 1963), 79–110; Hans Himmelheber, "Sculptors and Sculptures of the Dan," in *The Proceedings of the First International Congress of Africanists (Accra, 1962),* ed. Lalage Bown and Michael Crowder (Longmans, Green & Co., 1964), 243–55; Eberhard Fischer and Hans Himmelheber, *The Arts of the Dan in West Africa* (Museum Rietberg, 1984) (originally published in German as *Die Kunst der Dan* [Museum Rietberg, 1976]); and Robert Farris Thompson, *African Art in Motion: Icon and Act in the Collection of Katherine Coryton White,* exh. cat. (University of California Press, 1974), 159–65.

50 Harley, *Masks as Agents of Social Control,* 21, 23, 25, 27. In 1989, older Central Pende sculptors in Nioka-Munene (DR Congo) told me how, from the 1920s to the 1950s, they and their teachers fabricated names and dances for masks in order to pique the interest of Belgian clients. Although geographically distant from Harley's research center, my experience makes me wonder if the traders visiting Harley were motivated to invent different roles for each mask so as to appeal to Harley's unflagging interest in "function."

51 Harley, *Masks as Agents of Social Control,* 42. As it was further theorized, when masked figures enforce societal rules, the possibility of "sustained, divisive conflict is decreased by converting secular actions … into sacred, supra-social actions." Peter M. Weil, "The Masked Figure and Social Control: The Mandinka Case," *Africa* 41, no. 4 (1971): 279, 287.

52 Edward Alsworth Ross, "Social Control," *American Journal of Sociology* 1, no. 5 (1896): 518; and Edward Alsworth Ross, "Social Control: VIII. Art," *American Journal of Sociology* 3, no. 1 (1897): 64–78.

53 Roucek, *Social Control.*

54 The model of "social control" floated far from its source in American sociology and may have lasted the longest in African studies, where scholars' obsession with secrecy in the twentieth century has often distorted the ethnographic record. As many have observed, it is misleading to label organizations as "secret" when they enroll a full 50 percent of the population (for example, men's societies or women's societies).

55 Harley, *Masks as Agents of Social Control,* x–xi. For passages on judges, see x, 11, 14, 16, 17. Harley's intuition about the advantages of deniability in judicial settings parallels that of Andree, discussed above.

56 Harley, *Masks as Agents of Social Control,* vii, 11. Adams writes that "no evidence has emerged for Harley's vision of centralized, secret councils controlling all of Liberia." Marie Jeanne Adams, "Introduction," *Ethnologische Zeitschrift Zürich* 1 (1980): 10.

57 Harley, *Masks as Agents of Social Control,* 16.

58 Roy Sieber, "Masks as Agents of Social Control" [1962], in *The Many Faces of Primitive Art: A Critical Anthology,* ed. Douglas Fraser (Prentice Hall, 1966), 262. In 1957, Sieber received the first PhD in African art history from a US institution and went on to found one of the first graduate programs in African art history at Indiana University, where he trained a large number of museum professionals and academics.

59 Sieber, "Masks as Agents of Social Control," 257–58, 260–62.

60 Leon Siroto, "Masks and Social Organization Among the Bakwele People of Western Equatorial Africa" (PhD diss., Columbia University, 1969), 21, 25–26.

61 Siroto, "Masks and Social Organization," 5, 314. Homann roundly rejects a social control interpretation of mask violence in Bobo-Dioulasso ("When Muslims Masquerade," 78–117). She believes that there is pleasure in the panic surrounding the masks' use of whips, which is only possible because they are not used for discipline or coercion.

62 Leon Siroto, "*Gon:* A Mask Used in Competition for Leadership Among the Bakwele," in *African Art and Leadership,* ed. Douglas Fraser and Herbert M. Cole (University of Wisconsin Press, 1972), 57–76.

63 Hans Himmelheber and Eberhard Fischer prove outstanding exceptions. They ignored "social control" altogether to publish independent, field-based ethnography on Dan masking in the 1960s and 1970s, including Fischer, *Dan Artists* (2014 [1963]); Hans Himmelheber, "Die Geister und ihre irdischen Verkörperungen als Grundvorstellung in der Religion der Dan (Libera und Elfenbeinküste) unter Mitarbeit von Wowoa Tame-Tabmen, Ngor Diaple, Liberia," *Baessler-Archiv,* n.s., vol. 12 (1964): 161–263; and Fischer and Himmelheber, *The Arts of the Dan* (1984 [1976]). These texts probe masks in religious praxis as well as individual artistic creativity.

64 The exhibition *African Art in Motion* opened at the University of California, Los Angeles, Art Galleries, and traveled to the National Gallery of Art in Washington, DC, where it welcomed 323,785 visitors (5 May–22 September 1974). The installation "incorporated 5 audio-visual stations" (*African Art in Motion,* https://www.nga.gov/exhibitions /1974/african_motion.html), among the earliest use of video in an art museum in the United States. Importantly, this footage included performances by the judge Gaa-Wree-Wre and other Dan masqueraders.

65 Thompson, *African Art in Motion,* 159.

66 Thompson, *African Art in Motion,* 162–63.

67 Thompson, *African Art in Motion,* 165.

68 Henry John Drewal and Margaret Thompson Drewal, *Gẹlẹdẹ: Art and Female Power Among the Yoruba* (University of Indiana Press, 1983).

69 Jedrej, "Dan and Mende Masks," 72.

70 Daniel B. Reed, "'The Ge Is in the Church' and 'Our Parents Are Playing Muslim': Performance, Identity, and Resistance Among the Dan in Postcolonial Côte d'Ivoire,"

Ethnomusicology 49, no. 3 (2005): 361; see also Daniel B. Reed, *Dan Ge Performance: Masks and Music in Contemporary Côte d'Ivoire* (Indiana University Press, 2003), 96.

71 Reed, *Dan Ge Performance*, 97.

72 Monni Adams, "Agency and Control in Masked Festivals Among the Bo People, Southwestern Côte d'Ivoire," *Zeitschrift für ethnologie* 130, no. 2 (2005): 195–221.

73 Richard Schechner, *Performance Theory* (1988; rev. and expanded ed., Routledge, 2003), 287.

74 Babatunde Lawal, *The Gẹ̀lẹ̀dẹ́ Spectacle: Art, Gender, and Social Harmony in an African Culture* (University of Washington Press, 1996), xvii. He explicitly honors Griaule's model of "harmony."

75 Lawal, *The Gẹ̀lẹ̀dẹ́ Spectacle*, xxiv.

76 John Thabiti Willis, *Masquerading Politics: Kinship, Gender, and Ethnicity in a Yoruba Town* (Indiana University Press, 2018).

77 Z. S. Strother, *Inventing Masks: Agency and History in the Art of the Central Pende* (University of Chicago Press, 1998), 229–81. See also Paolo Israel, *In Step with the Times: Mapiko Masquerades of Mozambique* (Ohio University Press, 2014).

78 Nicolas Argenti, *The Intestines of the State: Youth, Violence, and Belated Histories in the Cameroon Grassfields* (University of Chicago Press, 2007), 187.

79 Argenti, *Intestines of the State*, 235.

80 Argenti, *Intestines of the State*, 4–5.

CHAPTER 3

1 Mircea Eliade, "Masks," in *Encyclopedia of World Art*, vol. 9 (McGraw-Hill, 1964), 524.

2 Henry Pernet, *Ritual Masks: Deceptions and Revelations*, trans. Laura Grillo (University of South Carolina Press, 1992), 117. Originally published in French as *Mirages du masque* (Labor et Fides, 1988). Although some recognized the boldness and erudition of Pernet's arguments—see, for example, Benjamin Ray, review of *Ritual Masks: Deceptions and Revelations* by Henry Pernet, *History of Religions* 35, no. 1 (1995): 95–96—his book was received with stony silence from most in the African art community.

3 Jean-Claude Schmitt, "Les masques, le diable, les morts," in *Le corps, les rites, les rêves, le temps* (Gallimard, 2001), 211, 220.

4 Schmitt, "Les masques, le diable, les morts," 217–20. Castle documents widespread references to "the diabolical origins" of masquerade in eighteenth-century Great Britain. Terry Castle, *Masquerade and Civilization* (Stanford University Press, 1986), 64.

5 For Carl Einstein's interest in metamorphosis, see Christa Lichtenstern, "Einsteins Begriff der 'metamorphotischen Identifikation' und sein Beobachtungen zur surrealistischen Kunst," in *Études Germaniques* (January/March 1998): 237–49; and Sebastian Zeidler, "Form as Revolt: Carl Einstein's Philosophy of the Real and the Work of Paul Klee," *Res: Anthropology and Aesthetics* 57–58 (2010): 229–63.

6 Emile Durkheim and Marcel Mauss, *Primitive Classification*, trans. Rodney Needham (University of Chicago Press, 1963), 6. Originally published in French as "De quelques formes primitives de classification," *L'année sociologique* 6 (1901–2): 1–72.

7   Pernet, *Ritual Masks,* 119.

8   Lucien Lévy-Bruhl, *How Natives Think,* trans. Lilian A. Clare (Ayer, 1926), 362. Originally published in French as *Les fonctions mentales dans les sociétés inférieures* (Presses universitaires de France, 1910). Lévy-Bruhl later rejected the concept of mystical participation, but the belief that "primitives" could not distinguish between the signifier and the signified laid the groundwork for the transformation hypothesis among his followers. Henry Pernet, "Masks," in *The Encyclopedia of Religion,* ed. Mircea Eliade, vol. 9 (Macmillan, 1987), 265.

9   Carl Einstein, "Negro Sculpture," trans. Charles W. Haxthausen and Sebastian Zeidler, *October* 107 (2004): 137. Originally published in German as *Negerplastik* (Verlag de Weissen Bücher, 1915).

10   Eckart von Sydow, *Die Kunst der Naturvölker und der Vorzeit* (Propyläen Verlag, 1923), 32: "Die Maske ist der Geist." Translation by Kim Richter.

11   Lucien Lévy-Bruhl, *Le surnaturel et la nature dans la mentalité primitive* (1931; Presses universitaires de France, 1963), 125 (my emphasis).

12   Pernet, *Ritual Masks,* 118–19.

13   Pernet puts on the table how rare it is for a scholar to have the language skills, ritual expertise, and field experience to evaluate beliefs about transformation: "Verification is far from easy since it is not only a matter of controlling facts, but also their interpretation" (*Ritual Masks,* 120).

14   Buraud's impact has not been acknowledged even though he was widely plagiarized. His book *Les masques* was reissued in 2014 in a beautiful edition with illustrations from the Musée du Quai Branly, Paris.

15   Georges Buraud, *Les masques* (Seuil, 1948), 98, as translated by Eliade, "Masks," 523.

16   David Wiles, *Mask and Performance in Greek Tragedy: From Ancient Festival to Modern Experimentation* (Cambridge University Press, 2007), 123.

17   Wiles, *Mask and Performance in Greek Tragedy,* 111–18.

18   Roland Barthes, "Le mythe de l'acteur possédé" [1958], in *Écrits sur le théâtre,* ed. Jean-Loup Rivière (Seuil, 2002), 234–37.

19   Roger Caillois, *Man, Play and Games,* trans. Meyer Barash (University of Illinois Press, 2001), 95. Originally published in French as *Jeux et les hommes: Le masque et le vertige* (Gallimard, 1958).

20   Caillois, *Man, Play and Games,* 95.

21   Caillois gnawed on the problem of how to distinguish truth from falsehood. As Pernet recognized, he proposes a chronological shift in consciousness: "The wearer is not taken in at the beginning, but he rapidly succumbs to the frenzy that transports him…. He then incarnates, temporarily, the frightening powers, he mimes them, he identifies with them, and soon alienated … he believes himself truly to be the god whose form he at first attempted to emulate with the help of a masterly or childish disguise … This is the victory of pretense: the simulation results in a possession that is not simulated." Pernet, *Ritual Masks,* 123–24 (translating and condensing Roger

Caillois, *Les jeux et les hommes [Le masque et le vertige]* [from the rev. and expanded ed., Gallimard, 1967], 188, 173–74).

22   Eliade, "Masks," col. 524. It is worth noting that Eliade's bibliography for his influential entry on the origins of masks in the *Encyclopedia of World Art* cites six works on Central European practices, Caillois's book *Man, Play and Games,* and only one work on Africa (Frobenius, "Die Masken und Geheimbünde Afrikas"); Eliade, "Masks," col. 568.

23   Ulli Beier was one of the first Africanists with field experience to associate masks with possession. Wishing to refute prominent Yoruba pastors in Nigeria who accused Egungun masked dancers of "'pretending' to be a spirit," Beier insisted that there was no chicanery—"every true Egungun will enter into a state of possession." The qualifier "true" was necessary because he admitted that "one finds today Eguns who are not actually achieving this religious experience." Ulli Beier, "The Egungun Cult Among the Yorubas," *Présence africaine,* n.s. (February–May 1958): 385.

24   Herbert M. Cole, "Introduction," in *I Am Not Myself: The Art of African Masquerade,* ed. Herbert M. Cole (Museum of Cultural History, University of California, Los Angeles [UCLA], 1985), 20. The echoes of Eliade and Caillois in the text are easy to hear. In 2005, Cole graciously agreed to be interviewed during my Theories of Masquerading seminar at UCLA and admitted that he had been reading Eliade. He stood by his theory, although he supported himself by referencing David Freedberg's *The Power of Images* rather than any African ethnography.

25   Susan E. Gagliardi has kindly sent me photos documenting the continuing influence of Cole's essays on the interpretation of masquerade in museum wall texts, including the permanent display of the Sainsbury Africa Galleries at the British Museum (July 2015) and the panel introducing the traveling exhibition *Disguise: Masks and Global African Art* at UCLA's Fowler Museum (2015-16).

26   Edward Lifschitz, "Hearing Is Believing: Acoustic Aspects of Masking in Africa," in *West African Masks and Cultural Systems,* ed. Sidney L. Kasfir (Musée royal de l'Afrique central, 1988), 221.

27   Pernet, *Ritual Masks,* 121, see also 133-35. Another skeptic is Kramer: "Masks were not employed in spirit possession, and, with some significant exceptions, spirit possession did not occur in masquerades." Fritz W. Kramer, *The Red Fez: Art and Spirit Possession in Africa,* trans. Malcolm Green (Verso, 1993), 161. Originally published in German as *Der rote Fes: Über Besessenheit und Kunst in Afrika* (Athenäum, 1987). Kramer draws on Leo Frobenius, *Kulturgeschichte Afrikas* (Erschienen im Phaidon-Verlag, 1933), 209-10, 295-97.

28   Z. S. Strother, *Inventing Masks: Agency and History in the Art of the Central Pende* (University of Chicago Press, 1998).

29   Pernet, *Ritual Masks,* 122.

30   The literature on animism in Amerindian societies has been able to take a different approach to the problem of transformation. Accepting that in animist thought "extraordinary beings … [show themselves] in the multiplication of identities in continuous transformation," Fausto has argued that the challenge for Amerindian art history was not mimesis (as in Europe) but "how to picture the transformational flux

that characterizes powerful beings." Carlos Fausto, "Whirlwinds of Images," in *Art Effects: Image, Agency, and Ritual in Amazonia,* trans. David Rodgers (University of Nebraska Press, 2020), 167; and Carlos Fausto, "Le masque de l'animiste: Chimères et poupées russes en Amérique indigene," *Gradhiva,* no. 13 (2011): 65.

31   Sidney L. Kasfir, "Masquerading as a Cultural System," in *West African Masks and Cultural Systems,* ed. Sidney L. Kasfir (Musée royal de l'Afrique central, 1988), 5. Kasfir also added body painting to the list, a position that John Picton rejected: Whereas masks distance the dancer from "one's usual social existence; body art effects transformation into one's usual social existence." John Picton, review of *West African Masks and Cultural Systems,* edited by Sidney L. Kasfir, *African Arts* 23, no. 1 (1989): 96.

32   Lisa Homann, "Controversy and Human Agency in 'Portrait Masks' from the Studio of André Sanou," *Africa* 88, no. 4 (2018): 771. Homann has been researching masquerade in Bobo-Dioulasso since 2006.

33   Jordan A. Fenton, *Masquerade and Money in Urban Nigeria: The Case of Calabar* (University of Rochester Press, 2022), 311–47.

34   Kenji Yoshida, "Masks and Transformation Among the Chewa of Eastern Zambia," *Senri Ethnological Studies* (Osaka) 31 (1991): 203.

35   Yoshida, "Masks and Transformation," 207.

36   Yoshida, "Masks and Transformation," 262.

37   When asked to define *hamba,* most people would demur and tell me to ask "the experts." *Hamba* is something like "faith" for Christians—it takes a host of theologians to interpret. Z. S. Strother, "From Performative Utterance to Performative Object: Pende Theories of Speech, Blood Sacrifice, and Power Objects," *Res: Anthropology and Aesthetics,* no. 37 (Spring 2000): 57–58.

38   Elisabeth L. Cameron, email message to author, 29 July 2008.

39   Michael Taussig, *Defacement: Public Secrecy and the Labor of the Negative* (Stanford University Press, 1999), 5 (emphasis in original).

40   Taussig, *Defacement,* 270.

41   Pernet, *Ritual Masks,* 122.

42   Gilbert Rouget, *Music and Trance: A Theory of the Relations Between Music and Possession,* trans. and revised by Brunhilde Biebuyck in collaboration with the author (University of Chicago Press, 1985), 56, 3. Originally published in French as *La musique et la transe: Esquisse d'une théorie générale des relations de la musique et de la possession* (Gallimard, 1980).

43   Rouget, *Music and Trance,* 26.

44   Cole, "Introduction," 20.

45   Rouget, *Music and Trance,* 26.

46   Judith Becker, *Deep Listeners: Music, Emotion, and Trancing* (Indiana University Press, 2004), 29.

47   Judith Becker, "Music and Trance," *Leonardo Music Journal* 4 (1994): 41.

48   Robin Horton, "The Kalabari Ekine Society: A Borderland of Religion and Art," *Africa* 33, no. 2 (1963): 95.

49   Phone conversations with Horton, who was in Buguma, Nigeria (2006), and London (11 October 2008). I thank Sokari Douglas Camp for connecting us.

50   Interpreting ritual praxis requires significant immersion in a cultural milieu. Picton studied a masquerade among the Ebira (Nigeria) in which relics (especially eyelashes) were removed from the corpse of a selected elder prior to burial and sewn into the costume in order to enable a performer to embody the identity of a deceased elder; however, even in this case Picton is able to document six other kinds of masquerading practiced among the Ebira, *none of which* involves the same concept of embodiment. John Picton, "Masks and Identities in Ebira Culture," in *Concepts of the Body/Self in Africa,* ed. Joan Maw (Institute für Afrikanistik und Ägyptologie der Universität Wien, 1992), 75–80. And he states firmly that "this is not a matter of possession (a phenomenon unknown in Ebira culture) but of the performer speaking as and with the authority of the deceased." Picton, "Masks and Identities," 76.

51   My emphasis. This paragraph is drawn from Jordan A. Fenton, "Expressive Currencies: Artistic Transactions and Transformations of Warrior-Inspired Masquerades in Calabar," *African Arts* 52, no. 1 (2019): 20, 25, 32nn25–26. Fenton's rich interpretation is based on over eight years of fieldwork. The skulls are willed to the Nnabo society by prominent members or by inductees who cannot otherwise afford the membership fees. Fenton, "Expressive Currencies," 32n24.

52   Anne-Marie Bouttiaux, "Sous l'apparence du masque, un espace de transgression," in *Le labyrinthe des apparences,* ed. Éric Clémens (Revue de l'Université de Bruxelles, 2000), 129n10.

53   Anne-Marie Bouttiaux, "Guro Masked Performers Serving Spirits and People," trans. Allen F. Roberts, *African Arts* 42, no. 2 (2009): 60. I write cautiously in the present tense as the impact of the Ivorian Civil War (2002–11) on Guro masquerade practices has yet to be assessed (Yann Petit, personal communications with author, 2024).

54   Bouttiaux, "Guro Masked Performers," 67.

55   Anne-Marie Bouttiaux, personal communication with author, 31 October 2011. The most detailed account is in Anne-Marie Bouttiaux, "La danse des hommes, la jubilation des esprits: Masques guro de la région de Zuenoula, Côte d'Ivoire" (PhD diss., Université Libre de Bruxelles, 2000).

56   Bouttiaux, "La danse des hommes"; and Anne-Marie Bouttiaux, "Porteur de *Zamble* en pays Guro: Les enjeux de la célébrité," *Art'in, revue d'arts plastiques et d'arts du spectacle (Université de Valenciennes)* 1, no. 1 (2001): 81. According to Bouttiaux, "All the dancers say they are possessed by Zamble, who enters through the top of the head when they are ready to enter the dance arena." She contrasts this form of trance with the complete and uncontrolled trance (*possession débridé*) experienced by (unmasked) women mediums (Bouttiaux, personal communication with author, 31 October 2011). I thank Dr. Bouttiaux for debating the issues with me and for generously sharing texts, photographs, and videos.

57   Bouttiaux, "Guro Masked Performers," 61.

58   Bouttiaux, "Porteur de *Zamble* en pays Guro," 80.

59   Bouttiaux, "Guro Masked Performers," 60 (emphasis in original). In sum, the Africanist literature offers little to compare with the fleshed-out study by John Emigh

of Hindu possession trance ("visitation") involving masks in Odisha and Bali. John Emigh, *Masked Performance* (University of Pennsylvania Press, 1996), 41–66. Emigh found that the performers of a small number of masks lost their sense of self and conscious control over their bodies and retained little memory of what transpired. Notably, the headpieces associated with trance experiences enjoyed a ritual life outside of performance, and I suspect this to be the case in West and Central Africa. The closest parallel in the Africanist literature to what Emigh describes is probably the "mediumistic" trance of Minyanka Komo performance, as described by Jespers: Philippe Jespers, "Le masque et la parole: Analyse d'un masque 'auditif' de la société initiatique du Komo Minyanka, Mali," in *Objets-Signes d'Afrique,* ed. Luc de Heusch (Musée royal de l'Afrique central, 1995), 51–54; and Philippe Jespers, "La puissance du masque: De l'audible au visible," in *Puissances de la voix: Corps sentant, corde sensible,* ed. Sémir Badir and Herman Parret (Presses universitaires de Limoges, 2001), 60, 63–67.

60   Eberhard Fischer, *Guro: Masks, Performances and Master Carvers in Ivory Coast* (Museum Rietberg, 2008), 285.

61   Anne-Marie Bouttiaux, "Du divertissement au sacrifice: Danses de masques guro de la region de Zuenoula, Côte d'Ivoire," in *La dynamique des masques en Afrique occidentale,* ed. Anne-Marie Bouttiaux (Musée royal de l'Afrique centrale, 2013), 129–35.

62   Bouttiaux, "Guro Masked Performers," 59, 64; Bouttiaux, "Du divertissement au sacrifice," 130; and Fischer, *Guro,* 285–86. It is more common than not for masqueraders in West and Central Africa to own amulets (or to bury medicine in the dance floor) to protect themselves from covert attacks motivated by jealousy. On the heavy impact of negotiating rivalry in the biography of champion dancers of Gyela or Gyela lu Zauli, see Fischer, *Guro,* 265–86; and Bouttiaux, "Du divertissement au sacrifice," 130, 135.

63   Fausto, "Le masque de l'animiste," 50–51; and Schmitt, "Les masques, le diable, les morts," 97.

64   Z. S. Strother, "Smells and Bells: The Role of Skepticism in Pende Divination," in *Insight and Artistry in African Divination,* ed. John Pemberton III (Smithsonian Institution Press, 2000), 99–115, plates 8–9; and Carlo Severi, "Memory, Reflexivity and Belief: Reflections on the Ritual Use of Language," *Social Anthropology* 10, no. 1 (2002): 26.

65   Severi, "Memory, Reflexivity and Belief," 28. Probst notes that the interlocking of emotional and cognitive processes in the reception of Nyau masks in Malawi. Feelings of astonishment and fear are punctured by "hesitation and indecision": "What appeared in encounters with the figures of *nyau* was on the one hand a sign of the existence of a world beyond the visible, and on the other the latent skepticism as to the validity of that sign." Peter Probst, "Sublime Images: Masked Performances and the Aesthetics of Belonging in Malawi," in *Masquerade: Essays on Tradition and Innovation Worldwide,* ed. Deborah Bell (McFarland, 2015), 89.

66   On the role of individuals, especially performers, see Strother, *Inventing Masks,* 23–43 (1998); Bouttiaux, "La danse des hommes" (2000); Bouttiaux, "Porteur de *Zamble* en pays Guro" (2001); Homann, "Controversy and Human Agency" (2018); Susan Elizabeth Gagliardi, "Art and the Individual in African Masquerades," *Africa* 88, no. 4 (2018): 702–17; and Fenton, *Masquerade and Money* (2022). Patrick McNaughton penned

the first monograph dedicated to the study of an individual masquerader, superstar Sidi Ballo in Mali. Patrick McNaughton, *A Bird Dance near Saturday City: Sidi Ballo and the Art of West African Masquerade* (Indiana University Press, 2008).

67 Richard Schechner, *Performance Theory* (1988; rev. and expanded ed., Routledge, 2003), 229.

68 Eli Bentor, "'Remember Six Feet Deep': Masks and the Exculpation of/from Death in Aro Masquerade," *Journal of Religion in Africa* 24, no. 4 (1994): 333–38; Nicolas Argenti, *The Intestines of the State: Youth, Violence, and Belated Histories in the Cameroon Grassfields* (University of Chicago Press, 2007), 20–21, 28; and Dunja Hersak, "On the Concept of Prototype in Songye Masquerades," *African Arts* 45, no. 2 (2012): 15–18. For example, Argenti draws on Mikhail Bakhtin and Jacques Derrida to argue that Oku masquerade "brings to life and transforms memories of extreme violence" (*Intestines of the State*, 28). Fenton concludes that masqueraders in Calabar engage in an "artistic transformation guided by human agency" (*Masquerade and Money*, 312).

69 Elizabeth Tonkin, "Masks and Powers," *Man*, n.s., vol. 14 (1979): 241.

70 Tonkin, "Masks and Powers," 242.

71 Tonkin, "Masks and Powers," 242; and Elizabeth Tonkin, "Masking and Masquerading, with Examples from West Africa," University of Birmingham Discussion Papers, series C, no. 36, Sociology and Politics (1979): 5.

72 George Lakoff and Mark Johnson, *Metaphors We Live By* (University of Chicago Press, 1980).

CHAPTER 4

1 Léopold Sédar Senghor, "The Spirit of Civilization, or the Laws of African Negro Culture," *Présence africaine*, no. 8–10 (June–November 1956): 57.

2 Modernist painters have been the most open to engaging emotion when musing on the impact of color, as when Pierre Matisse proclaimed that color may act "upon the inner sensibility like the sudden stroke of a gong." Ann Gibson, "Regression and Color in Abstract Expressionism: Barnett Newman, Mark Rothko, and Clyfford Still," *Arts Magazine* (March 1981): 149 (my emphasis).

3 Chike Aniakor, "Igbo Aesthetics: An Introduction," *Nigeria Magazine* 141 (1982): 12.

4 Senghor, "The Spirit of Civilization," 57.

5 Harris Memel-Fotê, "The Perception of Beauty in Negro-African Culture," in *Colloquium: Function and Significance of African Negro Art in the Life and for the People (March 30–April 8, 1966)* (Society of African Culture for the First World Festival of Negro Arts, 1968), 45–65; Sylvia Ardyn Boone, *Radiance from the Waters: Ideals of Feminine Beauty in Mende Art* (Yale University Press, 1986); and Wilfried Van Damme, "Beauty and Ugliness in African Art and Thought," in *The Language of Beauty in African Art*, ed. Constantine Petridis, exh. cat. (Art Institute of Chicago, 2022), 94–129.

6 I am grateful to Phyllis Hattis Rubin and Beatrice Rubin for driving many miles to allow me to examine this rare mask.

7   For full articulation of Pende theories of physiognomy, in the voices of the sculptors themselves, see Z. S. Strother, *Inventing Masks: Agency and History in the Art of the Central Pende* (University of Chicago Press, 1998), 101–53, 307–10.

8   Nzanda Gahondo, personal communication with author, Nioka-Munene, 1989. Nzando attributes the invention of Pulugunzu (facepiece, song, and dance) to the sculptor Maluba, who founded an important atelier at Nioka-Munene, where he died circa 1935. Pulugunzu did not have a long career perhaps because performers find that kaolin rubs off easily and stings the eyes. For this reason, white is usually applied sparingly on face masks.

9   The *mafuzo* masks expressed a real fear of being consumed, of being annihilated, during their heyday in the 1910s to 1930s and, as such, grant remarkable insight into the experience of being colonized. Some of the more fantastical forms have survived, mainly incorporated into daytime festivals, where they generate surprise and wonder. For a full history, see Strother, *Inventing Masks,* 229–63, 315–22.

10   Kassim Kone, personal communication with author, 9 March 2021; emails, 19 and 22 March 2021.

11   For more on some of the controversy that surrounds Senghor and emotion, see note 35 on p. 112.

12   Senghor, "The Spirit of Civilization," 57.

13   Catherine A. Lutz, *Unnatural Emotions: Everyday Sentiments on a Micronesian Atoll and Their Challenge to Western Theory* (University of Chicago Press, 1988); William M. Reddy, *The Navigation of Feeling: A Framework for the History of Emotions* (Cambridge University Press, 2001), ix–xi; and Lisa Feldman Barrett, *How Emotions Are Made: The Secret Life of the Brain* (Houghton Mifflin Harcourt, 2017).

14   Barrett, *How Emotions Are Made,* 15.

15   Reddy, *The Navigation of Feeling,* 12–13; and Barrett, *How Emotions Are Made,* chap. 3.

16   Reddy, *The Navigation of Feeling,* 8–12, 94–95; and Robert Boddice, *A History of Feelings* (Reaktion, 2019), 13–14.

17   Barrett, *How Emotions Are Made,* xi.

18   Barrett, *How Emotions Are Made,* 38–39.

19   Boddice, *A History of Feelings,* 10; see also Mark M. Smith, *Sensing the Past: Seeing, Hearing, Smelling, Tasting and Touching in History* (University of California Press, 2008).

20   All of the discussion from Drewal is from Henry John Drewal, "African Art and the Senses," *Sensory Studies* (2012), http://www.sensorystudies.org/sensorial-investigations/african-art-and-the-senses.

21   I thank Kathryn M. de Luna for a stimulating exchange on this topic (June 2019).

22   André Breton, "Phénix du Masque," *XXe Siècle,* n.s., no. 15 (1960): 60; and André Breton, *Oeuvres complètes* (Gallimard, 2008), 4:992. Reprintings of the text without the photographs have been misleading, as the suite of images conveys a central part of Breton's argument and explains his title, "Phoenix of the Mask": Breton expected the surrealists to bring a moribund European art form back to life.

23   Marcel Griaule, *Masques dogons* (1938; Institut d'ethnologie, 1983), 789–94.

24 Griaule, *Masques dogons,* 789.

25 Griaule, *Masques dogons,* 794.

26 Griaule, *Masques dogons,* 794.

27 Polly Richards, "The Dynamism of Dogon Masks and Mask Performances," in *ReCollecting Dogon,* ed. Paul R. Davis, https://www.menil.org/read/online-features /recollecting-dogon/dogon-now/dynamism-of-dogon-masks-polly-richards; and *Mask Stories,* directed by Polly Richards (Museum of African Art, 2013), https://vimeo.com /131739277.

28 Immanuel Kant, *Critique of the Power of Judgment,* trans. Paul Guyer (Cambridge University Press, 2000). Edmund Burke's text on the sublime is also considered to be a foundational text: "Astonishment … is the effect of the sublime in its highest degree." Edmund Burke, *A Philosophical Enquiry into the Origin of Our Ideas of the Sublime and Beautiful* [1757] (Columbia University Press, 1958), 53.

29 *Kinshasa Symphony,* directed by Claus Wischmann and Martin Baer (Sounding Images GmbH, Westdeutscher Rundfunk, Rundfunk Berlin-Brandenburg, 2010).

30 Aniakor, "Igbo Aesthetics," 12.

31 MacGaffey first referred to "astonishment" in 1988; however, as a social scientist, he was initially concerned to avoid "the distracting vocabularies of art and aesthetics." Wyatt MacGaffey, "Complexity, Astonishment and Power," *Journal of Southern African Studies* 14, no. 2 (1988): 190. He was freed to acknowledge that "sculptures admired for their art made better minkisi" via the work of Alfred Gell, who "defines artworks by their implication in social relations." Wyatt MacGaffey, "Astonishment and Stickiness in Kongo Art," *Res: Anthropology and Aesthetics* 39 (Spring 2001): 141, 148. As will become clear in the discussion of Pende masquerade, patrons are well aware of the social efficacy of aesthetic emotions.

32 In Central Africa, power objects are containers for animate energy dedicated to the accomplishment of a specific task.

33 Wyatt MacGaffey, "The Eyes of Understanding: Kongo Minkisi," in Wyatt MacGaffey and Michael D. Harris, *Astonishment and Power* (National Museum of African Art, 1994), 63.

34 William Holman Bentley, *Dictionary and Grammar of the Kongo Language, as Spoken at San Salvador, the Ancient Capital of the Old Kongo Empire, West Africa* (Baptist Missionary Society, 1887), 475 (my emphasis).

35 J. Decapmaker, "L'emploi du passif dans le langage des Bakongo," *Aequatoria* 17 (1954): 28.

36 Fu-Kiau Bunseki (1997), in Mary Nooter Roberts and Allen F. Roberts, *A Sense of Wonder: African Art from the Faletti Family Collection,* exh. cat. (Phoenix Art Museum, 1997), 34 (my emphasis).

37 MacGaffey, "Complexity, Astonishment and Power"; and Wyatt MacGaffey, "Franchising *Minkisi* in Loango: Questions of Form and Function," *Res: Anthropology and Aesthetics,* no. 65/66 (2014/2015): 155 (quotation). Probst slides the signification of *ngitukulu* from astonishment to fear or even terror, beyond what I believe is justified in Kikongo. See Peter Probst, "African Angst: On Nyau Masks, Figures of Evil, and the

Mediality of Terror," paper presented at Colloquium in Honor of Ute Luig, Free University of Berlin (2004), 4–5; and Peter Probst, "Schrecken und Staunen: Über Nyau-Maskender Chewa in Kontext der Konjunktur des Okkulten und der Medialisierung des Schreckens," in *Africa Screams,* ed. Tobias Wendl (Peter Hammer Verlag, 2004), 114.

38 William P. Murphy, "The Sublime Dance of Mende Politics: An African Aesthetic of Charismatic Power," *American Ethnologist* 25, no. 4 (1998): 566.

39 Murphy, "The Sublime Dance of Mende Politics," 563.

40 Murphy, "The Sublime Dance of Mende Politics," 574. Mary Nooter Roberts and Allan F. Roberts expanded on the interrelationship of wonder, the sublime, and the fantastic in African art. Roberts and Roberts, *A Sense of Wonder.*

41 The sudden appearance of a mask as tall as a palm tree is a well-known manifestation in West and Central Africa. I saw it at Gungu (DR Congo) in 1989. Strother, *Inventing Masks,* 242 (fig. 105).

42 Ute Röschenthaler, *Purchasing Culture: The Dissemination of Associations in the Cross River Region of Cameroon and Nigeria* (Africa World Press, 2011), 427.

43 Laurel Birch de Aguilar, *Inscribing the Mask: Interpretation of Nyau Masks and Ritual Performance Among the Chewa of Central Malawi* (University Press Fribourg, 1996), 15, 41. It is intriguing that the reaction of having the skin tighten in fear is reported primarily by people with a certain distance from the phenomenon, initiates who now live in urban centers, or uninitiated Malawians (Birch de Aguilar, *Inscribing the Mask,* 41n12).

44 Birch de Aguilar, *Inscribing the Mask,* 154.

45 Probst, "African Angst," 9–10.

46 Probst, "African Angst," 10; and Peter Probst, "Sublime Images: Masked Performances and the Aesthetics of Belonging in Malawi," in *Masquerade: Essays on Tradition and Innovation Worldwide,* ed. Deborah Bell (McFarland, 2015), 85.

47 Probst, "African Angst," 10–11; and Probst, "Schrecken und Staunen," 119–20.

48 Daniel B. Reed, *Dan Ge Performance: Masks and Music in Contemporary Côte d'Ivoire* (Indiana University Press, 2003), 1. The author integrates the study of music and masks into the Dan religious system throughout his book; see especially chapter 4, "What Is Ge?," 67–100. Yann Petit is currently studying the impact of the Ivorian Civil War (2002–11) on Dan masquerading practices. He notes that to this day many Dan people in Côte d'Ivoire resist translating *ge* or *gué* (pl. *genu*) as "masks" because they know that the French word (*masque*) usually signifies a facepiece and has a secular, even trivializing contemporary performance context. Yann Petit, email to author, 28 December 2024.

49 Reed, *Dan Ge Performance,* 78.

50 Reed, *Dan Ge Performance,* 78–79.

51 Mameri Tia, quoted in Reed, *Dan Ge Performance,* 88.

52 Kassim Kone, "Ugly as a *Kɔmɔ* Mask: An Aesthetics of Horror Among the Bamana," in *The Language of Beauty in African Art,* ed. Constantine Petridis, exh. cat. (Art Institute of Chicago, 2022), 256; see also Philippe Jespers, "La puissance du masque:

De l'audible au visible," in *Puissances de la voix: Corps sentant, corde sensible,* ed. Sémir Badir and Herman Parret (Presses universitaires de Limoges, 2001), 60.

53   Susan Elizabeth Gagliardi, "Seeing the Unseeing Audience: Women and West African Power Association Masquerades," *Africa* 88, no. 4 (2018): 750.

54   The following account is drawn from Kone, "Ugly as a *Kɔmɔ* Mask," and a class visit, 9 March 2021.

55   Komo was created by Bamana blacksmiths but has spread to several ethnic groups. Philippe Jespers was initiated into a Minyanka chapter of Komo in Mali and describes a different although equally haunting acoustic environment in which the performer's mirliton competes with the roar of a friction drum. He notes the ability of sounds to penetrate every corner of the community so that no one is able to escape the power of Komo. Jespers, "La puissance du masque," 2001.

56   "*Pensez aux masques Ntomo (initiation) des enfants. Ils déclenchent des émotions en fonction de la position du sujet: vieux, jeune, non-circoncis, circoncis. En fonction de cette position, ils peuvent ressentir de la peur, de la joie, de la nostalgie. Les nouveaux initiés apprécient leur nouvelle position d'autorité* ... c'est leur tour." Kone, personal communication with author, 9 March 2021.

57   Nick Routley, "A Visual Guide to Human Emotion," *Visual Capitalist,* 8 April 2021, https://www.visualcapitalist.com/a-visual-guide-to-human-emotion.

58   Senghor, "The Spirit of Civilization," 57.

59   Simon Ottenberg, "Illusion, Communication, and Psychology in West African Masquerades," *Ethos* 10, no. 2 (1982): 161.

60   Dangerously, there is also an assumption that "a ritual is also any *act* done *regularly,* usually without *thinking* about it," *Cambridge Dictionary,* under "ritual," https://dictionary.cambridge.org/us/dictionary/english/ritual (my emphasis). For a scholar's contrasting perspective on the difficulty of defining ritual practice, see Catherine Bell, *Ritual: Perspectives and Dimensions* (Oxford University Press, 1997).

61   On the passion, vibrancy, and creativity of "new" African masquerades, see Amanda M. Maples, Jordan A. Fenton, and Lisa Homann, eds., *New African Masquerades: Artistic Innovations and Collaborations,* exh. cat. (New Orleans Museum of Art, 2025).

62   The Pende material presented in chapters 4 and 5 dates from 1987–89, during which I observed 26 days of village masquerading and over 133 days of initiation masquerading, thanks to invitations to attend two boys' initiations (*mukanda*) in different regions. Follow-up trips in 2006 and 2023 and the research of Nzomba Dugo Kakema in 2018 have established the continuing importance of masquerades even as they evolve to satisfy a population that would now overwhelmingly self-identify as Christian. See Strother, *Inventing Masks;* and Z. S. Strother and Nzomba Dugo Kakema, "The Role of Masks in the Eastern Pende Mukanda," in *Congo as Fiction: Art Worlds Between Past and Present,* ed. Nanina Guyer and Michaela Oberhofer (Museum Rietberg, 2020), 254–72.

63   For an in-depth exegesis of the Pende religious system, see Z. S. Strother, "From Performative Utterance to Performative Object: Pende Theories of Speech, Blood

Sacrifice, and Power Objects," *Res: Anthropology and Aesthetics,* no. 37 (Spring 2000): 49–71.

64 Like most speakers of Bantu languages, Kipende speakers do not have a word for "ancestor." Igor Kopytoff, "Ancestors as Elders in Africa," *Africa* 41, no. 2 (1971): 129–42. When pressed to be precise, they refer to the "maternal uncles who have already died" (*malemba afile kale*).

65 Regularly, if less frequently, masquerades are woven into investiture rituals for new chiefs and into the coming-out ceremony for boys' initiations, and they are used as petitions for the healing of the chief. All involve a sacrificial meal near the chief's *kibulu* (ritual house), overseen by the chief, his counselors, and the performers. I witnessed each of these circumstances in the late 1980s on multiple occasions except for those dances once organized to petition the dead to heal a community in times of pandemic. As such, Eastern Pende practice contradicts Van Beek and Leyten's conclusion that "masks only rarely function in healing ceremonies, rarely in sacrifices, and hardly ever in cyclical, agricultural or rain rituals." Walter E. A. Van Beek and Harrie Leyten, *Masquerades in African Society: Gender, Power, and Identity* (James Currey, 2023), 45.

66 "*[Dans le Kasaï on fait] danser les masques a doublée roles: 1) Communier avec les Vumbi pour obtenir la bénédiction et le bonheur 2) Divertissement.*" Nzomba Dugo Kakema, personal communication with author, 22 August 2019.

67 I am deeply thankful for several conversations with Deniz Hughes about music, most recently on 30 August 2024. There is evidence for the conflicting emotions that Hughes highlights in the work of scholars focused on masked performers, such as Anne-Marie Bouttiaux, "La danse des hommes, la jubilation des esprits: Masques guro de la région de Zuenoula, Côte d'Ivoire" (PhD diss., Université Libre de Bruxelles, 2000); Anne-Marie Bouttiaux, "Sous l'apparence du masque, un espace de transgression," in *Le labyrinthe des apparences,* ed. Eric Clemens (Revue de l'Université de Bruxelles, 2000), 115–32; Anne-Marie Bouttiaux, "Porteur de *Zamble* en pays Guro: Les enjeux de la célébrité," *Art'in, revue d'arts plastiques et d'arts du spectacle (Université de Valenciennes)* 1, no. 1 (2004): 77–85; Patrick McNaughton, *A Bird Dance near Saturday City: Sidi Ballo and the Art of West African Masquerade* (Indiana University Press, 2008); and Jordan A. Fenton, *Masquerade and Money in Urban Nigeria: The Case of Calabar* (University of Rochester Press, 2022).

68 It can be a struggle to find an inspirational lead drummer because some Christian churches ban their drummers from participating in masked dances. In particular, the Pentecostals offer weekly employment and are eager to hire skilled musicians. It is impossible for a drummer to pass up weekly work for occasional work in a masquerade.

69 I thank Chief Kingange (Kaluma a Mbangu) for his gracious hospitality.

70 In December 1987, Pumbu was danced following ceremonies to petition the dead for the cure of the mortal illness of Chief Kombo-Kiboto (Mukanzo a Kilumbu). Following Kombo's death, it was danced again in February 1988 to celebrate the inauguration of his successor. Chief Kingange was unusually fond of Pumbu and would often have him close masquerades organized to thank the dead for good harvests or hunts.

71 The threat of killing gives the day its edge, and no one advertises that the goat or chicken slaughtered by Pumbu serves as a thank-you dinner for the lead dancers and special guests.

72 Nzomba Dugo Kakema, personal communication with author, 22 August 2019.

73 Central Pende interviewed in 2006 reported not having the leisure, well-being, or financial resources to organize dances of masks as they had in the past. Kwilu province has yet to recover from the economic collapse triggered by the slow slide of Mobutu Sese Seko from power, 1990–97. Eastern Pende, located in a mining zone, have been more sheltered by having access to the diamond economy.

74 Strother, *Inventing Masks,* 229–63.

75 Gatemo Pumbu, Gimasa Gabate, and Muwawa a Bungu, Nioka-Kakese, 28 April 1989. Also, Khoshi Mahumbu and Masuwa, Nioka-Munene, 1989.

76 "*Gusuanguluisa mila yakhadi tshitshitshiala.*" Mukedi, April 1989.

77 It is appropriate to address Congolese by their first name unless they have adopted a French first name, in which case the Congolese name takes the place of a surname.

78 Scientists today would say that it releases endorphins.

79 Léon de Sousberghe, *L'art pende* (Académie royale de Belgique, 1959); Muyaga Gangambi, *Les masques pende de Gatundo* (Centre d'êtudes ethnologiques, 1974); and Strother, *Inventing Masks.*

80 The oldest term seems to be "masks of beauty." The Kipende word for beauty (*ginango*) has lost out to the Kikongo loan word *kiese,* translated as happiness.

81 In 1989, elders across a wide range of Central Pende communities took pleasure in sharing vivid memories of masks (such as Pumbu or Pulugunzu; see fig. 21) that had once aroused fear and consternation. However, I did not personally witness any fearful reactions during Central Pende performances (in contrast to what was still an animated reality among Eastern Pende). The few surviving *mbuya jia mafuzo* provoked some wonder and curiosity but no stampedes.

82 Strother, *Inventing Masks,* 46–51; Reed, *Dan Ge Performance,* 144–48; and Lisa Homann, "Alluring Obscurity: Dancing Nocturnal White Masks in Southwestern Burkina Faso," *Res: Anthropology and Aesthetics,* no. 65/66 (2014/2015): 171–73. Beginning with Frobenius (see fig. 12), European researchers have attempted to categorize masks by their visual properties—their materials or styles. The anthropologist Léon de Sousberghe tried to divide Pende masks (face fragments) into categories by materials—wood or raffia—and was forced to admit that his categories did not conform to any local reality (de Sousberghe, *L'art pende*). For example, initiation masks may be made from either material. After a valiant effort to develop a typology for a plethora of Bobo masks in Burkina Faso, Le Moal threw up his hands, admitting that any analysis of Bobo masks must begin with the work's "biography" rather than the materials. Guy Le Moal, *Les Bobo: Nature et fonction des masques* (1980; Musée royal de l'Afrique central, 1999), 111–12. Page references are to the 1999 edition.

Van Beek and Leyten speculate that there might have been an evolution from leaves to fibers to cloth but admit that most masking societies make use of a mix of materials (*Masquerades in African Society,* 54–55).

83 Seminar on Masks and Emotions, Université de Kinshasa, 6 July 2023.

84 Van Beek and Leyten, *Masquerades in African Society,* 149–80.

85 Charles Sikitele (now Sikitele Gize), excerpts from "Les Souvenirs," in *Prix de Poésie Sébastien Ngonso* (Université Lovanium, 1968), 34–36. I thank Professor Sikitele for his warm welcome and for his gift of a rare edition of his poems.

86 Sikitele Gize, personal communication with author, 8 July 2023.

87 Strother, *Inventing Masks,* 23–44; Bouttiaux, "Porteur de *Zamble*"; McNaughton, *A Bird Dance;* Lisa Homann, "Controversy and Human Agency in 'Portrait Masks' from the Studio of André Sanou," *Africa* 88, no. 4 (2018): 768–801; and Fenton, *Masquerade and Money.*

CHAPTER 5

1 See chapter 4 for a discussion of conflicting emotions in masquerade, inspired by conversation with Deniz Hughes, 30 August 2024.

2 Karl Heinz Bohrer, *Suddenness: On the Moment of Aesthetic Appearance,* trans. Ruth Crowley (Columbia University Press, 1994). Originally published in German as *Plötzlichkeit: Zum Augenblick des ästhetischen Scheins* (Suhrkamp, 1981). See also Peter Probst, "Schrecken und Staunen: Über Nyau-Maskender Chewa in Kontext der Konjunktur des Okkulten und der Medialisierung des Schreckens," in *Africa Screams,* ed. Tobias Wendl (Peter Hammer Verlag, 2004), 119.

3 Monni Adams, "'It Opens Your Mouth!': Forest Spirit Identities in Public Display and Private Discussion; Masking and Rhetoric in Canton Boo, Southwestern Côte d'Ivoire," *Archiv für Völkerkunde* 56 (2006): 12 (my emphasis). For in-depth documentation and insightful analysis of this phenomenon, see Lisa Homann, "When Muslims Masquerade: *Lo Gue* Performance in Southwestern Burkina Faso" (PhD diss., University of California, Los Angeles, 2011), for example, p. 86.

4 A string of exclamations of surprise and amazement challenge performers to rise to the level of Ngoma, a renowned dancer: Wow, wow, wow, Ngoma! (2×) Wow! Ngoma came with style (2×). *Mawe, Mawe, Mawe, Ngoma!* (2×) *Mawe! Ngoma wajile mu lulendo* (2×).

5 Bohrer, *Suddenness,* vii.

6 André Breton, "Phénix du Masque," *XXe Siècle,* n.s., no. 15 (1960): 55–63. Reprinted with only one photo in André Breton, *Oeuvres complètes,* vol. 4 (Gallimard, 2008), 990–94, 1427.

7 Cari Meltzer, personal communication with author, continued in email, 20 July 2020.

8 Anthony Vidler, *The Architectural Uncanny* (MIT Press, 1992), 23.

9 Vidler, *The Architectural Uncanny,* 23.

10 In Vidler, *The Architectural Uncanny,* 222.

11 Simon Ottenberg, "Illusion, Communication, and Psychology in West African Masquerades," *Ethos* 10, no. 2 (1982): 160–61.

12 Terry Castle, *Masquerade and Civilization* (Stanford University Press, 1986), 4–5. For interview-based research investigating the "double consciousness" of British actors,

see William Archer, "Masks or Faces?" [1888], in *The Paradox of Acting; Masks or Faces?* (Hill and Wang, 1957), 184–200.

13 Adams, "'It Opens Your Mouth!,'" 10, 22.

14 Julie Taymor (with Alexis Greene), *The Lion King: Pride Rock on Broadway* (Disney Editions, 1997), 29.

15 Taymor, *Lion King,* 144.

16 Taymor, *Lion King,* 124.

17 Taymor, *Lion King,* 29; see also 144.

18 Carlos Fausto, "Le masque de l'animiste: Chimères et poupées russes en Amérique indigène," *Gradhiva,* no. 13 (2011): 52.

19 John Rudlin, *Commedia dell'Arte: An Actor's Handbook* (Routledge, 1994), 4.

20 For a vivid phenomenological analysis of the surprise, suspense, anxiety, terror, humor, and exhilaration associated with the unpredictability of masks on tour in Bobo-Dioulasso, Burkina Faso, see Homann, "When Muslims Masquerade," chap. 2. "Even though attendees know what to expect, they never know when or where, or to whom it will happen." Homann, "When Muslims Masquerade," 103.

21 Elisabeth L. Cameron, personal communication with author.

22 Vidler, *The Architectural Uncanny,* 57.

23 Siona Wilson, email responding to one of my lectures, 21 February 2005.

24 Michael Taussig, *Defacement: Public Secrecy and the Labor of the Negative* (Stanford University Press, 1999), 257 (my emphasis).

25 Taussig, *Defacement,* 104, 127, 147. I thank Susan E. Gagliardi for bringing this text to my attention.

26 Taussig, *Defacement,* 102–42.

27 Taussig, *Defacement,* 129.

28 Taussig, *Defacement,* 127, 147.

29 The camps are organized every twelve to fifteen years. Nzomba Dugo Kakema collected important information on the initiations held in 2018, which confirmed the contemporaneity of what is described above. Z. S. Strother and Nzomba Dugo Kakema, "The Role of Masks in the Eastern Pende Mukanda," in *Congo as Fiction: Art Worlds Between Past and Present,* ed. Nanina Guyer and Michaela Oberhofer (Museum Rietberg, 2020), 254–72.

30 Strother and Nzomba Dugo Kakema, "The Role of Masks in the Eastern Pende Mukanda," 270–71. Ottenberg was a pioneer in recognizing the importance of childhood masquerades, inspired by his interest in psychoanalysis. Ottenberg, "Illusion, Communication, and Psychology," 170–75.

31 Quoted by Constance Classen, *The Deepest Sense: A Cultural History of Touch* (University of Illinois Press, 2012), 132.

32 Johann Gottfried Herder, *Sculpture: Some Observations on Shape and Form from Pygmalion's Creative Dream*, ed. and trans. Jason Gaiger (University of Chicago, 2002). Originally published in 1778.

33 Vidler, *The Architectural Uncanny.*

34 Eastern Pende men tend to dismiss the significance of the *mukanda* masks. With a wave of the hand, they claim that they serve only as "police" (*pulushi*). It is hard for an outsider to agree, given their importance in socialization. For example, they set the stage for the reception of the community masks, which rarely chase and which arouse different aesthetic emotions.

35 Ernst Theodor Wilhelm Hoffmann, "The Uncanny Guest," in *The Tales of Hoffmann* (Heritage Press, 1943), 278–79. Translation of Ernst Theodor Wilhelm Hoffmann, "Der unheimliche Gast."

36 Hoffmann, "The Uncanny Guest," 281.

37 Hoffmann, "The Uncanny Guest," 283–84.

38 Hoffmann, "The Uncanny Guest," 279–80.

39 Hoffmann, "The Uncanny Guest," 279 (emphasis in original).

40 Nicolas Argenti, "Ephemeral Monuments, Memory and Royal Sempiternity in a Grassfields Kingdom," in *The Art of Forgetting,* ed. Adrian Forty and Susanne Küchler (Berg, 1999), 45.

41 Argenti, "Ephemeral Monuments, Memory and Royal Sempiternity," 43 (my emphasis).

42 Argenti, "Ephemeral Monuments, Memory and Royal Sempiternity," 40.

43 Argenti, "Ephemeral Monuments, Memory and Royal Sempiternity," 40, 51n36, 51n37.

44 Sigmund Freud, "The Uncanny" [1919], in *Writings on Art and Literature* (Stanford University Press, 1997), 193.

Selected Bibliography

Achebe, Chinua. "The Igbo World and Its Art." In *Hopes and Impediments,* 62–67. Doubleday, 1988.

Adams, Marie Jeanne. "Introduction." *Ethnologische Zeitschrift Zürich* 1 (1980): 9–12.

Adams, Monni. "Agency and Control in Masked Festivals Among the Bo People, Southwestern Côte d'Ivoire." *Zeitschrift für ethnologie* 130, no. 2 (2005): 195–221.

———. "Both Sides of the Collecting Encounter: The George W. Harley Collection at the Peabody Museum of Archaeology and Ethnology, Harvard University." *Museum Anthropology* 32, no. 1 (2009): 17–32.

———. "'It Opens Your Mouth!': Forest Spirit Identities in Public Display and Private Discussion; Masking and Rhetoric in Canton Boo, Southwestern Côte d'Ivoire." *Archiv für Völkerkunde* 56 (2006): 1–30.

———. "Women and Masks Among the Western Wè of Ivory Coast." *African Arts* 19, no. 2 (1986): 46–55, 90.

Alcott, Louisa May. *Behind a Mask* [1866]. In *Alternative Alcott,* edited by Elaine Showalter, 95–202. Rutgers University Press, 1988.

Andree, Richard. "Die Masken." In *Ethnographische Parallelen und Vergleiche,* 107–65. 2nd ed. Leipzig, Veit & Comp., 1889.

———. "Die Masken in der Völkerkunde." *Archiv für Anthropologie* 16 (1886): 477–506.

Aniakor, Chike. "Igbo Aesthetics: An Introduction." *Nigeria Magazine* 141 (1982): 3–15.

Archer, William. *Masks or Faces?* [1888]. In *The Paradox of Acting by Denis Diderot and Masks or Faces? by William Archer,* 75–226. Hill and Wang, 1957.

Argenti, Nicolas. "Ephemeral Monuments, Memory and Royal Sempiternity in a Grassfields Kingdom." In *The Art of Forgetting,* edited by Adrian Forty and Susanne Küchler, 21–52. Berg, 1999.

———. *The Intestines of the State: Youth, Violence, and Belated Histories in the Cameroon Grassfields.* University of Chicago Press, 2007.

Bakhtin, Mikhail. *Rabelais and His World.* Indiana University Press, 1984. Originally published in Russian in 1965.

Barrett, Lisa Feldman. *How Emotions Are Made: The Secret Life of the Brain.* Houghton Mifflin Harcourt, 2017.

Barthes, Roland. *Camera Lucida.* Hill and Wang, 1980.

———. "Le mythe de l'acteur possédé." In *Écrits sur le théâtre,* edited by Jean-Loup Rivière, 234–37. Seuil, 2002. Originally published in 1958 in the journal *Théâtre d'Aujourd'hui.*

Bastian, Adolf. "Masken und Maskerein." *Zeitschrift für Völkerpsychologie* 14 (1883): 335–58.

Becker, Judith. *Deep Listeners: Music, Emotion, and Trancing.* Indiana University Press, 2004.

———. "Music and Trance." *Leonardo Music Journal* 4 (1994): 41–51.

Bédouin, Jean-Louis. *Les masques.* Presses universitaires de France, 1961.

Beier, Ulli. "The Egungun Cult Among the Yorubas." *Présence africaine,* n.s. (February–May 1958): 33–36.

Bell, Catherine. *Ritual: Perspectives and Dimensions.* Oxford University Press, 1997.

Belting, Hans. "Towards an Anthropology of the Image." In *Anthropologies of Art,* edited by Mariët Westermann, 41–58. Sterling and Francine Clark Art Institute, 2005.

Bentley, William Holman. *Dictionary and Grammar of the Kongo Language, as Spoken at San Salvador, the Ancient Capital of the Old Kongo Empire, West Africa.* Baptist Missionary Society, 1887.

Bentor, Eli. "'Remember Six Feet Deep': Masks and the Exculpation of/from Death in Aro Masquerade." *Journal of Religion in Africa* 24, no. 4 (1994): 333–38.

Birch de Aguilar, Laurel. *Inscribing the Mask: Interpretation of Nyau Masks and Ritual Performance Among the Chewa of Central Malawi.* University Press Fribourg, 1996.

Boddice, Robert. *A History of Feelings.* Reaktion, 2019.

Bohrer, Karl Heinz. *Suddenness: On the Moment of Aesthetic Appearance.* Translated by Ruth Crowley. Columbia University Press, 1994. Originally published in 1981 as *Plötzlichkeit: Zum Augenblick des ästhetischen Scheins* by Suhrkamp.

Boone, Sylvia Ardyn. *Radiance from the Waters: Ideals of Feminine Beauty in Mende Art.* Yale University Press, 1986.

Bouttiaux, Anne-Marie. "La danse des hommes, la jubilation des esprits: Masques guro de la région de Zuenoula, Côte d'Ivoire." PhD diss., Université Libre de Bruxelles, 2000.

———. "Du divertissement au sacrifice: Danses de masques guro de la région de Zuenoula, Côte d'Ivoire." In *La dynamique des masques en Afrique occidentale,* edited by Anne-Marie Bouttiaux, 116–40. Musée royal de l'Afrique centrale, 2013.

———. "Guro Masked Performers Serving Spirits and People." Translated by Allen F. Roberts. *African Arts* 42, no. 2 (2009): 56–67.

———. "Porteur de *Zamble* en pays Guro: Les enjeux de la célébrité." *Art'in, revue d'arts plastiques et d'arts du spectacle (Université de Valenciennes)* 1, no. 1 (2001): 77–85.

———. "Sous l'apparence du masque, un espace de transgression." In *Le labyrinthe des apparences,* edited by E. Clemens, 115–32. Revue de l'Université de Bruxelles, 2000.

Brandl, Flora. "Mask Metaphors in the German Language and Austrian Vernacular." Manuscript from the seminar Masquerade: Rhetoric/Theory/Practice, Columbia University, Fall 2020.

Breton, André. "Phénix du masque." *XXe Siècle,* n.s., no. 15 (1960): 55–63. Reprinted in 2008 with only one photo in vol. 4 of *Oeuvres complètes* by Gallimard, 990–94, 1427.

Bruce, Vicki, and Andy Young. *In the Eye of the Beholder: The Science of Face Perception.* Oxford University Press, 1998.

Buraud, Georges. *Les masques.* Seuil, 1948. Reissued in 2014 by Musée du Quai Branly.

Burke, Edmund. *A Philosophical Enquiry into the Origin of Our Ideas of the Sublime and Beautiful.* Columbia University Press, 1958. Originally published in 1757.

Butler, Judith. *Gender Trouble: Feminism and the Subversion of Identity.* Routledge, 1990.

Caillois, Roger. *Man, Play and Games.* Translated by Meyer Barash. University of Illinois Press, 2001. Originally published in 1958 as *Jeux et les hommes (Le masque et le vertige)* by Gallimard. Original English translation in 1961 by The Free Press of Glencoe, Inc.

Cameron, Elisabeth L. "Women = Masks: Initiation Arts in North-Western Province, Zambia." *African Arts* 31, no. 2 (1998): 50–61, 93.

Carlson, Amanda B. "In the Spirit and in the Flesh: Women, Masquerades, and the Cross River." *African Arts* 52, no. 1 (2019): 46–61.

Castle, Terry. *Masquerade and Civilization.* Stanford University Press, 1986.

Classen, Constance. *The Deepest Sense: A Cultural History of Touch.* University of Illinois Press, 2012.

Clifford, James. "Power and Dialogue in Ethnography: Marcel Griaule's Initiation." In *The Predicament of Culture: Twentieth-Century Ethnography, Literature and Art,* 55–91. Harvard University Press, 1988. Originally published in 1983.

Cole, Herbert M. *African Arts of Transformation.* University of California, Santa Barbara, Art Gallery, 1970. Exhibition catalog.

———. "Introduction." In *I Am Not Myself: The Art of African Masquerade,* edited by Herbert M. Cole, 55–91. Museum of Cultural History, University of California, Los Angeles, 1985. Exhibition catalog.

Crawley, A. E. "Mask." In *Encyclopedia of Religion and Ethics,* vol. 8, edited by James Hastings, 483–87. Charles Scribner's Sons, 1916.

Davis, Paul R., ed. *ReCollecting Dogon.* Menil, 2017. https://www.menil.org/read/online-features/recollecting-dogon.

Decapmaker, J. "L'emploi du passif dans le langage des Bakongo." *Aequatoria* 17 (1954): 1, 28–30.

de Sousberghe, Léon. *L'art pende.* Académie royale de Belgique, 1959.

Diagne, Souleymane Bachir. "Négritude." In *The Stanford Encyclopedia of Philosophy,* edited by Edward N. Zalta and Uri Nodelman. Metaphysics Research Lab, Philosophy Department, Stanford University, 2018. https://plato.stanford.edu /archives/sum2018/entries/negritude.

Diawara, Manthia. "The African Public Intellectual: The Negritude of Léopold Sédar Senghor." In *Dak'Art. Afrique: Miroir?,* 200-205. Biennale de l'Art African Contemporain, 2008. Exhibition catalog.

———. "The 1960s in Bamako: Malick Sidibé and James Brown." In *Everything but the Burden: What White People Are Taking from Black Culture,* edited by Greg Tate, 164-90. Broadway Books, 2003.

Dieterlen, Germaine. "Masks and Mythology Among the Dogon." *African Arts* 12, no. 3 (1989): 34-43, 87-88.

———. "Mythologie, histoire et masques." *Journal de la Société des Africanistes* 59, no. 1-2 (1989): 7-38.

———. "Symbolisme du masque en Afrique occidentale." In *Le masque,* 49-55. Musée Guimet, 1960. Exhibition catalog.

Doquet, Anne. *Les masques dogon: Ethnologie savante et ethnologie autochtone.* Karthala, 1999.

Drewal, Henry John. "African Art and the Senses." *Sensory Studies* (2012). http://www .sensorystudies.org/sensorial-investigations/african-art-and-the-senses.

Drewal, Henry John, and Margaret Thompson Drewal. *Gẹlẹdẹ: Art and Female Power Among the Yoruba.* University of Indiana Press, 1983.

Durkheim, Emile, and Marcel Mauss. *Primitive Classification.* Translated by Rodney Needham. University of Chicago Press, 1963. Originally published as "De quelques formes primitives de classification," *L'année sociologique* 6 (1903): 1-72.

Einstein, Carl. "Negro Sculpture." Translated by Charles W. Haxthausen and Sebastian Zeidler. *October* 107 (2004): 122-45. Originally published in 1915 as *Negerplastik* by Verlag de Weissen Bücher.

Eliade, Mircea. "Masks." In *Encyclopedia of World Art,* vol. 9, 520-25. McGraw-Hill, 1964.

Emigh, John. *Masked Performance.* University of Pennsylvania Press, 1996.

Fausto, Carlos. "Le masque de l'animiste: Chimères et poupées russes en Amérique indigène." *Gradhiva,* no. 13 (2011): 48-67.

———. "Whirlwinds of Images." In *Art Effects: Image, Agency, and Ritual in Amazonia,* translated by David Rodgers, 123-71, 322-26. University of Nebraska Press, 2020.

Fenton, Jordan A. "Expressive Currencies: Artistic Transactions and Transformations of Warrior-Inspired Masquerades in Calabar." *African Arts* 52, no. 1 (2019): 18-33.

——. *Masquerade and Money in Urban Nigeria: The Case of Calabar*. University of Rochester Press, 2022.

Fischer, Eberhard. *Dan Artists: The Sculptors Tame, Si, Tompieme and Sõn; Their Personalities and Work*. Scheidegger & Spiess, 2014. Originally published as "Künstler der Dan," *Baessler Archiv,* n.s., 10, no. 2 (1963): 161–263.

——. *Guro: Masks, Performances and Master Carvers in Ivory Coast*. Museum Rietberg, 2008.

Fischer, Eberhard, and Hans Himmelheber. *The Arts of the Dan in West Africa*. Museum Rietberg, 1984. Originally published in 1976 as *Die Kunst der Dan*.

Fo, Dario. *The Tricks of the Trade*. Translated by Joe Farrell. Edited by Stuart Hood. Routledge, 1991. Originally published in 1987 as *Manuale minimo dell'attore* by Einaudi.

Freud, Sigmund. "The Uncanny" [1919]. In *Writings on Art and Literature* (Stanford University Press, 1997). Reproduced from *The Standard Edition of the Complete Psychological Works of Sigmund Freud,* edited by James Strachey, 193–233, 277–78.

Frobenius, Leo. *Auf dem Wege nach Atlantis*. Edited by Herman Frobenius. Vita Deutsches Verlagshaus, 1911.

——. *Kulturgeschichte Afrikas*. Erschienen im Phaidon-Verlag, 1933.

——. "Die Masken und Geheimbünde Afrikas." In *Nova Acta: Abhandlungen der Kaiserlichen Leopoldinisch-Carolinischen Deutschen Akademie der Naturforscher* 74, no. 1 (1898): 1–278, 14 plates, 33 black-and-white illustrations.

——. "Les masques et les sociétés secrètes d'Afrique" [1898]. In *Masques,* translated by Alfred Schwartz, 241–393. Musée Dapper, 1995. The ethnological presentation (part 2) of Frobenius's 1898 text is published with reproductions of some of the original illustrations (mixed with others).

——. *Und Afrika sprach …* 3 vols. Vita, 1912–13.

Gagliardi, Susan Elizabeth. "Art and the Individual in African Masquerades." *Africa* 88, no. 4 (2018): 702–17.

——. "Seeing the Unseeing Audience: Women and West African Power Association Masquerades." *Africa* 88, no. 4 (2018): 744–67.

Gibson, Ann. "Regression and Color in Abstract Expressionism: Barnett Newman, Mark Rothko, and Clyfford Still." *Arts Magazine* (March 1981): 144–53.

Green, Sandra E. *Gender, Ethnicity, and Social Change on the Upper Slave Coast: A History of the Anlo-Ewe*. Heinemann, 1996.

Griaule, Marcel. *Conversations with Ogotemmêli: An Introduction to Dogon Religious Ideas*. Translated by Ralph Butler. Revised by Audrey I. Richards and Beatrice Hooke. Oxford University Press, 1965. Originally published in 1948 as *Dieu d'eau: Entretiens avec Ogotemmêli*.

———. *Masques dogons.* Institut d'ethnologie, 1983. Originally published in 1938.

Griaule, Marcel, and Germaine Dieterlen. *The Pale Fox.* Translated by Stephen C. Infantino. Continuum Foundation, 1986. Originally published in 1965 as *Le renard pâle* by Institut d'ethnologie.

Harley, George. *Masks as Agents of Social Control in Northeast Liberia.* Knaus Reprint Corp., 1968. Originally published in 1950 by Peabody Museum of Archaeology and Ethnology.

Harris, Cheryl I. "Whiteness as Property." *Harvard Law Review* 106, no. 8 (1993): 1707–91.

Heintze, Beatrix, ed. *Max Buchners Reisen nach Zentralafrika, 1878–1882.* Rüdiger Köppe, 1999.

Hersak, Dunja. "On the Concept of Prototype in Songye Masquerades." *African Arts* 45, no. 2 (2012): 12–23.

Himmelheber, Hans. "Die Geister und ihre irdischen Verkörperungen als Grundvorstellung in der Religion der Dan (Libera und Elfenbeinküste) unter Mitarbeit von Wowoa Tame-Tabmen, Ngor Diaple, Liberia." *Baessler-Archiv,* n.s., vol. 12 (1964): 161–263.

———. "Personality and Technique of African Sculptors." In *Technique and Personality,* edited by Margaret Mead, 79–110. Museum of Primitive Art, 1963.

———. "Sculptors and Sculptures of the Dan." In *The Proceedings of the First International Congress of Africanists (Accra, 1962),* edited by Lalage Bown and Michael Crowder, 243–55. Longmans, Green & Co., 1964.

Hoffmann, Ernst Theodor Wilhelm. "The Uncanny Guest." In *The Tales of Hoffmann,* 277–314. Heritage Press, 1943. Originally published in 1820 as "Der unheimliche Gast."

Homann, Lisa. "Alluring Obscurity: Dancing Nocturnal White Masks in Southwestern Burkina Faso." *Res: Anthropology and Aesthetics,* no. 65/66 (2014/2015): 158–78.

———. "Controversy and Human Agency in 'Portrait Masks' from the Studio of André Sanou." *Africa* 88, no. 4 (2018): 768–801.

———. "When Muslims Masquerade: *Lo Gue* Performance in Southwestern Burkina Faso." PhD diss., University of California, Los Angeles, 2011.

Horton, Robin. "The Kalabari Ekine Society: A Borderland of Religion and Art." *Africa* 33, no. 2 (1963): 94–113.

Israel, Paolo. *In Step with the Times: Mapiko Masquerades of Mozambique.* Ohio University Press, 2014.

Jedrej, M. C. "Dan and Mende Masks: A Structural Comparison." *Africa* 56, no. 1 (1986): 71–80.

Jentsch, Ernst. "On the Psychology of the Uncanny." *Angelaki* 20 (1995): 7–16. Originally published in 1906 as "Zur Psychologie des Unheimlichen," *Psychiatrisch-Neurologische Wochenschrift* 8, no. 22 (1906): 195–98; 8, no. 23 (1906): 203–5.

Jespers, Philippe. "Le masque et la parole: Analyse d'un masque 'auditif' de la société initiatique du Komo Minyanka, Mali." In *Objets-Signes d'Afrique,* edited by Luc de Heusch, 37–56. Musée royal de l'Afrique central, 1995.

———. "La puissance du masque: De l'audible au visible." In *Puissances de la voix: Corps sentant, corde sensible,* edited by Sémir Badir and Herman Parret, 51–69. Presses universitaires de Limoges, 2001.

Kaiser, Franz-W., and Iba Ndiaye. "Conversation." In *Iba Ndiaye: Painter Between Continents,* edited by Okwui Enwezor and Franz-W. Kaiser, 45–61. Adam Biro, 2002.

Kant, Immanuel. *Critique of the Power of Judgment.* Translated by Paul Guyer. Cambridge University Press, 2000.

Kasfir, Sidney L. "Masquerading as a Cultural System." In *West African Masks and Cultural Systems,* edited by Sidney L. Kasfir, 1–16. Musée royal de l'Afrique central, 1988.

Keita, D., M. M. Tessougue, and Y. Fane. "Patrimoine culture Malien sabordé au nom d'un Islam puritain." *Annales de l'Université Ouaga I Pr Joseph KI-ZERBO,* series A, vol. 25 (2018): 1–27.

Kofman, Sarah. *The Childhood of Art: An Interpretation of Freud's Aesthetics.* Translated by Winifred Woodhull. Columbia University Press, 1988. Originally published in 1970 as *L'enfance de l'art* by Payot.

Kone, Kassim. "Ugly as a *Kɔmɔ* Mask: An Aesthetics of Horror Among the Bamana." In *The Language of Beauty in African Art,* edited by Constantine Petridis, 244–49. Art Institute of Chicago, 2022. Exhibition catalog.

Kopytoff, Igor. "Ancestors as Elders in Africa." *Africa* 41, no. 2 (1971): 129–42.

Kramer, Fritz W. *The Red Fez: Art and Spirit Possession in Africa.* Translated by Malcolm Green. Verso, 1993. Originally published in 1987 as *Der rote Fes: Über Besessenheit und Kunst in Afrika* by Athenäum.

Lakoff, George, and Mark Johnson. *Metaphors We Live By.* University of Chicago Press, 1980.

Lawal, Babatunde. *The Gèlèdé Spectacle: Art, Gender, and Social Harmony in an African Culture.* University of Washington Press, 1996.

Leiris, Michel. "Masques dogon." *Minotaure,* no. 2 (1 June 1933): 45–51.

Le Moal, Guy. *Les Bobo: Nature et fonction des masques.* Musée royal de l'Afrique central, 1999. Originally published in 1980 by ORSTOM.

Lévi-Strauss, Claude. "The Many Faces of Man." *World Theatre* 10, no. 1 (1961): 11–20.

Lévy-Bruhl, Lucien. *How Natives Think.* Translated by Lilian A. Clare. Ayer, 1926. Originally published in 1910 as *Les fonctions mentales dans les sociétés inférieures* by Presses universitaires de France.

———. *Le surnaturel et la nature dans la mentalité primitive.* Presses universitaires de France, 1963. Originally published in 1931 by F. Alcan.

Lifschitz, Edward. "Hearing Is Believing: Acoustic Aspects of Masking in Africa." In *West African Masks and Cultural Systems,* edited by Sidney L. Kasfir, 221–29. Musée royal de l'Afrique central, 1988.

Lott, Eric. *Love and Theft: Blackface Minstrelsy and the American Working Class.* Oxford University Press, 1993.

Lutz, Catherine A. *Unnatural Emotions: Everyday Sentiments on a Micronesian Atoll and Their Challenge to Western Theory.* University of Chicago Press, 1988.

MacGaffey, Wyatt. "Astonishment and Stickiness in Kongo Art." *Res: Anthropology and Aesthetics* 39 (Spring 2001): 137–50.

———. "Complexity, Astonishment and Power." *Journal of Southern African Studies* 14, no. 2 (1988): 188–203.

———. "The Eyes of Understanding: Kongo Minkisi." In *Astonishment and Power,* by Wyatt MacGaffey and Michael D. Harris, 20–103. National Museum of African Art, 1994.

———. "Franchising *Minkisi* in Loango: Questions of Form and Function." *Res: Anthropology and Aesthetics,* no. 65/66 (2014/2015): 148–57.

Maertens, Jean-Thierry. *Le masque et le miroir: Essai d'anthropologie des revêtements faciaux.* Aubier Montaigne, 1978.

Maples, Amanda M., Jordan A. Fenton, and Lisa Homann, eds. *New African Masquerades: Artistic Innovations and Collaborations.* New Orleans Museum of Art, 2025. Exhibition catalog.

Marchand, Suzanne. "Leo Frobenius and the Revolt Against the West." *Journal of Contemporary History* 32, no. 2 (1997): 153–70.

Mbembe, Achille. "The Aesthetics of Vulgarity." In *On the Postcolony,* 102–41. University of California Press, 2001. Originally published as "Provisional Notes on the Postcolony," *Africa* 62, no. 1 (1992): 3–37.

McEvilley, Thomas. "An Interview with Moustapha Dimé." In *Fusion: West African Artists at the Venice Biennale,* 32–53. Prestel, 1993. Exhibition catalog.

McNaughton, Patrick. *A Bird Dance near Saturday City: Sidi Ballo and the Art of West African Masquerade.* Indiana University Press, 2008.

Memel-Fotê, Harris. "The Perception of Beauty in Negro-African Culture." In *Colloquium: Function and Significance of African Negro Art in the Life and for the People (March 30–April 8, 1966),* 45–65. Society of African Culture for the First World Festival of Negro Arts, 1968.

Mercer, Kobena, and Isaac Julien. "True Confessions." In *Black Male: Representations of Masculinity in Contemporary American Art,* edited by Thelma Golden, 191–200. Whitney Museum of Art, 1994. Exhibition catalog.

Murphy, William P. "The Sublime Dance of Mende Politics: An African Aesthetic of Charismatic Power." *American Ethnologist* 25, no. 4 (1998): 563–82.

Muyaga Gangambi. *Les masques pende de Gatundo.* Centre d'êtudes ethnologiques, 2nd series, vol. 22, 1974.

Nietzsche, Friedrich. *The Birth of Tragedy.* Translated by Clifton P. Fadiman. Dover Publications, 1995. Originally published in 1872 as *Die Geburt der Tragödie aus dem Geiste der Musik* by Verlag von E. W. Fritzsch.

Nunley, John W. *Moving with the Face of the Devil.* University of Illinois Press, 1987.

Oguibe, Olu. "Beyond Death and Nothingness." *African Arts* 31, no. 1 (1998): 48–55, 96.

O'Neill, Eugene. "Memoranda on Masks." In *Playwrights on Playwriting: The Meaning and Making of Modern Drama from Ibsen to Ionesco,* edited by Toby Cole, 65–69. Hill and Wang, 1960. Originally published in 1932 in *American Spectator.*

Ottenberg, Simon. "Illusion, Communication, and Psychology in West African Masquerades." *Ethos* 10, no. 2 (1982): 149–85.

Otto, Rudolf. *The Idea of the Holy: An Inquiry into the Non-Rational Factor in the Idea of the Divine and Its Relation to the Rational.* Translated by John W. Harvey. Oxford University Press, 1958. Originally published in 1917 as *Das Heilige: Über das Irrationale in der Idee des Göttlichen und sein Verhältnis zum Rationalen* by Trewendt et Garnier.

Peek, Philip M. "The Sounds of Silence: Cross-World Communication and the Auditory Arts in African Societies." *American Ethnologist* 21, no. 3 (1994): 474–94.

Perchuk, Andrew, and Helaine Posner. *The Masculine Masquerade: Masculinity and Representation.* MIT Press, 1995.

Pernet, Henry. "Masks." In *The Encyclopedia of Religion,* vol. 9, edited by Mircea Eliade, 259–69. Macmillan, 1987. Second revised edition edited by Lindsay Jones, 5764–72. Thomson Gale, 2005.

———. *Ritual Masks: Deceptions and Revelations.* University of South Carolina Press, 1992. Originally published in 1988 as *Mirages du masque* by Labor et Fides.

Picton, John. "Masks and Identities in Ebira Culture." In *Concepts of the Body/Self in Africa,* edited by Joan Maw, 67–86. Institut für Afrikanistik und Ägyptologie der Universität Wien, 1992.

———. "On Placing Masquerades in Ebira." *African Languages and Cultures* 2, no. 1 (1989): 73–92.

———. Review of *West African Masks and Cultural Systems,* edited by Sidney L. Kasfir. *African Arts* 23, no. 1 (1989): 95–96.

———. "What's in a Mask?" *African Languages and Cultures* 3, no. 2 (1990): 181–202.

Probst, Peter. "African Angst: On Nyau Masks, Figures of Evil, and the Mediality of Terror." Manuscript from Colloquium in Honor of Ute Luig, Free University of Berlin, 2004.

———. "Picture Dance: Reflections on *Nyau* Image and Experience." *Iwalewa Forum* 1/2000, 17–32.

———. "Schrecken und Staunen: Über Nyau-Maskender Chewa in Kontext der Konjunktur des Okkulten und der Medialisierung des Schreckens." In *Africa Screams,* edited by Tobias Wendl, 115–25. Peter Hammer Verlag, 2004.

———. "Sublime Images: Masked Performances and the Aesthetics of Belonging in Malawi." In *Masquerade: Essays on Tradition and Innovation Worldwide,* edited by Deborah Bell, 84–90. McFarland, 2015.

Radar, Edmond. *Invention et métamorphose des signes.* Éditions Klincksieck, 1978.

Ranger, Terence. *The Invention of Tribalism in Zimbabwe.* Mambo Press, 1985.

Rank, Otto. *The Double.* New American Library, 1971.

Ray, Benjamin. Review of *Ritual Masks: Deceptions and Revelations,* by Henry Pernet. *History of Religions* 35, no. 1 (1995): 95–96.

Reddy, William M. *The Navigation of Feeling: A Framework for the History of Emotions.* Cambridge University Press, 2001.

Reed, Daniel B. *Dan Ge Performance: Masks and Music in Contemporary Côte d'Ivoire.* Indiana University Press, 2003.

———. "'The Ge Is in the Church' and 'Our Parents Are Playing Muslim': Performance, Identity, and Resistance Among the Dan in Postcolonial Côte d'Ivoire." *Ethnomusicology* 49, no. 3 (2005): 347–67.

Richards, Polly, director. *Mask Stories.* Museum for African Art and the National Museum of Mali, Bamako, 2013.

Ripa, Cesare. *Baroque and Rococo Pictorial Imagery: The 1758–60 Hertel Edition of Ripa's "Iconologia."* Translated by Edward A. Maser. Dover Publications, 1971.

Rivière, Joan. "Womanliness as a Masquerade." *International Journal of Psycho-Analysis* 10 (1929): 303–13.

Roberts, Mary Nooter, and Allen F. Roberts. *A Sense of Wonder: African Art from the Faletti Family Collection.* Phoenix Art Museum, 1997. Exhibition catalog.

Röschenthaler, Ute M. "Honoring Ejagham Women." *African Arts* 31, no. 2 (1998): 38–49, 92–93.

———. *Die Kunst der frauen: Zur Komplementarität von Nacktheit und Maskierung bei den Ejagham im Südwesten Kameruns.* Verlag für Wissenschaft und Bildung, 1993.

———. *Purchasing Culture: The Dissemination of Associations in the Cross River Region of Cameroon and Nigeria,* 215–76, 426–31. Africa World Press, 2011.

Ross, Edward Alsworth. "Social Control." *American Journal of Sociology* 1, no. 5 (1896): 513–35.

———. *Social Control: A Survey of the Foundations of Order.* Macmillan, 1901.

———. "Social Control: VIII. Art." *American Journal of Sociology* 3, no. 1 (1897): 64–78.

Roucek, Joseph. *Social Control.* D. Van Nostrand Co., 1947. Reprint, 1949. 2nd ed., 1956.

Rouget, Gilbert. *Music and Trance: A Theory of the Relations Between Music and Possession.* Translated and revised by Brunhilde Biebuyck in collaboration with the author. University of Chicago Press, 1985. Originally published in 1980 as *La musique et la transe: Esquisse d'une théorie générale des relations de la musique et de la possession* by Gallimard.

Routley, Nick. "A Visual Guide to Human Emotion." *Visual Capitalist,* 8 April 2021. https://www.visualcapitalist.com/a-visual-guide-to-human-emotion.

Rudlin, John. *Commedia dell'Arte: An Actor's Handbook.* Routledge, 1994.

Schechner, Richard. "Julie Taymor: From Jacques Lecoq to 'The Lion King': An Interview." *The Drama Review* 43, no. 3 (1999): 36–55.

———. *Performance Theory.* 1988. Revised and expanded edition, Routledge, 2003.

Schindler, Ines, et al. "Measuring Aesthetic Emotions: A Review of the Literature and a New Assessment Tool." PLOS ONE 12, no. 6 (2017): e0178899. https://doi.org/10.1371/journal.pone.0178899.

Schmitt, Jean-Claude. "Les masques, le diable, les morts." In *Le corps, les rites, les rêves, le temps,* 211–37. Gallimard, 2001.

Senghor, Léopold Sédar. "Emotion" (1962). In *Prose and Poetry,* edited and translated by John Reed and Clive Wake, 34–35. Heinemann, 1976.

———. "The Lessons of Leo Frobenius." In *Leo Frobenius on African History, Art and Culture: An Anthology,* edited by Eike Haberland, translated by Patricia Crampton, vii–xiii. M. Wiener, 2007. Originally published in 1973.

———. "No. 30 Composantes de l'oeuvre africaine." In *Léopold Sédar Senghor: Enregistrements historiques,* edited by Philippe Sainteny. Frémeaux et Associés, 2006.

———. "Préface." In *Ethnologiques: Hommages à Marcel Griaule,* edited by Solange de Ganay, Annie Lebeuf, and Jean-Paul Lebeuf, v–vii. Hermann, 1987.

———. "The Spirit of Civilization, or the Laws of African Negro Culture." *Présence africaine,* no. 8–10 (June–November 1956): 51–64.

Severi, Carlo. "Memory, Reflexivity and Belief: Reflections on the Ritual Use of Language." *Social Anthropology* 10, no. 1 (2002): 23–40.

Sieber, Roy. "Masks as Agents of Social Control." In *The Many Faces of Primitive Art: A Critical Anthology,* edited by Douglas Fraser, 257–63. Prentice-Hall, Inc., 1966. Originally published in 1962 in *African Studies Bulletin* 5, no. 2 (1962): 8–13.

Sikitele, Charles [now Sikitele Gize]. Excerpts from "Les Souvenirs." In *Prix de Poésie Sébastien Ngonso,* 29–36. Université Lovanium, 1968.

Siroto, Leon. "*Gon:* A Mask Used in Competition for Leadership Among the Bakwele." In *African Art and Leadership,* edited by Douglas Fraser and Herbert M. Cole, 57–76. University of Wisconsin Press, 1972.

———. "Masks and Social Organization Among the Bakwele People of Western Equatorial Africa." PhD diss., Columbia University, 1969.

Smith, Mark M. *Sensing the Past: Seeing, Hearing, Smelling, Tasting and Touching in History.* University of California Press, 2008.

Soyinka, Wole. *The Burden of Memory, The Muse of Forgiveness.* Oxford University Press, 1999.

———. *Myth, Literature and the African World.* Cambridge University Press, 1976.

Streck, Bernhard. "Leo Frobenius." In *Masques,* 247–57. Musée Dapper, 1995. Exhibition catalog.

Strother, Z. S. "Dancing a Topic to Death: After 100 Years of Research, What Do We Really Know About Masquerade in Africa?" Manuscript from the symposium Visualizing Africa: New Perspectives on Art, History, and Culture, University of Michigan, Ann Arbor, 14 September 2002.

———. "From Performative Utterance to Performative Object: Pende Theories of Speech, Blood Sacrifice, and Power Objects." *Res: Anthropology and Aesthetics,* no. 37 (Spring 2000): 49–71.

———. *Inventing Masks: Agency and History in the Art of the Central Pende.* University of Chicago Press, 1998.

———. "Smells and Bells: The Role of Skepticism in Pende Divination." In *Insight and Artistry in African Divination,* edited by John Pemberton III, 99–115, plates 8–9. Smithsonian Institution Press, 2000.

Strother, Z. S., and Nzomba Kakema Dugo. "The Role of Masks in the Eastern Pende Mukanda." In *Congo as Fiction: Art Worlds Between Past and Present,* edited by Nanina Guyer and Michaela Oberhofer, 254–72. Museum Rietberg, 2020.

Taussig, Michael. *Defacement: Public Secrecy and the Labor of the Negative.* Stanford University Press, 1999.

Taymor, Julie (with Alexis Greene). *The Lion King: Pride Rock on Broadway.* Disney Editions, 1997.

Tchimou, Famedji-Koto. *Langage de la danse chez les Dogons.* L'Harmattan, 1995.

Thompson, Robert Farris. *African Art in Motion: Icon and Act in the Collection of Katherine Coryton White.* University of California Press, 1974. Exhibition catalog.

Tonkin, Elizabeth. "Masking and Masquerading, with Examples from West Africa." University of Birmingham Discussion Papers, series C, no. 36, Sociology and Politics (August 1979).

——. "Masks and Powers," *Man,* n.s., vol. 14 (June 1979): 237–48.

Vail, Leroy, ed. *The Creation of Tribalism in Southern Africa.* University of California Press, 1989.

Van Beek, Walter E. A. "Dogon Restudied (A Field Evaluation of the Work of Marcel Griaule)." *Current Anthropology* 32, no. 3 (1991): 139–67.

——. "Enter the Bush: A Dogon Mask Festival." In *Africa Explores,* edited by Susan Vogel, 56–73. Center for African Art, 1991.

Van Beek, Walter E. A., and Harrie M. Leyten. *Masquerades in African Society: Gender, Power, and Identity.* James Currey, 2023.

Van Damme, Wilfried. "Beauty and Ugliness in African Art and Thought." In *The Language of Beauty in African Art,* edited by Constantine Petridis, 94–129. Art Institute of Chicago, 2022. Exhibition catalog.

Vidler, Anthony. *The Architectural Uncanny.* MIT Press, 1992.

von Sydow, Eckart. *Die Kunst der Naturvölker und der Vorzeit.* Propyläen Verlag, 1923.

Weil, Peter M. "The Masked Figure and Social Control: The Mandinka Case," *Africa* 41, no. 4 (1971): 279–93.

——. "Women's Masks and the Power of Gender in Mande History." *African Arts* 31, no. 2 (1998): 28–37, 88–90, 94–95.

Wilde, Oscar. "The Critic as Artist" [1891]. In *Intentions: The Decay of Lying; Pen, Pencil, and Poison; The Critic as Artist; The Truth of Masks,* 93–217. Brentano's, 1905.

Wiles, David. *Mask and Performance in Greek Tragedy: From Ancient Festival to Modern Experimentation.* Cambridge University Press, 2007.

Willis, John Thabiti. *Masquerading Politics: Kinship, Gender, and Ethnicity in a Yoruba Town.* Indiana University Press, 2018.

Yoshida, Kenji. "Masks and Transformation Among the Chewa of Eastern Zambia." *Senri Ethnological Studies* (Osaka) 31 (1991): 203–73.

Research Note
and Acknowledgments

When I returned home in September 1989 after thirty-two months of immersive study of both ritual and secular masquerade in Zaïre (now Democratic Republic of the Congo), funded by the US Information Agency (Fulbright Predoctoral Grants), I was startled by the vehemence of scholars in the United States who viewed African masks as tools of transformation related to beliefs in spirit possession. In DR Congo, Khoshi Mahumbu, Malenge Mundugu Mukhokho, and Masuwa Léon had pushed me to acknowledge dancers as the inventors of masks. The performers subsequently interviewed unanimously explained that they were seeking fame and emphasized their role not only in generating a new "idea," a new concept, but also in supervising a collaborative process through which a master sculptor, drummers, and sometimes singers worked together to achieve their vision.[1]

An invitation in 2002 from Raymond Silverman to reflect on the "state of the field" for his symposium, Visualizing Africa, at the University of Michigan prompted me to think about the disconnect between my experience and the literature, which I addressed in my paper "After 100 Years of Research, What Do We Really Know About Masquerade in Africa?" Feedback from Siona Wilson and others following a subsequent talk, "Lying Masks," at the Institute of Fine Arts, New York University, in 2005, spurred me to flesh out my proposition that face masks can trigger a sense of the uncanny because they literally double the face. The Experience and Use of Wonder, a symposium organized by David Doris in 2008 at the University of Michigan, inspired me to engage the field of emotion, as interlocutors in DR Congo had already urged me to do. As ideas matured, colleagues at Indiana University, Harvard University, Emory University, Museu Nacional—Universidade Federal do Rio de Janeiro, Howard University, the University of California, Los Angeles, and the University of California, Santa Barbara debated and helped me fine-tune my positions, which reached a mature expression in the Getty Research Institute Council Lecture titled "Masks and the Uncanny, in Africa and Beyond" (2017).

The gestation period has been significant, and I am deeply indebted for lengthy and sometimes impassioned debates about masked performance, emotions, historiography, trance, popular culture, and German language sources with Monni Adams, Anne-Marie Bouttiaux, Fiona Brandl, Elisabeth L. Cameron, Herbert Cole, Grace Dingledine, Carlos Fausto, Jordan A. Fenton, Eberhard Fischer, Susan E. Gagliardi, Jonathan Hay, Lisa Homann, Robin Horton, Deniz Hughes, Kassim Kone, Steven Levine, Patrick McNaughton, Cari Meltzer, Megan Metcalf, Andrew Perchuk, Henry Pernet, Daniel Reed, Kim Richter, and Julie Taymor. I also thank Katie Van Heest and Laura Santiago for their incomparable editing prowess. At the Getty Research Institute, Michele Ciaccio showed remarkable patience over the years and I am grateful for her openness to consider multiple requests to rethink the format of the text, which were ably executed by designer Jon Grizzle. Karen Ehrmann worked magic in procuring many of the images, and Victoria Gallina made them all that they can be.

Interlocutors in the field, who are named in the text itself, pushed me to move out of my comfort zone as an art historian to think about emotions released through masked performance. I was honored to be able to present the central argument of this text in a seminar at the Université de Kinshasa, in the Faculté des Lettres et Sciences Humaines at the invitation of Professors Placide Mumbembele and Kiangu Sindani (6 July 2023). Various reactions arising from that experience have been noted in the text. The acclaimed historian Sikitele Gize brought the meeting to a close, announcing, "I was marked by the masks," recalling the depth of emotion that he experienced during a masquerade organized in 1966 in the wake of brutal postcolonial repression. It is hoped that testimonies like Sikitele's from audience-participants will make concrete the thesis of this text, crystallized by Professor Kassim Kone in his aphorism: "The function of masks is to trigger the emotions."

NOTES

1   Z. S. Strother, *Inventing Masks: Agency and History in the Art of the Central Pende* (University of Chicago Press, 1998).

Illustration Credits

The following sources have granted permission to reproduce illustrations in this volume.

Figs. 1, 25, 26. Photo © Z. S. Strother.

Fig. 2. Fonds Marcel-Griaule, LESC / CNRS, Université Paris Nanterre.

Figs. 3, 6, 7, 23. Photo © Lisa Homann.

Figs. 4, 32. bpk Bildagentur / Ethnologisches Museum / Staatliche Museen / Hans-Joachim Koloss / Art Resource, NY.

Fig. 5. Photo © Martha G. Anderson.

Fig. 8. Photo © Ute Röschenthaler.

Fig. 9. Album / Alamy Stock Photo.

Fig. 10. Purchased with funds from the North Carolina Museum of Art Foundation, Art Trust Fund, 2007.2 / a-d.

Fig. 11. Xseon / Shutterstock.com.

Fig. 16. Museum Purchase, Museum Improvements-Collections Fund, 1936–1937, Peabody Museum of Archeology and Ethnology. George W. Harley collection. Photo: Hillel Burger.

Fig. 17. Image by Robert Farris Thompson. From Robert Farris Thompson, *African Art in Motion*, exh. cat. (University of California Press, 1974), 161 (plate 198).

Fig. 18. Bibliothèque nationale de France.

Fig. 19. Photo © Eberhard Fischer.

Fig. 20. Photo © Zoro bi Irié, during the 2009 Royal Museum for Central Africa (Tervuren, Belgium) mission in Côte d'Ivoire, led by Anne-Marie Bouttiaux as head of the Ethnography Division.

Fig. 21. Photo © Visko Hatfield.

Fig. 22. Author wearing face mask of *Pulugunzu* while photographed at home by Beatrice Rubin, July 24, 2023.

Fig. 24. Drawing by Philippe Jespers. Used by permission.

Fig. 27. Eliot Elisofon Photographic Archives, National Museum of African Art, Smithsonian Institution. EEPA EECL 4247.

Fig. 28. Photo © Joan Marcus.

Fig. 29. Photo © Elisabeth L. Cameron.

Fig. 30. © Martin Gusinde / Anthropos Institute / Editions Xavier Barral.

Fig. 31. Photo © Z. S. Strother. Photographed with the permission of Chief Kende Kakele (Katshivi Koji).

African Masks and Emotions publishes the Getty Research Institute Council Lecture delivered by Z. S. Strother on 12 October 2017.

This publication is supported by the Getty Research Institute Council.

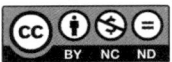
Published by the Getty Research Institute, Los Angeles
Getty Publications
1200 Getty Center Drive, Suite 500
Los Angeles, California 90049-1682
getty.edu/publications

Laura Santiago, *Editor*
Jon Grizzle, *Designer*
Victoria Gallina, *Production*
Karen Ehrmann, *Image and Rights Acquisition*

Distributed in the United States and Canada by the University of Chicago Press

Distributed outside the United States and Canada by Yale University Press, London

This publication was peer reviewed through a single-masked process in which the reviewers remained anonymous.

Type composed in Lygia and Lygia Sans

Printed in China

Library of Congress Cataloging-in-Publication Data
Names: Strother, Z. S., author.
Title: African masks and emotions : in theory and in practice / Z. S. Strother.
Description: Los Angeles: Getty Research Institute, [2026] | Includes bibliographical references. | Summary: "Z. S. Strother uses ethnographic studies of individual mask cultures in Africa to dispute the assumptions that masks universally hide, reveal, or transform"—Provided by publisher.
Identifiers: LCCN 2025013665 (print) | LCCN 2025013666 (ebook) | ISBN 9781606069936 (paperback) | ISBN 9781606069943 (pdf) | ISBN 9781606069950 (epub)
Subjects: LCSH: Masks, African—Psychological aspects. | Masks, African—Social aspects. | Masquerades—Africa.
Classification: LCC GN645 .S76 2026 (print) | LCC GN645 (ebook) | DDC 391.4/34019—dc23/eng/20250615
LC record available at https://lccn.loc.gov/2025013665
LC ebook record available at https://lccn.loc.gov/2025013666

Authorized Product Safety Representative in the European Union: Easy Access System Europe, Mustamäe tee 50, 10621 Tallinn, Estonia, gpsr.requests@easproject.com

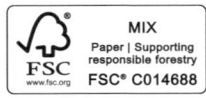